Office 2000
fast&easy™

Send Us Your Comments

To comment on this book or any other PRIMA TECH title, visit our reader response page on the Web at **www.prima-tech.com/comments**.

How to Order

For information on quantity discounts, contact the publisher: Prima Publishing, P.O. Box 1260BK, Rocklin, CA 95677-1260; (916) 632-4400. On your letterhead, include information concerning the intended use of the books and the number of books you wish to purchase. For individual orders, visit PRIMA TECH's Web site at **www.prima-tech.com**.

Office 2000

fast&easy™

Diane Koers

A DIVISION OF PRIMA PUBLISHING

A Division of Prima Publishing

Prima Publishing and colophon are registered trademarks of Prima Communications, Inc. PRIMA TECH and Fast & Easy are trademarks of Prima Communications, Inc., Rocklin, California 95677.

Publisher: Stacy L. Hiquet

Associate Publisher: Nancy Stevenson

Managing Editor: Dan J. Foster

Senior Editor: Kelli R. Crump

Senior Acquisitions Editor: Deborah F. Abshier

Project Editor: Rebecca I. Fong

Assistant Project Editor: Estelle Manticas

Editorial Assistant: Brian Thomasson

Technical Reviewer: Ray Link

Copy Editor: Judy Ohm

Interior Layout: Marian Hartsough

Cover Design: Prima Design Team

Indexer: Katherine Stimson

Microsoft, Windows, Windows NT, Outlook, PowerPoint, PhotoDraw, MSN, and FrontPage are trademarks or registered trademarks of Microsoft Corporation.

Important: If you have problems installing or running Microsoft Office, go to Microsoft's Web site at **www.microsoft.com**. Prima Publishing cannot provide software support.

Prima Publishing and the author have attempted throughout this book to distinguish proprietary trademarks from descriptive terms by following the capitalization style used by the manufacturer.

Information contained in this book has been obtained by Prima Publishing from sources believed to be reliable. However, because of the possibility of human or mechanical error by our sources, Prima Publishing, or others, the Publisher does not guarantee the accuracy, adequacy, or completeness of any information and is not responsible for any errors or omissions or the results obtained from the use of such information. Readers should be particularly aware of the fact that the Internet is an ever-changing entity. Some facts may have changed since this book went to press.

ISBN: 0-7615-1762-6

Library of Congress Catalog Card Number: 98-68147

Printed in the United States of America

99 00 01 02 03 DD 10 9 8 7 6 5 4 3 2 1

To Ira

I know you'll always be good to her

Acknowledgments

I am deeply grateful to the many people at Prima Publishing who worked on this book. Thank you for all the time you gave and for your assistance.

To Debbie Abshier for the opportunity to write this book and her confidence in me. To Judy Ohm and Ray Link for their assistance in making this book technically and grammatically correct, and to Rebecca Fong for all her patience and guidance.

Lastly, a big hug and kiss to my husband, Vern, for his never-ending patience during those very late nights spent writing this book.

About the Author

DIANE KOERS owns and operates All Business Service, a software training and consulting business formed in 1988 that services the central Indiana area. Her area of expertise has long been in the word processing, spreadsheet and graphics area of computing as well as providing training and support for Peachtree Accounting software. Diane's authoring experience includes Prima's *Lotus 1-2-3 97 Fast & Easy*, *WordPerfect 8 Fast & Easy*, *Windows 98 Fast & Easy*, and *Works 4.5 Fast & Easy* and has co-authored Prima Tech's *The Essential Windows 98 Book.* She has also developed and written software training manuals for her clients' use.

Active in church and civic activities, Diane enjoys spending her free time traveling and playing with her grandson and her three Yorkshire Terriers.

Contents at a Glance

Contents

PART IV
USING POWERPOINT 177

Introduction

This *Fast & Easy* guide from Prima Publishing will help you master Microsoft Office 2000, whether you are computer challenged or a sophisticated power user. This book uses a step-by-step approach, illustrations, and easy instructions to complete a task.

Office 2000 is a powerful and popular suite of programs that will support many aspects of your everyday work style. For example, information is provided to help you write a letter, create a spreadsheet, produce a professional-looking presentation, and manage your schedule and electronic mail.

Each of the individual programs interacts with the other programs in the suite. For example, you may need to prepare a business report in Word that contains graphs and charts based on data you enter in an Excel spreadsheet. Perhaps later, after you have delivered your report (possibly using Outlook's e-mail), you may need to prepare and schedule a PowerPoint presentation. In addition, you'll learn how to use Office 2000 products to interact with the Internet.

You'll quickly be able to tap into the program's user-friendly integrated design and feature-rich environment.

Who Should Read This Book?

This manual can be used by those who have never used the Office programs before as well as those who are new to this version of Office.

The easy-to-follow, highly visual nature of this book makes it the perfect learning tool. Computer terms and phrases are clearly explained in non-technical language, and expert tips and shortcuts help you achieve quality results.

By using *Office 2000 Fast & Easy* as a step-by-step reference, any level of user can look up steps for a task quickly without having to plow through pages of descriptions.

Added Advice to Make You a Pro

You'll notice that this book uses steps and keeps explanations to a minimum to help you learn faster. Included in the book are a few elements that provide some additional comments without encumbering your progress through the steps:

- **Tips** offer shortcuts when performing an action, or a hint about a feature that might make your work in Office applications quicker and easier.
- **Notes** give you a bit of background or additional information about a feature, or advice about how to use the feature in your day-to-day activities.

In addition, two helpful appendixes will show you how to install Microsoft Office and how to use one of the time saving wizards that are included in Office!

Read and enjoy this Fast & Easy book. It certainly is the fastest and easiest way to learn Microsoft Office 2000.

PART I

Getting Started

1

Welcome to Office 2000

As confusing as computers are today, not understanding the basic elements you see onscreen can be frustrating. What's a dialog box? Where is that pop-up menu coming from? The good thing about Microsoft Office products is that the elements are the same in each program. Throughout Part I, you will learn the common ways you can approach tasks, regardless of the Office program you are using or the document in which you are working. The basic premise of each Fast & Easy Guide is that people learn best by doing. In this chapter, you'll learn how to:

- Start and exit an Office 2000 program
- Identify common screen elements

Starting a Program

Starting a program (also called an *application*) is simple to do—and it's the necessary first step toward getting anything done. Because computers can be set up differently, you might not see the icons on your Desktop or the menu choices on the Programs menu that you see in this example.

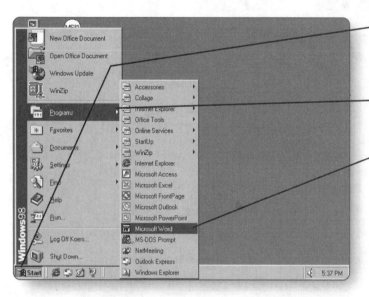

1. Click on the **Start button** on the Windows Taskbar. The Start menu will appear.

2. Click on **Programs**. The Programs menu will appear.

3. Click on the Office **program name** that you want to start. The Welcome screen for the program will appear briefly before the main program window opens.

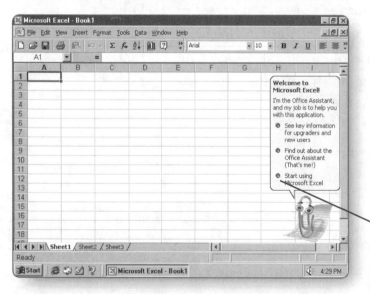

If this is your first time using a program, the Office Assistant appears with a balloon welcoming you. For example, if you are using Excel for the first time, the balloon says, "Welcome to Excel." For more information about working with Office Assistant, see Chapter 4, "Getting Help with Office."

4. Click on the **blue button** next to "Start using Microsoft Excel" (or the appropriate program name).

TIP

If you're asked for a user name, type your name and initial in the dialog box and click on OK.

Identifying Common Screen Elements

All Office 2000 programs contain common screen elements. You'll learn more about the following elements as you work in individual programs in this book:

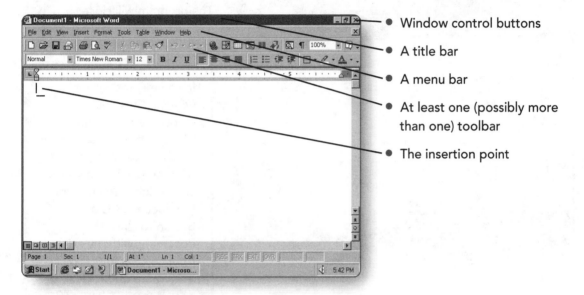

- Window control buttons
- A title bar
- A menu bar
- At least one (possibly more than one) toolbar
- The insertion point

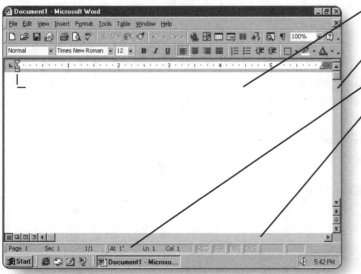

- The working area (also called the document area)
- A vertical scroll bar
- A status bar
- A horizontal scroll bar

The insertion point appears in different locations in the various Office programs. On your screen, it flashes. The insertion point represents the location at which text will appear when you start typing. As you type, the insertion point moves to the right.

Exiting a Program

When you no longer want to work in a program, you should follow the proper procedure for exiting the program to ensure that you don't damage files.

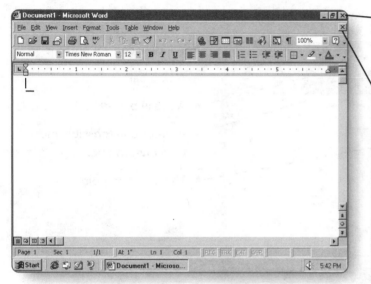

1. **Click** on the **Close button**. The program will close.

TIP

In some cases, you might notice a Close button below the application's Close button. This second Close button controls the document in which you are working. You can use the document Close button to close the document without exiting from the program. You'll learn more about closing documents in Chapter 3, "Finding Common Ways to Work in Documents."

NOTE

If you do any work in a document, a dialog box will appear asking whether you want to save your work. In Chapter 3, "Finding Common Ways to Work in Documents," you'll learn how to save documents.

2

Choosing Commands

You use commands to communicate with programs—
commands are your way of telling a program what you want it
to do. Most often, you issue commands by choosing them from
menus, but you also can issue commands using toolbars and
shortcut menus. In this chapter, you'll learn how to:

- Use the menu and keyboard to choose commands
- Make selections in dialog boxes
- Work with shortcut menus and toolbars

Discovering Personalized Menus

All Windows programs use menus to select from, but Office 2000 has added a function called *personalized menus*. When the menu is first accessed, only the most common features are displayed. If you pause the mouse pointer over the main menu selection, or move it down to the double arrows at the bottom of a menu, the menu will expand to include all available features for that menu.

In this chapter, we'll use the Microsoft Word application. Start Word by clicking on the Start Button and choosing Programs, Microsoft Word.

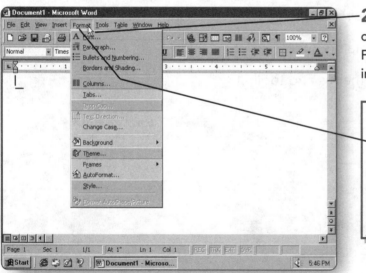

1. Click on **Format**. The Format menu will appear with nine options.

2. Pause the **mouse pointer** over the Format menu. The Format menu will expand to include more items.

TIP

Click on the main menu selection (Format, in this example) to close a menu without making any selection.

When you see a right-pointing arrowhead in a menu, it means another menu is available.

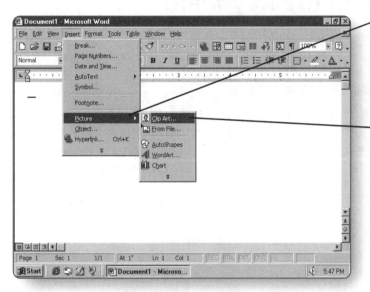

3. Move the **mouse pointer** down the menu to select any item with an arrow. The item will be highlighted and a submenu will appear.

4. Move the **mouse pointer** to the right of your selection in step 3. The first item in the submenu will be highlighted.

5. Click on a **selection** in the submenu. The feature associated with that menu item will be activated.

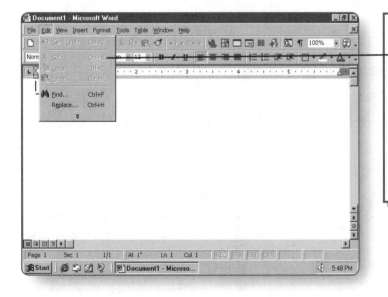

NOTE

Some options in the menu may appear dimmed, meaning that they are not available at this time. You probably need a document open or text selected before you can use items that are dimmed.

Choosing Commands with the Keyboard

If you're not comfortable with using the mouse, you can also open menus and choose commands using the keyboard.

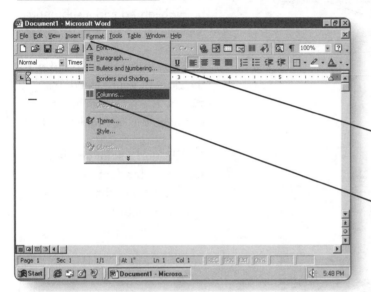

1. **Press** the **Alt key** on your keyboard. The menu bar will become active and a gray box will appear around the word "File" on the menu bar.

2. **Press** the **underlined letter** of a menu name. The menu will appear.

3. **Press** the **underlined letter** of a command name. The command will execute.

Using Shortcut Menus

Shortcut menus contain a limited number of commands. The commands you see on a shortcut menu depend on what you're doing at the time you open the shortcut menu. You always press the right mouse button to open a shortcut menu.

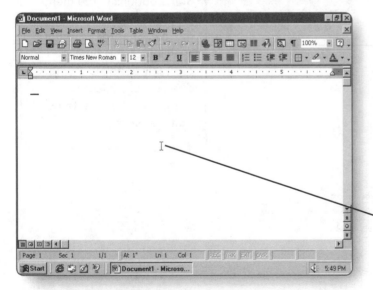

1. **Move** the **mouse pointer** into the document area. The pointer will appear as an I-beam.

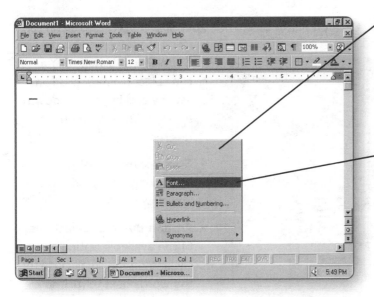

2. Press the **right mouse button** (right-click). The mouse pointer will change to an arrow and the shortcut menu for regular text will appear in the working area of the document.

3. Click on a **menu selection**. The menu action will be taken.

Working with Dialog Boxes

TIP

Press the Esc key or click on the working area to close a shortcut menu without choosing a command.

Many selections in the menu are followed by three periods, called *ellipses*. Selections followed by ellipses indicate that, if you select one of these items, a dialog box will appear with the next group of options. The Page Setup menu selection will display an example of a dialog box.

1. Click on **File**. The File menu will appear.

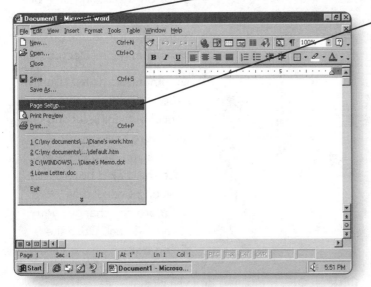

2. Click on **Page Setup**. The Page Setup dialog box will open.

Options have been grouped together by tabs in the dialog box. In this example, you can select from these groups: Margins, Paper Size, Paper Source, or Layout.

Depending on the dialog box, several types of selections will display.

3. Click on **Paper Size**. The Paper Size tab will display on top.

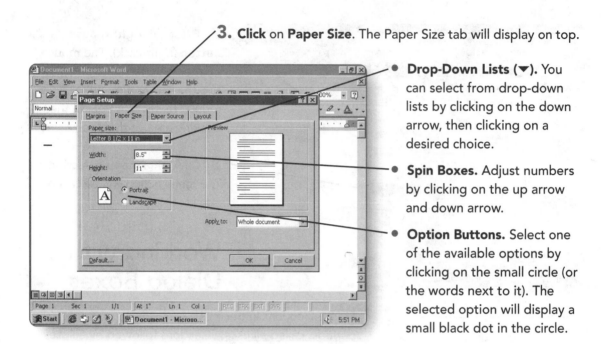

- **Drop-Down Lists (▼).** You can select from drop-down lists by clicking on the down arrow, then clicking on a desired choice.

- **Spin Boxes.** Adjust numbers by clicking on the up arrow and down arrow.

- **Option Buttons.** Select one of the available options by clicking on the small circle (or the words next to it). The selected option will display a small black dot in the circle.

4. Click on **Layout**. The Layout tab will come to the top of the stack.

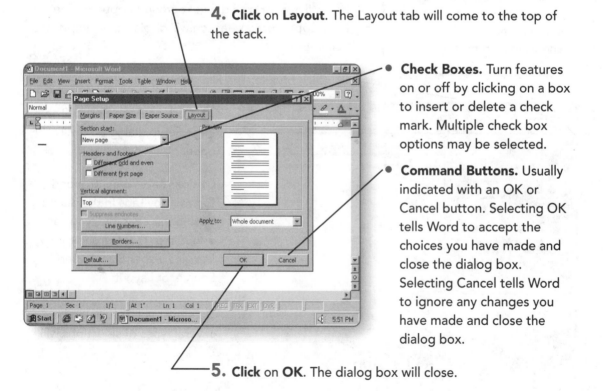

- **Check Boxes.** Turn features on or off by clicking on a box to insert or delete a check mark. Multiple check box options may be selected.

- **Command Buttons.** Usually indicated with an OK or Cancel button. Selecting OK tells Word to accept the choices you have made and close the dialog box. Selecting Cancel tells Word to ignore any changes you have made and close the dialog box.

5. Click on **OK**. The dialog box will close.

3

Finding Common Ways to Work in Documents

Office 2000 programs let you perform tasks in the same way, regardless of the program in which you are working. In this chapter, you'll learn how to:

- Preview a document before printing
- Print, save, and close a document
- Open an existing document
- Start a new document
- Fix mistakes

Previewing a Document

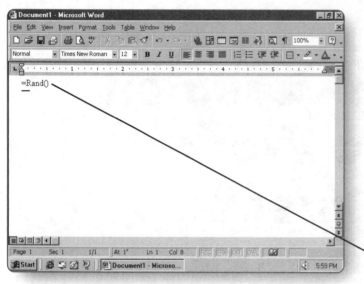

Print Preview is available in Word and Excel (in PowerPoint, you can view slides as you create them) and is most helpful when you're trying to make sure information is aligned as you want it. What you see (and the rest of the tasks we cover in this chapter) would be more meaningful if you had some text onscreen, so we'll start by letting Word add some random text.

1. Type =Rand(). The insertion point will move to the right as you type.

2. Press the **Enter key.** The text you typed will be replaced with several copies of the sentence "The quick brown fox jumps over the lazy dog."

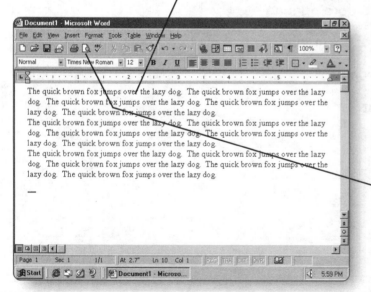

NOTE

The text you typed was actually a formula that Word 2000 recognizes as meaning, "Enter some sample text."

3. Click on the **Print Preview button.** Word will switch to Print Preview mode, in which you can see the layout and appearance of your document as it will appear when printed.

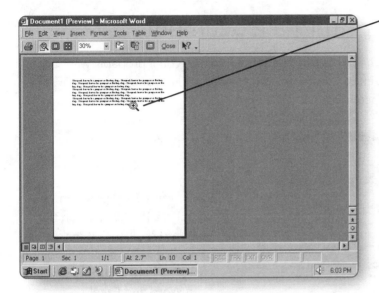

4. **Move** the **mouse pointer** over the document onscreen. The pointer will change to a magnifying glass.

5. **Click** on the **document**. It will enlarge (zoom) so you can actually read the text.

NOTE

You must click on the portion of the document you want to enlarge.

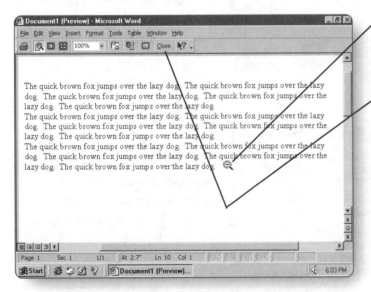

6. **Click** on the **document** again to return the document to regular size.

7. **Click** on **Close**. The document will return to its previous view.

Printing a Document

When your document is complete, you'll probably want to print it. You can send it to your printer for a hard copy of the document.

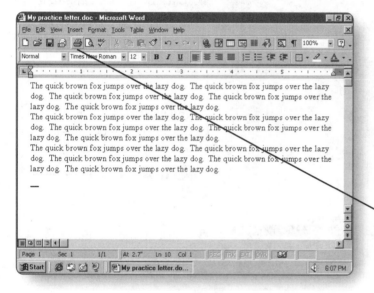

Printing from the Toolbar

Each Office 2000 program contains a Print button on the Standard toolbar that makes printing easy. In addition, you can print from Print Preview in both Word and Excel.

1. Click on the **Print button**. One copy of the entire document will be printed.

Printing from the Menu

When electing to print from the menu, a dialog box will appear in which you can determine exactly what to print, which printer to use or how many copies to print.

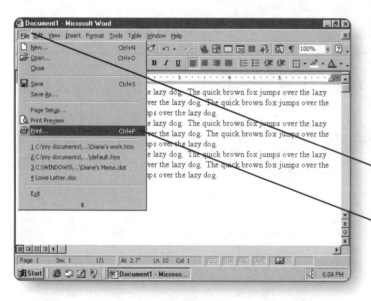

1. Click on **File**. The File menu will appear.

2. Click on **Print**. The Print dialog box will open.

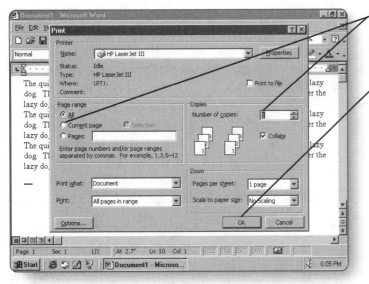

3. Make any desired **changes** in the Print dialog box. The options will be selected.

4. Click on **OK**. The document will be printed.

Saving Your Document

Anyone who uses a computer has probably lost data at one time or another. If you haven't been saving to disk regularly, it only takes a few seconds to lose hours of work. Word has built-in features to help protect you against this eventuality. However, you still need to save.

Saving a Document the First Time

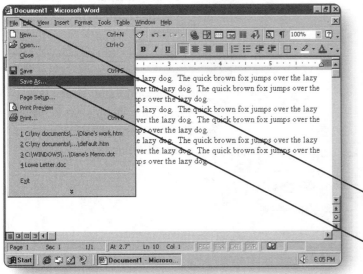

When you first create a document, it has no name. If you want to use that document later, it must have a name so Word can find it. Word asks for a name the first time you save the document, and then puts the name in the Title Bar at the very top of the screen.

1. Click on **File**. The File menu will appear.

2. Click on **Save As**. The Save As dialog box will open.

3. **Type** a **name** for your file in the File name: text box. The file name will be displayed.

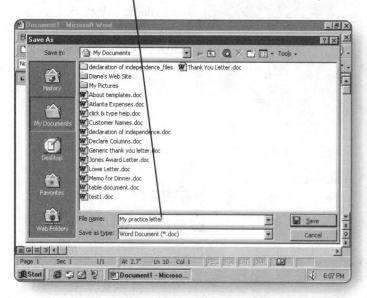

NOTE

Filenames can be up to 256 characters in length and can include most characters on your keyboard, including spaces.

NOTE

The Save in: drop-down list box lists folder options where you can save the document. The default folder that appears is "My Documents." If you don't want to save it to this folder, or if you want to save your document to another disk, you can select another one. Click on the down arrow to browse.

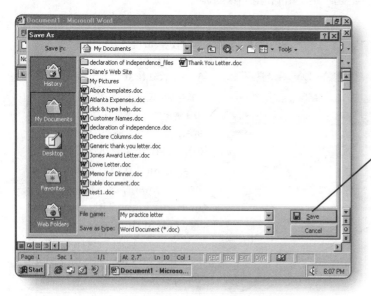

4. **Click** on **Save**. Your document will be saved and the name you specified will appear in the title bar.

Resaving a Document

As you continue to work on your document, you should resave it every ten minutes or so to help ensure that you do not lose any changes.

1. Click on the **Save button**. The document will be resaved with any changes. No dialog box will appear because the document is resaved with the same name and in the same folder as previously specified.

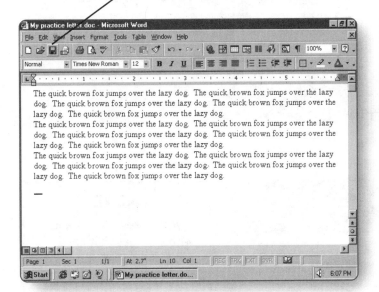

Closing a Document

When you are finished working on a document, you should close it. *Closing* is the equivalent of putting it away for later use. When you close a document, you are only putting the document away—not the program. The application, Word, for example, is still active and ready to work for you.

1. Click on **File**. The File menu will appear.

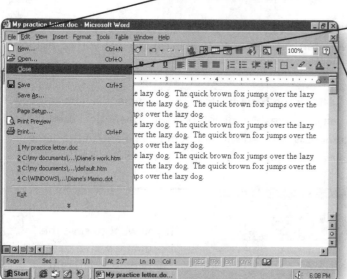

2a. Click on **Close**. The document will be put away.

OR

2b. Click on the **Close Button**. The document will be closed. By choosing this method, you combine steps 1 and 2.

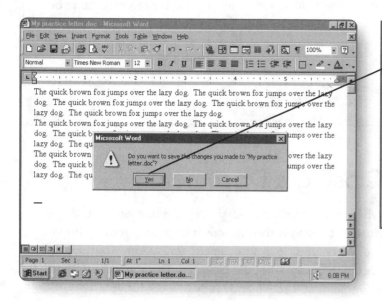

NOTE

If you close a document with changes that have not been saved, the application will prompt you with a dialog box. Choose Yes to save the changes or No to close the file without saving the changes.

Opening an Existing Document

Opening a document is putting a copy of that file up into the computer's memory and onto your screen so that you can work on it. If you make any changes, be sure to save the file again.

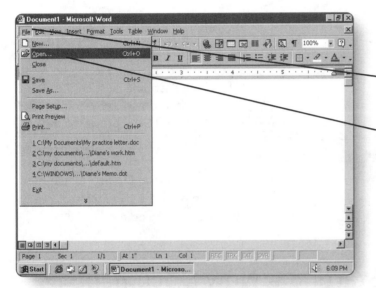

1. **Click** on **File**. The File menu will appear.

2. **Click** on **Open**. The Open dialog box will open.

TIP

Optionally, click on the Open button on the toolbar.

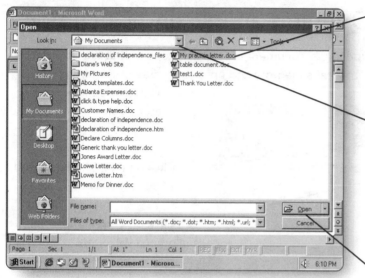

3. Click on the **file name** you wish to open. The file name will be highlighted.

NOTE

If your file is located in a different folder than the one displayed in the Look in: list box, click on the drop-down arrow to navigate to the proper folder.

4. Click on **Open**. The file will be placed on your screen, ready for you to edit.

Starting a New Document

When a Word, Excel or PowerPoint session is first started, a blank document appears ready for you to use. However, during the course of using Word you may need another blank document. Creating a new document is only a mouse click away!

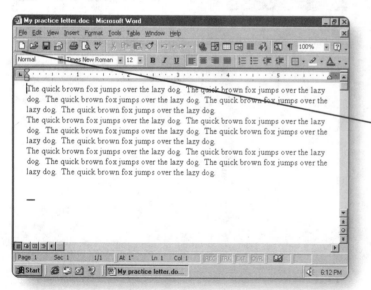

1. Click on the **New button**. A new screen will appear.

The title of the new document will depend on how many documents you've created during this session.

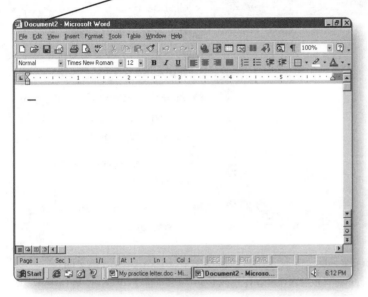

Using the Standard Toolbar

There are several buttons on the standard toolbar that are common to the Office application.

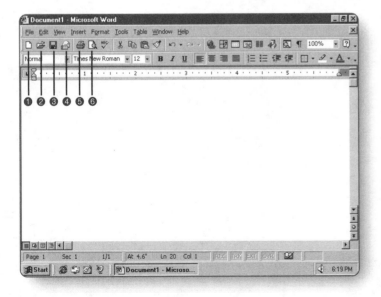

The following table lists these common buttons and their function:

❶ **New**. Delivers a new blank document

❷ **Open**. Opens a previously created document

❸ **Save**. Saves a document

❹ **E-mail**. E-mails a document

❺ **Print**. Prints a document

❻ **Print Preview**. Shows a document in full page

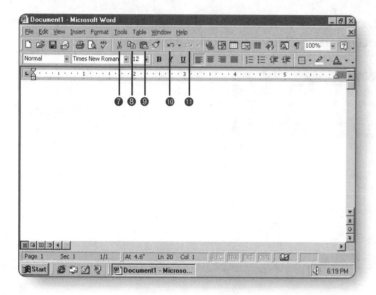

⓻ Cut. Removes selected information to the Windows clipboard

⓼ Copy. Duplicates selected information to the Windows clipboard

⓽ Paste. Copies information on the Windows clipboard to the current document

⓾ Undo. Reverses the last action taken

⓫ Redo. Reverses the most recent Undo step

You've already seen several of these icons used in this chapter. The remaining functions will be discussed in later chapters.

4

Getting Help with Office

Although you'll find many answers to your questions in this book, sometimes you need additional information. Microsoft supplies you with several types of assistance. In this chapter, you'll learn how to:

- Work with the Office Assistant
- Use the Help menu
- Get help on the Web

Using the Office Assistant

When you opened an Office 2000 application for the first time, what you probably noticed first was that cute little paper clip trying to get your attention. That's Clippit the Office Assistant, Office 2000's Help feature.

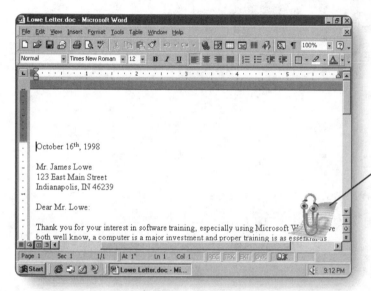

Asking the Assistant for Help

What sets Office Assistant apart from other help features is that you can use simple, everyday language to ask for help.

1. Click anywhere on the Office Assistant. A balloon will appear asking, "What would you like to do?" with an insertion point flashing in the white text box.

TIP

Pressing F1 also brings up the Assistant query window.

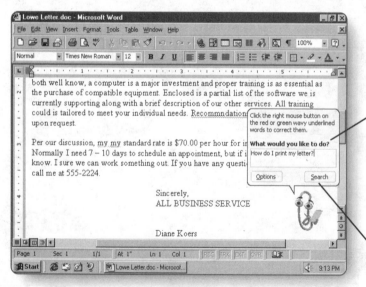

2. Type a **question** or just a word or two of what you need assistance with. An example might be: "How do I print my letter?" The text will appear in the white text box.

3. Click on **Search**. A new window will appear with more choices related to your topic.

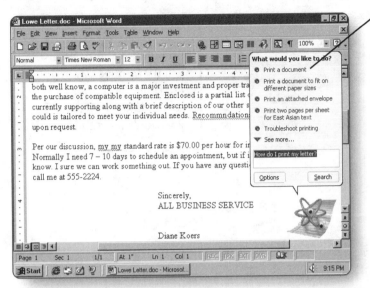

4. Click on a **topic**. The help information window will appear on your screen.

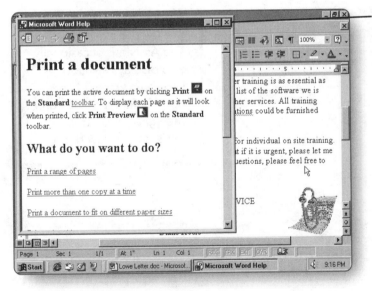

5. Click on the help **close box** when you are finished reading the help topic. The help window will close and the original window will return to full size.

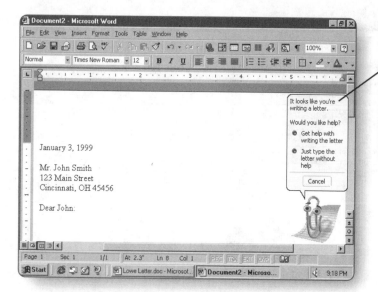

NOTE

Sometimes the Assistant will try to guess what you are doing and offer assistance. Click on Cancel if you don't want the help.

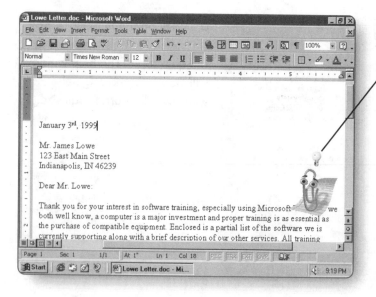

NOTE

The Assistant occasionally also displays a yellow light bulb when it has a tip on a feature. Click on the light bulb in the Assistant to view the tip.

Choosing a Different Assistant

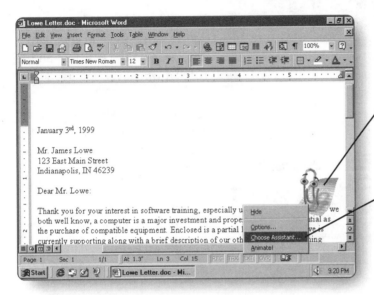

Is Clippit getting a little dull or just not your style? There is a way to select a different icon for Office Assistant.

1. Right-click while the pointer is positioned on top of the Assistant. A shortcut menu will appear.

2. Click on **Choose Assistant**. The Office Assistant dialog box will appear with the Gallery tab displayed.

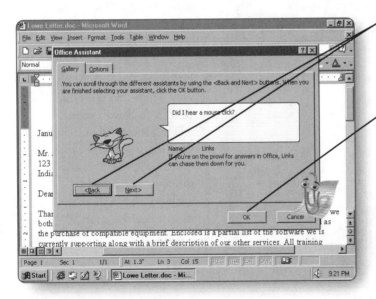

3. Click on **Back** or **Next** to view other Assistants. A picture and description of the available assistants will appear.

4. Click on **OK** when you see the one you want. The Office Assistant dialog box will close and you'll have a new helper!

NOTE

Depending upon the options selected when Office was installed, you may be prompted to insert your Office CD.

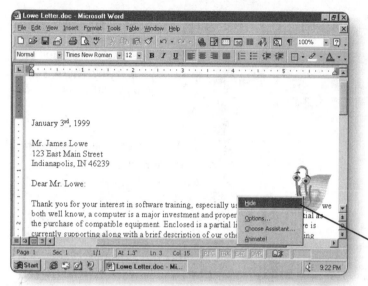

Hiding the Assistant

The Office Assistant is cute, but sometimes it's just in your way. You can hide the assistant and recall it whenever you need it.

1. Right-click while the pointer is positioned on top of the Assistant. A shortcut menu will appear.

2. Click on **Hide**. The Office Assistant will disappear.

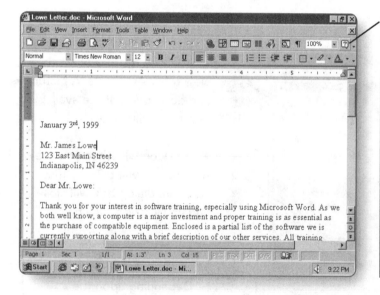

3. Click on the **Help button**. The Assistant will reappear.

NOTE

If the Assistant is in the way when you are typing text in your document, it will automatically move as your insertion point gets close to it. You can also move it manually by clicking on it and dragging it to a new location.

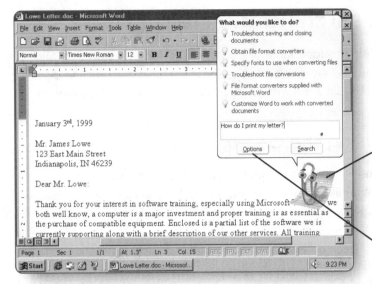

Turning Off the Assistant

If you find that you don't use the Assistant and don't want to see it, you can turn it off.

1. Click anywhere on the Office Assistant. The "What would you like to do?" balloon will appear.

2. Click on **Options**. The Office Assistant dialog box will open.

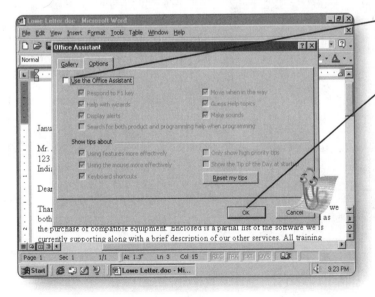

3. Click on **Use the Office Assistant**. The check mark from the box will be removed.

4. Click on **OK**. The Office Assistant will be turned off until you manually choose to use it again.

TIP

Click on Help and choose Use Office Assistant to return the Assistant to an active status.

Searching the Help File

Help includes Table of Contents and Index features to help you find an answer. To use these features, turn off the display of the Office Assistant as explained in the previous section.

Using the Contents Tab

The Help Contents feature presents Help information in a folder-like format, making it easy for you to browse available topics.

1. Click on **Help**. The Help menu will appear.

2. Click on **Microsoft Word Help**. The Microsoft Word Help window will open. If you're working in Excel or another Office application, the menu will list the Help for that application.

3. Click on the **Contents tab.** The Contents tab will come to the front.

4. Double-click on a **general topic.** The topic folder will open.

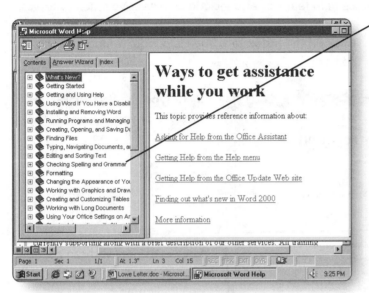

> ### NOTE
>
> A *general topic* has specific topics and is signified by a red book, whereas a *specific topic* is indicated by a yellow paper with a question mark on it. Some general topics may have other general topics listed under them.

5. Click on the **specific topic** that you want to view. The specific topic will be highlighted.

The information for that topic will be displayed in the Help window.

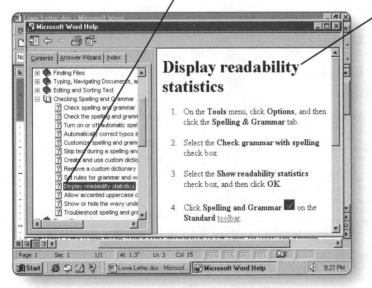

Using the Index Tab

Office help features also include an extensive index of topics.

1. Click on the **Index tab.** The Help Index window will come to the front.

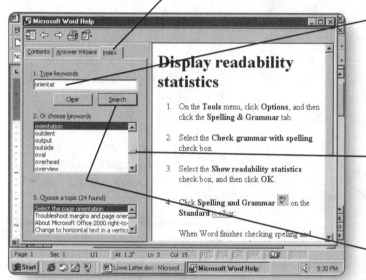

2a. Type the **first characters** or **word** of your keyword. The keywords will jump alphabetically to the word that you typed.

OR

2b. Scroll through the **list of keywords** until you can click on your keyword. The keyword will be highlighted.

3. Click on **Search**. A list of topics will appear under the keyword list.

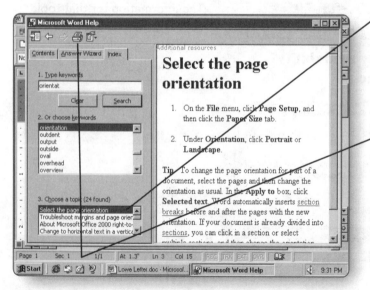

4. Click on a **topic**. The information will be displayed in the Help window.

TIP

Click on the Print button to print a displayed topic.

---

5. Click on the **Close button.** The Help window will close.

Using What's This?

There are so many items on an Office application screen, it's hard to remember what each item is or does. Use the What's this? feature to identify the various buttons and components.

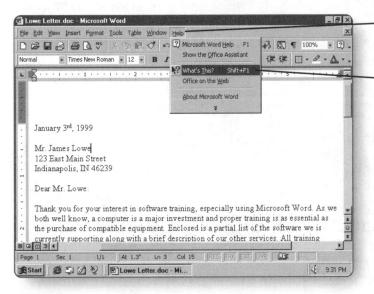

1. Click on **Help**. The Help menu will appear.

2. Click on **What's This?** The mouse pointer will change to a pointer with a question mark.

TIP

Pressing Shift+F1 is another way to access the What's This? feature.

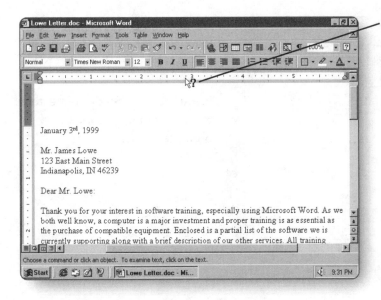

3. Position the **pointer** over any button or item on the screen. The mouse pointer will continue to display the question mark pointer.

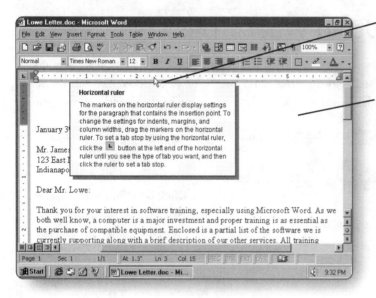

4. **Click** the **mouse**. A detailed information screen will appear and explain the item's function.

5. **Click anywhere** on the document window. The What's This box will close.

Getting Help on the Web

If you have access to the Internet, Microsoft includes some wonderful assistance from its Web site.

1. **Click** on **Help**. The Help menu will appear.

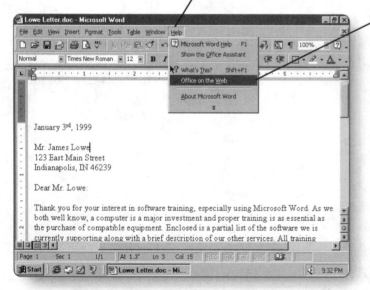

2. **Click** on **Office on the Web**. Your Web browser program will launch.

If you are not already connected to the Internet, you will be prompted to do so.

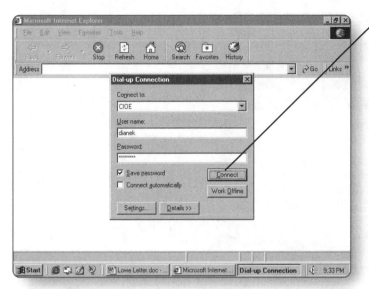

3. Click on **Connect**. Your Internet connection will be established and the Microsoft Office home page will be displayed.

NOTE

Web pages change frequently. The Web page that you see may not be the same one displayed in this book.

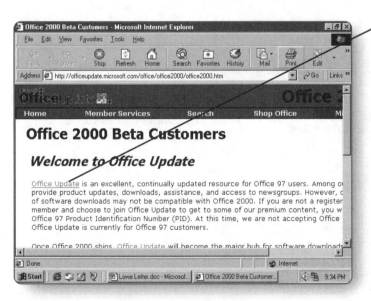

4. Follow the **instructions** on the screen to access various help topics.

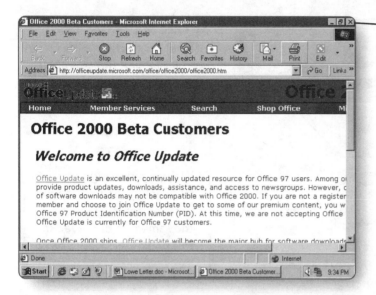

5. Click on the **Close button**. The Internet Explorer window will close.

When you have completed accessing the Web help, you'll want to close Internet Explorer.

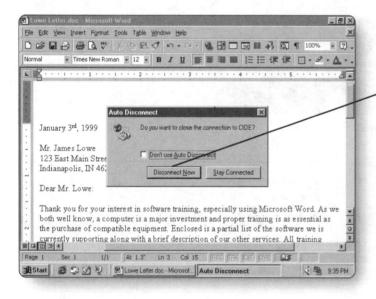

You may be prompted to disconnect from your Internet Service Provider (ISP).

6. Click on **Disconnect Now**. The connection to the ISP will close.

Part I Review Questions

1. How do you start an Office 2000 program? *See "Starting a Program" in Chapter 1*

2. Why should you follow proper procedures to exit an Office 2000 program? *See "Exiting a Program" in Chapter 1*

3. What are personalized menus? *See "Discovering Personalized Menus" in Chapter 2*

4. How do you display a shortcut menu? *See "Using Shortcut Menus" in Chapter 2*

5. What must you do to access a drop-down list in a dialog box? *See "Working with Dialog Boxes" in Chapter 2*

6. What must you specify when saving a document? *See "Saving a Document the First Time" in Chapter 3*

7. What happens when you try to close a document with changes that have not been saved? *See "Closing a Document" in Chapter 3*

8. Name three toolbar buttons that are common to the Office applications. *See "Using the Standard Toolbar" in Chapter 3.*

9. What is the Office Assistant? *See "Using the Office Assistant" in Chapter 4*

10. What happens to the mouse pointer when you click on What's This? from the Help menu? *See "Using What's This?" in Chapter 4*

PART II

Using Word

5

Learning Word Basics

When you first start any Office program, including Word, you need to learn how to enter and manipulate information. If you don't have Word open on your screen, follow the steps in Chapter 1, "Welcome to Office 2000," to open Word. In this chapter, you'll learn how to:

- Type, delete, and select text
- Insert special characters
- Use Undo and Redo
- Move around in a document
- Create a bulleted list and a numbered list

Typing Text

Notice that there is a flashing vertical bar on your screen. This is called the *insertion point*. It marks the location where text will appear when you type.

If you type a few lines of text, you'll notice that you don't need to press the Enter key at the end of each line. The program automatically moves down or wraps to the next line for you. This feature is called *word wrap*. You only press the Enter key to start a new paragraph.

1. Type some **text**. The text will display on the screen.

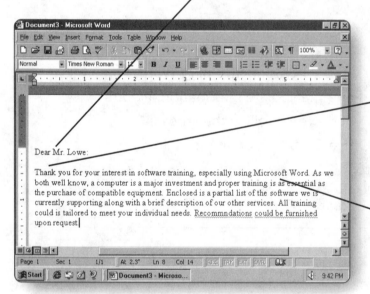

2. Press the **Enter key**. The insertion point will move down to the next line.

3. Press the **Enter key** again. The insertion point will move down another line, creating a blank line between your paragraphs.

4. Type a **paragraph** of text. Don't press Enter; just keep typing until you have several lines of text. Word's text wrap feature will take care of moving the insertion point down to the next line when necessary.

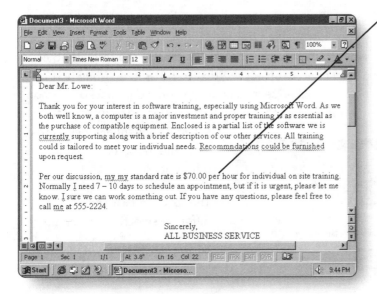

5. Continue typing text until your document is complete. The text you type will display on the screen.

Inserting, Selecting, and Deleting Text

Editing text with Word is a breeze. Need extra words? Just type them in. Need to delete words? Just highlight them and press the Delete key.

Inserting Text

Word begins in *insert* mode. This means that when you want to add new text to a document, simply place the insertion point where you want the new text to be and start typing.

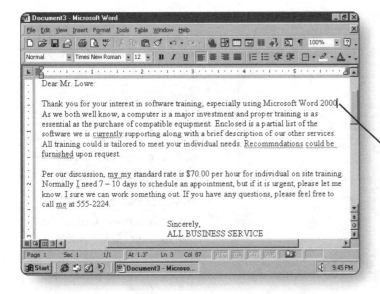

1. Click the **mouse pointer** directly in front of the word in the body of the document where you want new text to appear. The blinking insertion point will appear.

2. Type any **new word** or **phrase**, adding a space before or after as necessary. The new text is inserted into the document. Word will push the existing text to the right and keeps moving it over or down to make room for the new text.

Selecting Text

In order to move, copy, delete, or change the formatting of text, you need to select the text to be edited. When text is selected, it will appear as light type on a dark background on your screen—just the reverse of unselected text. You can only select a sequential block of text at a time, not bits of text in different places.

The following list shows different selection techniques:

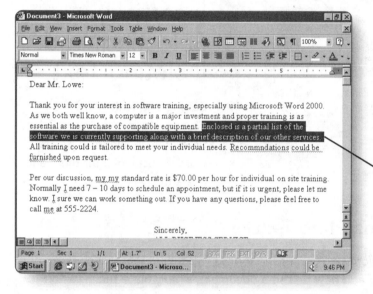

- To select one word, double-click on the word.

- To select a sentence, hold down the Ctrl key and click anywhere on the sentence.

- To select an entire paragraph, click three times (triple-click) anywhere in the paragraph.

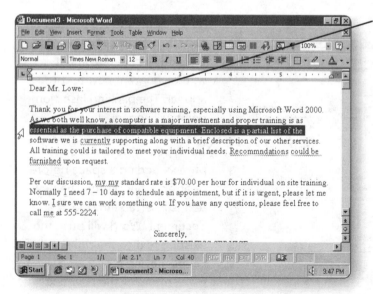

- To select a single line of text, click once in the left margin with the mouse arrow next to the line to be selected.

- To select a block of text, click at the beginning of the text, hold the mouse button down, and drag across the balance of the text to be selected.

- To select the entire document, press Ctrl+A or choose Edit, Select All.

TIP

To deselect text, click anywhere in the document where the text is not highlighted.

Deleting Text

You can delete unwanted text one character, one word, one paragraph at a time; or any combination of the above. Two common keys used to delete text are the Backspace and the Delete key. Pressing the Backspace key will delete one character at a time to the left of the insertion point, whereas pressing the Delete key will delete one character at a time to the right of the insertion point.

TIP

An easy way to remember which direction the Backspace key will delete is to look at the arrow printed on the Backspace key (most keyboards). The arrow points to the left, indicating this is the direction the characters will be deleted.

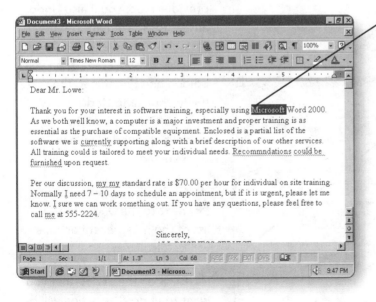

1. Select the **text** to be deleted. The text will be highlighted.

2. Press the **Delete key**. The text will be deleted.

Using Undo and Redo

If you want to restore text that you deleted, or reverse an action recently taken, use the Undo feature of Word. You're one click away from reversing your previous action.

1. **Click** on the **Undo button**. The last action taken will be reversed.

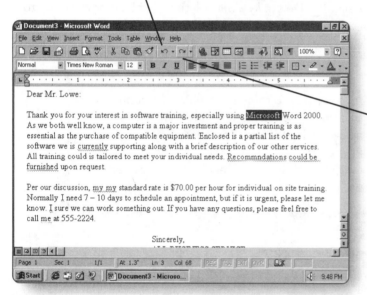

If you chose to undo an action and then decided that you liked it better the way you had it, choose the Redo feature.

2. **Click** on the **Redo button**. The Undo action will be reversed.

Word keeps track of several steps that you have recently taken. When you Undo a previous step, you'll also Undo any actions taken after that step. For example, you changed the case of some text, then you bolded and underlined the text. If you choose to Undo the Change Case action, the bolding and underlining will also be reversed.

3. **Click** on the **down arrow** (▼) next to the Undo button. A list of the most recent actions will be displayed.

4. **Click** on the **action** that you want to undo. The action will be reversed as well as all actions above it on the list.

Inserting Special Characters or Symbols

Word includes hundreds of special characters and symbols for you to include in your document. Symbols include things like copyright or trademark symbols, stars, check marks or airplanes.

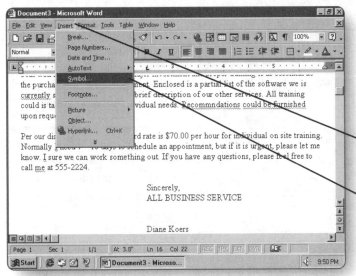

1. **Click** the **mouse** where you want the special character to appear. The blinking insertion point will appear.

2. **Click** on **Insert**. The Insert menu will appear.

3. **Click** on **Symbol**. The Symbol dialog box will open.

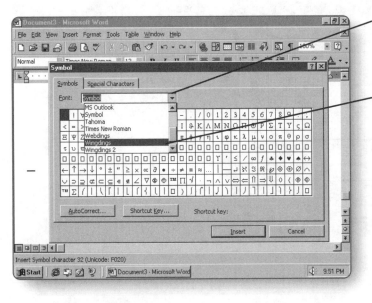

4. **Click** on the **down arrow** (▼) next to the Font: list box. A list of fonts will appear.

5. **Click** on a **font**. The symbols available for that font will display.

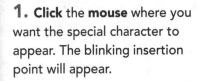

TIP

For a large variety of unusual characters, look at the Monotype Sorts or the Wingdings fonts.

6. Click on a **character**. A magnified version of the symbol will appear.

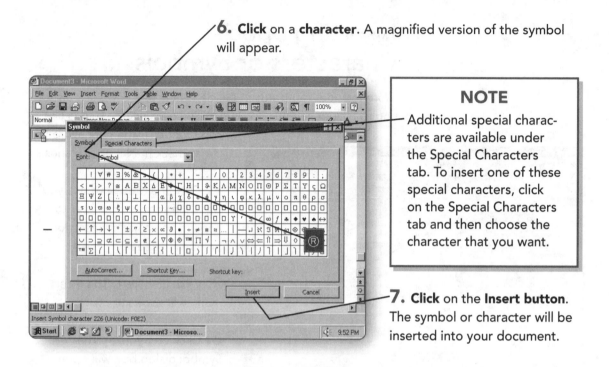

NOTE

Additional special characters are available under the Special Characters tab. To insert one of these special characters, click on the Special Characters tab and then choose the character that you want.

7. Click on the **Insert button**. The symbol or character will be inserted into your document.

8. Click on the **Close button**. The Symbol dialog box will close.

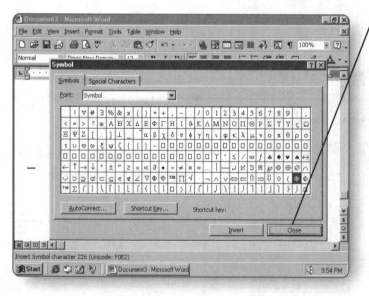

Moving Around in a Document

In order to work with your document, you'll need to place the insertion point. There are two methods to move around the Word screen: using the keyboard or the mouse. With Word 2000, there is a new feature called Click and Type.

Using Click and Type

If you prefer using the mouse rather than the keyboard to move around the screen, you can position the insertion point with the mouse and double-click where you would like to enter text.

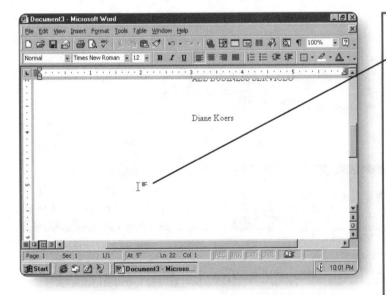

TIP

Before double-clicking the mouse, pay close attention to the position of the lines surrounding the pointer. If the lines are to the right of the I-beam, the text you type will be flow to the right of the insertion point. If the lines are to the left, the text will flow to the left of the insertion point. If the lines are under the I-beam, the text will be centered at the insertion point.

1. Double-click the **mouse pointer** anywhere on the white text area of the screen. A blinking insertion point will appear.

2. Type text. The text will appear where you clicked the insertion point.

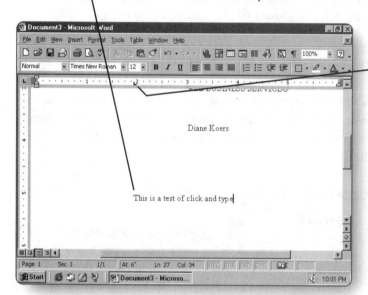

NOTE

Word is actually placing a tab stop at the position of the double-click. Tabs are covered later in this chapter.

3. Double-click the **mouse pointer** at a different location in the white text area. The insertion point will move to that location.

Using the Scroll Bars

Two scroll bars are in the document window—a vertical scroll bar and a horizontal scroll bar. Displaying text by using the scroll bars does not, however, move the insertion point. You'll need to click the mouse wherever you'd like the insertion point to be located.

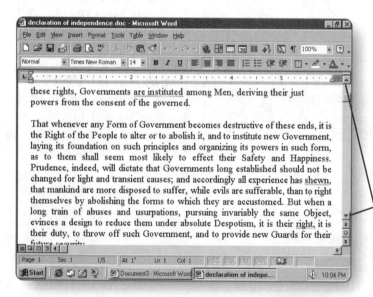

1a. Click on the **arrow** at either end of the vertical scroll bar. This will move the document up or down in the window.

OR

1b. **Click** on the **arrow** at either end of the horizontal scroll bar. This will move the document left or right.

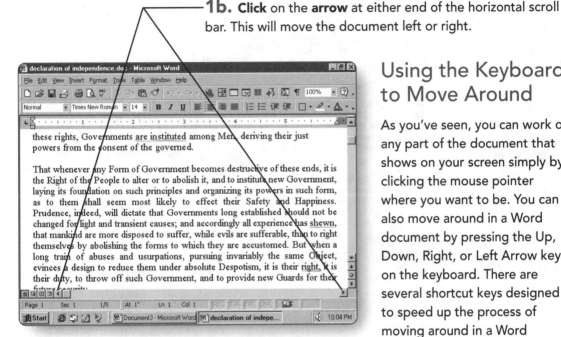

Using the Keyboard to Move Around

As you've seen, you can work on any part of the document that shows on your screen simply by clicking the mouse pointer where you want to be. You can also move around in a Word document by pressing the Up, Down, Right, or Left Arrow keys on the keyboard. There are several shortcut keys designed to speed up the process of moving around in a Word document. The following table illustrates these shortcut keys.

To Move	Do This
A word at a time	Press Ctrl+Right Arrow or Ctrl+Left Arrow
A paragraph at a time	Press Ctrl+Up Arrow or Ctrl+Down Arrow
A full screen up at a time	Press the PageUp key
A full screen down at a time	Press the PageDown key
To the beginning of a line	Press the Home key
To the end of a line	Press the End key
To the top of the document	Press Ctrl+Home
To the bottom of the document	Press Ctrl+End
To a specified page number	Press Ctrl+G, then enter the page number

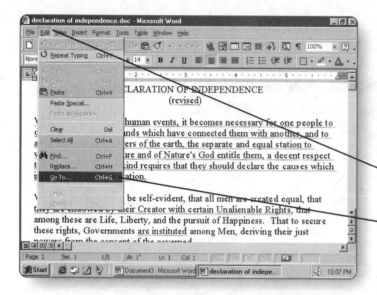

Using the Go To Command

If you have a rather lengthy document, use the Go To command to jump to a specific location in the document.

1. **Click** on **Edit**. The Edit menu will appear.

2. **Click** on **Go To**. The Go To page of the Find and Replace dialog box will appear.

TIP

Press Ctrl+G to quickly display the Go To page of the Find and Replace dialog box.

NOTE

The Go To command is one of those commands that may not display immediately upon choosing the Edit menu. Hold the mouse over the Edit menu for a few seconds to display the full Edit menu.

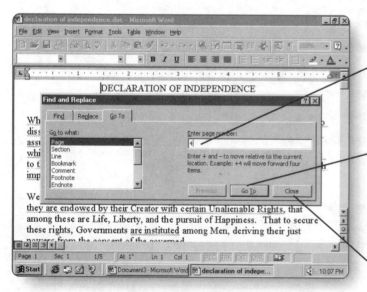

3. **Type** the **page number** you'd like to display. The number will appear in the Enter Page Number: text box.

4. **Click** on the **Go To button**. The specified page will be displayed. The insertion point will be located at the beginning of the specified page.

5. **Click** on the **Close button**. The Go To dialog box will close.

6

Formatting a Word Document

Word includes several features to assist you in making your text look just the way you want it. You can change fonts and sizes, align text on a page or even create bulleted or numbered lists. In this chapter, you'll learn how to:

- Change fonts, font sizes, and font appearances
- Arrange text on a page
- Move and copy text and formatting
- Create a bulleted list and a numbered list

Enhancing Text

Enhancing text is the process of changing its appearance. For example, you can change fonts or point sizes or add embellishments, such as boldface, italic, or underline.

Changing the Font

The *font* is the typeface of the text. Windows comes with a variety of fonts, and Office adds some additional fonts. Other programs installed on your computer might also install fonts.

1. **Select** some **text** in the document. The text will be highlighted.

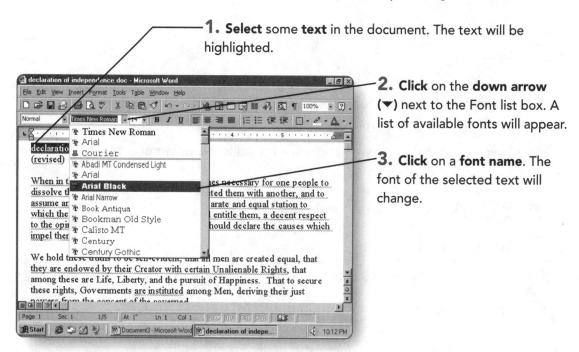

2. **Click** on the **down arrow** (▼) next to the Font list box. A list of available fonts will appear.

3. **Click** on a **font name**. The font of the selected text will change.

Changing the Font Size

The *font size* controls how large the font appears. Each font can be used in a number of different sizes. Font sizes are measured in *points*, and a point is actually ½ of an inch.

1. **Select** some **text** in the document. The text will be highlighted.

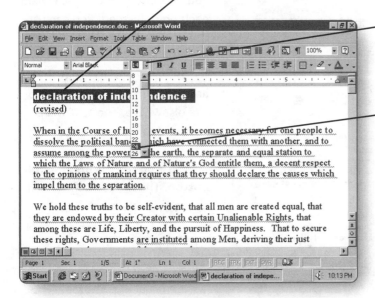

2. **Click** on the **down arrow** (▼) next to the Font Size list box. A list of available font sizes will appear.

3. **Click** on a **font size**. The size of the selected text will change.

Applying Bold, Italic, or Underline

Applying formatting attributes like **bold**, *italic* or <u>underline</u> will call attention to particular parts of your text. You can easily access these choices with the Word toolbar.

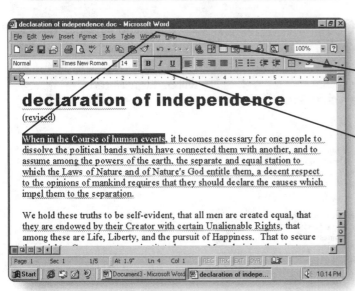

1. **Select** the **text** to be formatted. The text will be highlighted.

2. **Click** on the appropriate **toolbar button**: either **B** for bold, *I* for italic, or <u>U</u> for underline, or any combination of the three. The formatting will be applied. You can repeat the above steps to remove the attribute.

Copying Formatting to Another Selection

If you spend several minutes setting up just the right formatting for a heading that will appear multiple times in a long document, you don't want to have to try to remember your selections and repeat them each time. Instead, you can use the Format Painter tool.

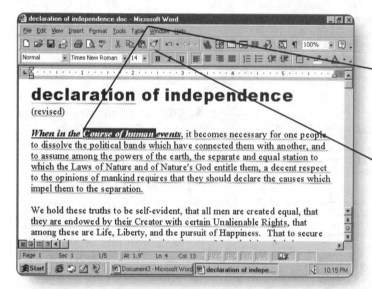

1. Select any of the **text** that has the formatting you want to use elsewhere. The text will be highlighted.

2. Click on the **Format Painter button**. The mouse pointer will change to a paintbrush.

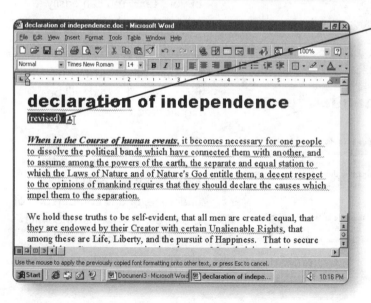

3. Press and **hold** the **mouse button** and **drag** over the text to be formatted. The new text will be highlighted.

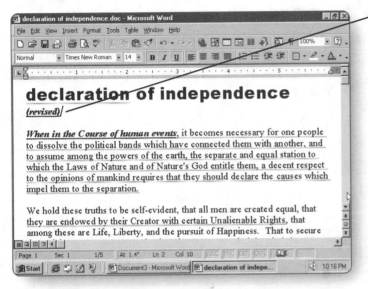

4. Release the **mouse button**. The new text will have the attributes of the original text.

TIP

To keep the Format Painter function on for repeated use, click twice on the Format Painter button. When finished using the Format Painter function, click on the button again to turn it off.

Changing Text Case

When you need to change the capitalization case of text, Word provides an easy way to change it without retyping.

1. Select the **text** to be changed. The text will be highlighted.

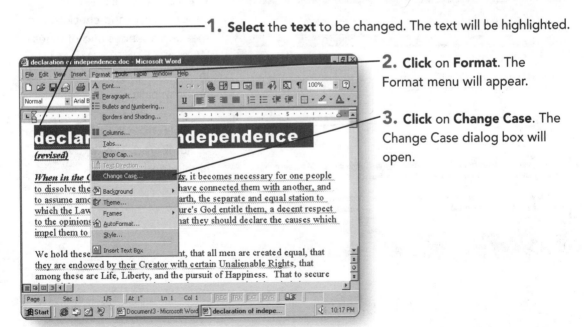

2. Click on **Format**. The Format menu will appear.

3. Click on **Change Case**. The Change Case dialog box will open.

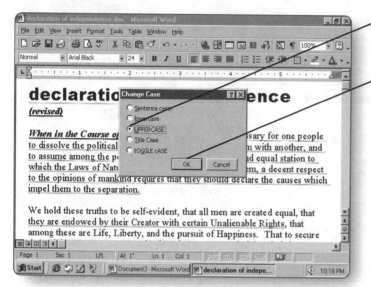

4. Click on a **case option**. The option will be selected.

5. Click on **OK**. The text will be modified.

Working with Bulleted or Numbered Lists

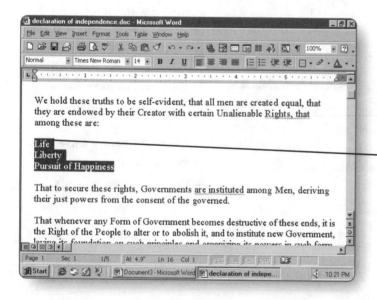

Everyone uses lists—from shopping lists and checklists to meeting agendas and outlines. Word can help you format lists in your documents automatically.

1. Select the **list** to be bulleted or numbered. The text will be highlighted.

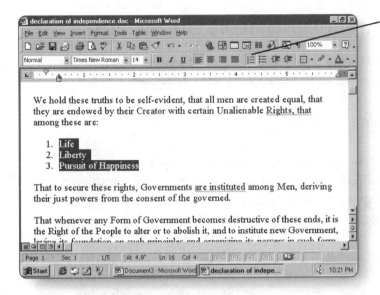

2a. **Click** on the **Numbering button** on the toolbar. Numbers will be applied to the list.

OR

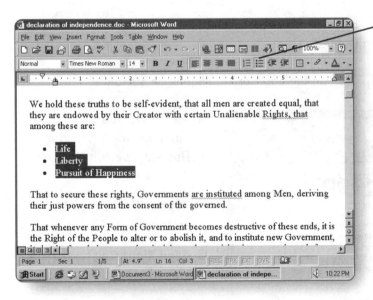

2b. **Click** on the **Bullets button** on the toolbar. Bullets will be applied to the lists.

TIP

Repeat the above steps to remove the bullets or numbering.

Arranging Text on a Page

Arranging text includes indenting text and modifying line spacing, as well as aligning text horizontally.

Aligning Text

Alignment arranges the text to line up at one or both margins, or centers it across the page. Like line spacing, alignment is usually applied to an entire paragraph or document.

You can align paragraphs of text to the left, right, or center. You can also *justify* your text, which means that the text will be evenly spaced across the page from the left edge to the right edge.

1. **Select** the **text** that you want to align. The text will be highlighted.

2. **Click** on the appropriate **alignment button**:

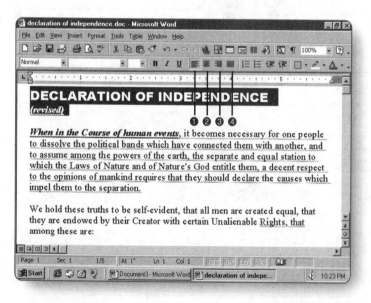

❶ **Align Left**. The text will be aligned at the left margin. This is the default choice in Word.

❷ **Center**. The text will be centered.

❸ **Align Right**. The text will be aligned at the right margin.

❹ **Justify**. The text will be evenly spaced across the page.

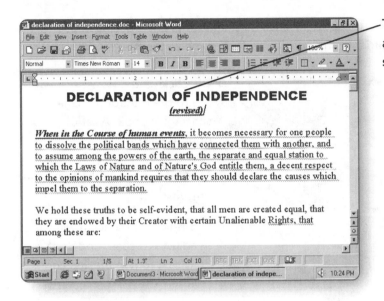

The selected text will realign according to the option you selected.

Changing Line Spacing

Line spacing is the amount of vertical space between each line of text. You might want to change line spacing when you want to make a document easier to read, for example, or for a draft so that the reader has room to make changes.

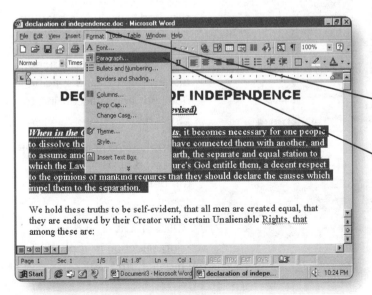

1. Select the **text** in which you want to change the line spacing. The text will be highlighted.

2. Click on **Format**. The Format menu will appear.

3. Click on **Paragraph**. The Paragraph dialog box will open.

4. If necessary, **click** on the **Indents and Spacing tab**. The Indents and Spacing tab will come to the front.

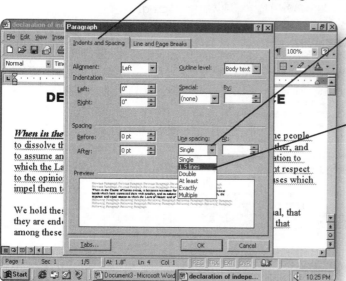

5. **Click** on the **down arrow** (▼) to the right of the Line spacing: list box. A list of options will display.

6. **Click** on one of the following **options**:

- **Single**. Line spacing will adjust to accommodate the largest font in the line and a little extra.

- **1.5 lines**. Line spacing will be set 1½ times that of single spacing.

- **Double**. Line spacing will be twice that of single spacing.

- **At Least**. Line spacing adjusts to the minimum required to include a graphic or large letter in a line.

- **Exactly**: All lines are a fixed distance apart. Line spacing does not adjust according to font size.

- **Multiple**: Line spacing will be increased or decreased by the percentage that you specify.

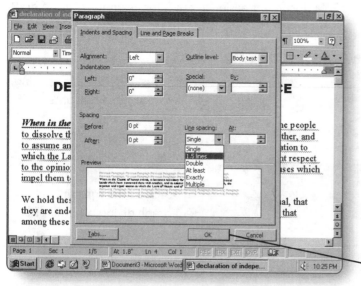

7. **Click** on **OK**. The new spacing selection is applied to the highlighted text.

TIP

Shortcut keys to set line spacing are Ctrl+1 for single spacing, Ctrl+2 for double spacing and Ctrl+5 for 1.5 line spacing.

Indenting Text

To draw the reader's attention to certain text, you sometimes want to indent that text so it doesn't line up with the left margin. Word includes a toolbar button to help you quickly indent your text.

1. Select the **text** to be indented. The text will be highlighted.

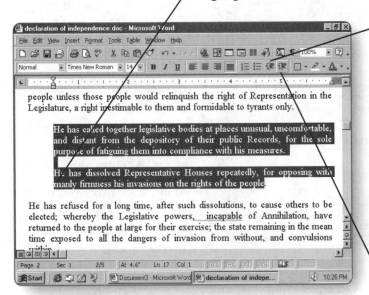

2. Click on the **Increase Indent button**. The selected text will move ½ inch from the left margin.

TIP

Each time you click on the increase indent button, the text will indent an additional ½ inch.

3. Click on the **Decrease Indent button**. The selected text will move ½ inch closer to the left margin.

Working with Tabs

If you press the Tab key to move across the page, you'll notice that Word has default stops set every ½ inch.

Setting Tabs

You can set tabs at particular points along the ruler so that when you press the Tab key, the cursor moves to that point automatically, instead of stopping every five spaces.

1. Click the **mouse pointer** on the Tab button at the left end of the ruler to select from the following alignments:

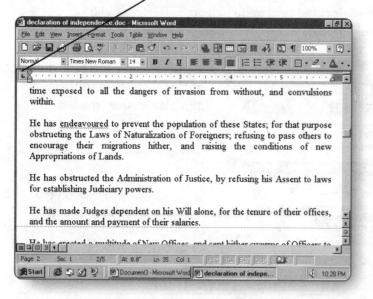

- **Left**. The Tab button is already set to the left tab symbol, an "L." Text will appear with the left edge of the text at the tab.

- **Center**. Click one time to display the center tab symbol. An upside down "T" will appear. Text will center around a center tab.

- **Right**. Click two times to display the right tab symbol. A backward "L" will appear. Text will appear with the right edge of the text at the tab.

- **Decimal**. Click three times to display the decimal tab symbol. An upside-down "T" with a dot on the right will appear. Decimal points, such as dollars and cents, align to the tab. The decimal tab is selected in this example.

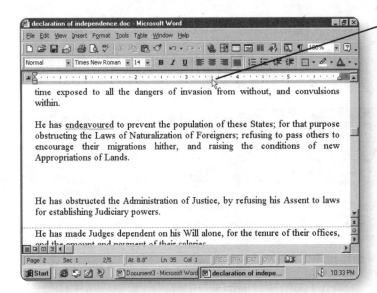

2. **Click** on the **ruler** to set the tab for the current paragraph or any currently selected text. A left, right, center, or decimal tab symbol will appear in the ruler at the spot you selected.

3. **Click** in the **paragraph** and **press** the **Tab key**. This moves the insertion point to the tab where you want the text to appear.

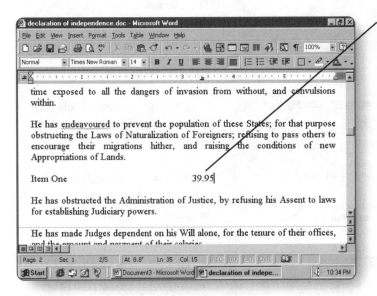

4. **Type** some **text**. The text will conform to the chosen tab. This example shows the decimal tab alignment.

Moving Tabs

If you don't like the position where you placed the tab stop, you can easily move it!

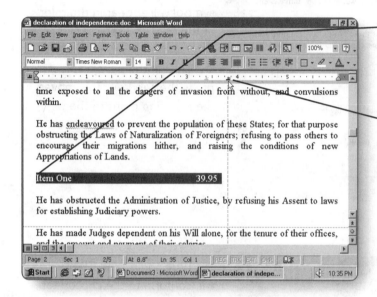

1. **Select** the **paragraphs** that have a tab that needs to be moved. The text will be highlighted.

2. **Drag** the **current tab setting** to the new desired location on the ruler bar. A vertical dotted line indicates the new tab position.

3. **Release** the **mouse button**. The tab will be reset and any text will be moved.

Deleting Tabs

Deleting an unwanted tab stop is an easy process when using Word's ruler.

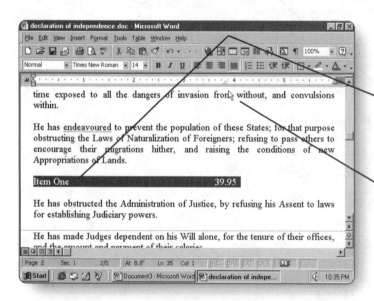

1. **Select** the **paragraphs** that have a tab that needs to be deleted. The text will be highlighted.

2. **Drag** the **current tab setting** off the ruler, into the body of the document. A vertical dotted line will appear.

3. **Release** the **mouse button**. The tab will be deleted.

Moving or Copying Text

Windows includes a feature called the *Clipboard*, which lets you hold information temporarily. Microsoft Word, as well as the other Office applications, uses the Clipboard feature very effectively to move or copy text from one place to another.

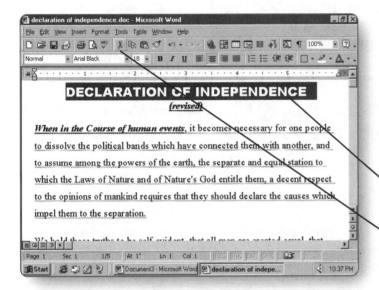

Moving Text

The feature used to move text from one place to another is called *cut and paste*. With cut and paste, the original text is deleted and placed in the new location.

1. Select the **text** to be moved. The text will be highlighted.

2. Click the **Cut button**. The text will be removed from the document, and will be stored on the Windows Clipboard.

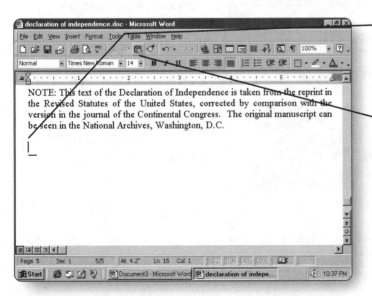

3. Click the **mouse** where you want the text to be located. The blinking insertion point will appear.

4. Click the **Paste button**. The text will be placed at the new location.

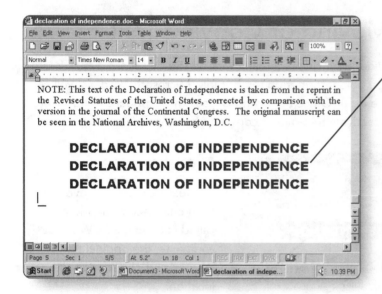

NOTE

Text or objects placed on the Windows Clipboard remain on the Clipboard even after it's been pasted into a new location. You can paste the same text again and again. It will remain on the Clipboard until other text or objects are placed on the Clipboard, or until the computer is restarted.

Copying Text

The process of copying text will leave the original text in its original location while a copy of it is placed on the Windows Clipboard.

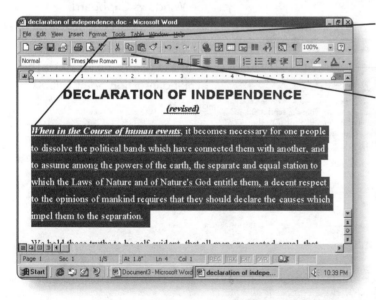

1. **Select** the **text** to be copied. The text will be highlighted.

2. **Click** the **Copy button**. The text will be stored on the Windows Clipboard. It doesn't appear that anything happened, but it did.

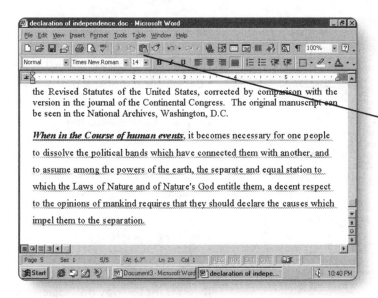

3. Click the **mouse** where you want the text to be located. The blinking insertion point will appear.

4. Click on the **Paste button**. The text will be placed at the new location.

Using Drag-and-Drop

Another method of moving text from one location to another is to use the Drag-and-Drop method. The Drag-and-Drop method works best for a small amount of text to be moved a short distance.

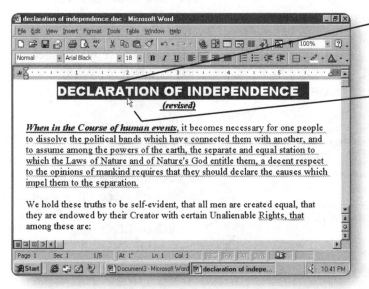

1. Select the **text** to be moved. The text will be highlighted.

2. Position the **mouse pointer** on top of the highlighted text. The white mouse arrow will point to the left.

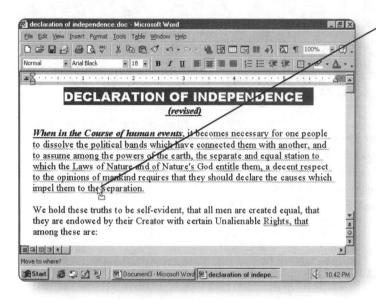

3. Hold down the **mouse button** and **drag** the **mouse** to the desired location. A small box will appear at the bottom of the mouse arrowhead and a gray line will indicate the position of the text.

4. Release the **mouse button**. The text will be moved.

Using Collect and Paste

If you want to copy nonadjacent items from one or more documents and place them together on the Clipboard, Word has a new feature called *Collect and Paste* to help you do this quickly and easily. To use the Collect and Paste feature, each item is appended to the Clipboard contents, and then inserted as a group in a new location or document. To use the Collect and Paste feature, you'll need to display the Clipboard toolbar.

TIP

To copy text with drag-and-drop, hold down the Ctrl key before dragging the selected text. Release the mouse button before releasing the Ctrl key.

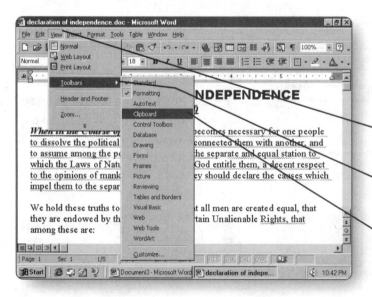

1. Click on **View**. The View menu will appear.

2. Click on **Toolbars**. The Toolbars submenu will appear.

3. Click on **Clipboard**. The Clipboard toolbar will display.

4. Select the **first block of text** to be copied to the Clipboard. The text will be highlighted.

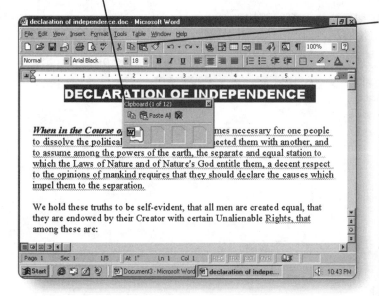

5. Click on the **Copy button**. The selection will be copied to the Clipboard.

6. Repeat steps 1 and 2 for each additional item you want to copy to the Clipboard. Each item will appear on the Clipboard toolbar.

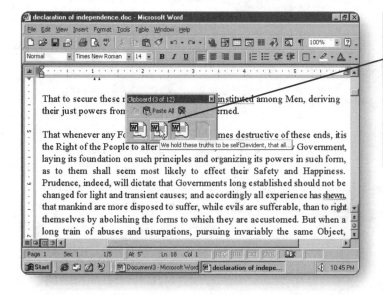

7. **Click** on the **mouse** where you want to insert the Clipboard contents. The blinking insertion point will appear.

8. **Click** on the **Paste All button**. The contents of the Clipboard will be placed in the document.

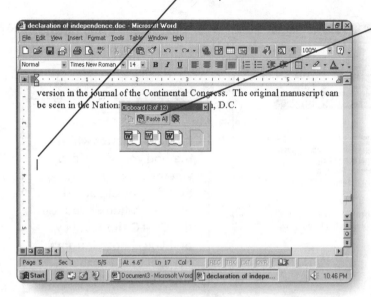

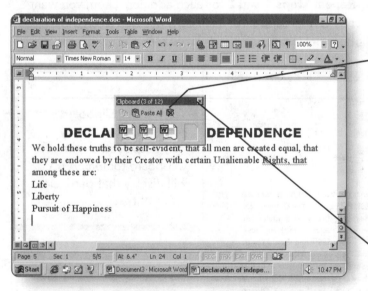

If you are finished with the collect and paste feature, you may find it helpful to put the Clipboard toolbar away.

9. **Click** on the **Close Button**. The Clipboard toolbar will disappear.

7

Improving Your Writing

Whatever you're writing, spelling or grammatical errors can ruin the impression that you're trying to create. Word has spelling and grammar checkers correct these errors and several other tools to improve your writing. In this chapter, you'll learn how to:

- Use AutoCorrect and AutoFormat
- Find and replace text
- Find and correct spelling and grammatical errors
- Use the Thesaurus

Working with AutoCorrect

AutoCorrect is a great feature. If you type something wrong, Word automatically corrects it. Or, if you type "(c)" and Word interprets it as a copyright symbol, it will insert ©.

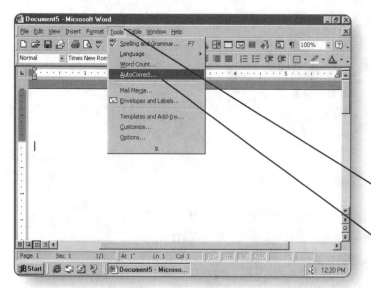

Adding AutoCorrect Entries

If you know that you commonly make the same typing mistake, such as "clcik" when it should be "click," you can instruct Word to fix it for you.

1. **Click** on **Tools**. The Tools menu will appear.

2. **Click** on **AutoCorrect**. The AutoCorrect dialog box will open with the AutoCorrect tab in front.

3. **Type** your **common mistake** in the Replace: text box. The text will display.

4. **Click** in the **With: text box**. A blinking insertion point will display.

5. **Type** the **correct version**. The text will display.

6. **Click** on **Add**. The word will be added to your permanent AutoCorrect list.

7. **Click** on **OK**. The dialog box will close.

Now, Word automatically corrects your mistake each time you type it.

Deleting AutoCorrect Entries

What if you're typing an article on common misspellings and you *want* to type the word "teh" or you want to use "(c)" to indicate a heading in a report, but Word keeps changing this to a copyright symbol?

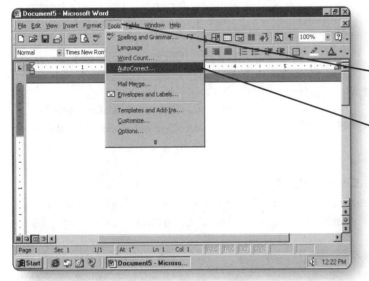

1. Click on **Tools**. The Tools menu will appear.

2. Click on **AutoCorrect**. The AutoCorrect dialog box will appear with the AutoCorrect tab in front.

3. Click on an **entry** from the AutoCorrect list. The entry will appear in the Replace: and With: text boxes.

4. Click on **Delete**. The entry will be deleted.

5. Click on **OK.** The AutoCorrect dialog box will close.

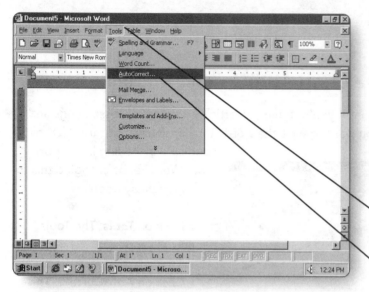

Exploring Auto-Format as You Type

Word can also format text as you are typing it. This can include automatically creating bulleted and numbered lists or replacing fractions with fraction characters.

1. Click on **Tools**. The Tools menu will appear.

2. Click on **AutoCorrect**. The AutoCorrect dialog box will open.

3. Click on the **AutoFormat As You Type tab.** The AutoFormat As You Type tab will come to the front. More automatic features will be available from this tab.

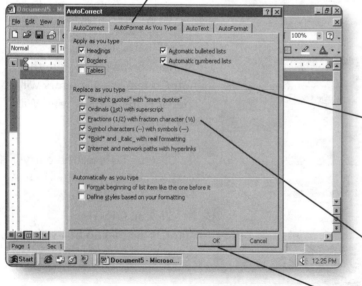

4. Click on any **option** that you want to apply. A selected option will have a check mark in the box next to it. You'll notice options such as the following:

- Word can generate automatic bulleted or numbered lists (refer to Chapter 6, "Formatting a Word Document," for more information on this feature).

- Word can apply "smart quotes," change 1st to 1st, make 1/2 into ½, and more!

5. Click on **OK**. The Auto-Correct dialog box will close.

Using Find and Replace

Find and Replace are real time savers. You can quickly find out if you covered a topic in a lengthy report, and you can change names, dates, and prices throughout documents with just a few keystrokes.

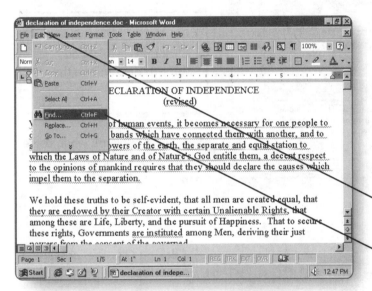

Using Find

Word's Find command is useful to seek out text in a document that you may have trouble visually locating. The Find command does not change any text, it simply locates and highlights it for you.

1. Click on **Edit**. The Edit menu will appear.

2. Click on **Find**. The Find and Replace dialog box will open.

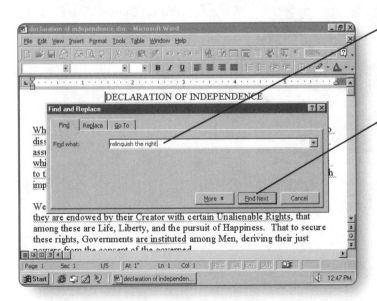

3. Type the **word** or **phrase** that you want to search for. The typed text will appear in the Find what: text box.

4. Click on **Find Next.** Word will take you to the first occurrence of the word or phrase that you're looking for.

The first occurrence of the word or phrase is highlighted.

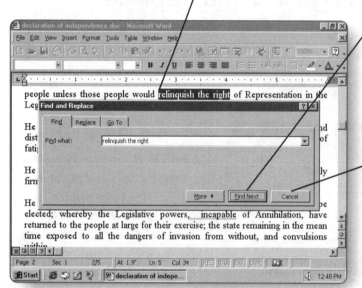

5. **Click** on **Find Next** again. Word will take you to the next occurrence of the word or phrase that you're looking for.

TIP

Click on Cancel if you want to discontinue the search.

Word will notify you when there are no more occurrences of the search text.

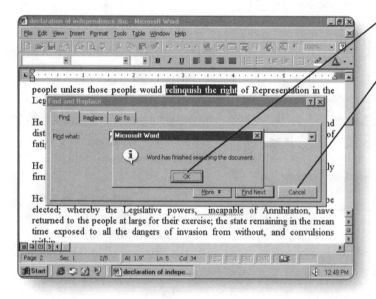

6. **Click** on **OK**. The message box will close.

7. **Click** on **Cancel**. The Find and Replace dialog box will close.

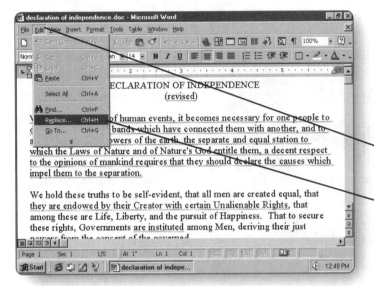

Using Replace

If you want to locate text and change it to something else, let Word do it for you with the Replace feature.

1. Click on **Edit**. The Edit menu will appear.

2. Click on **Replace**. The Find and Replace dialog box will open.

3. Type the **text** for the search. The text will appear in the Find what: text box.

4. Click in the **Replace with: text box**. The blinking insertion point will appear.

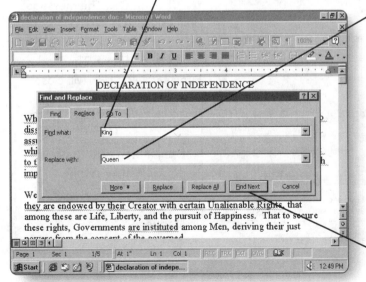

5. Type a **replacement word** or phrase. The text will appear in the Replace with: text box.

TIP

To delete the "found" text, leave the Replace with: box empty. You'll be replacing the found text with nothing.

6. Click on **Find Next**. Word will highlight the first match.

7. Choose one of the **following**:

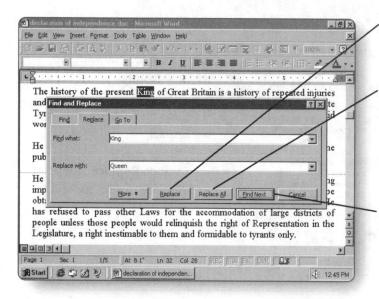

- **Replace.** The text will be replaced and Word will highlight the next text match.

- **Replace All.** All occurrences of the found text will be replaced with the replace text and you will be notified of the total number of replacements.

- **Find Next.** Word will not make any changes to this occurrence and will jump to the next occurrence of the text.

Word will notify you when there are no more occurrences of the search text.

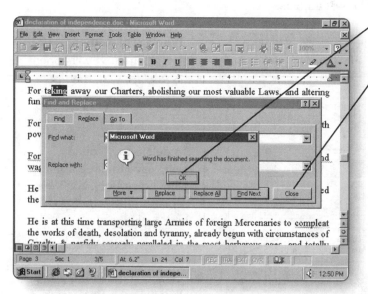

8. Click on **OK**. The message box will close.

9. Click on **Close**. The Find and Replace dialog box will close.

TIP

Use caution with Replace All. Note that in this example, "taking" would be replaced with "taqueen."

Correcting Spelling and Grammatical Errors

Word has built-in dictionaries and grammatical-rule sets to check your document. Word can identify possible problems as you type, and it also can run a special spelling and grammar check to provide you with more information about the problems and tools for fixing them. These features aren't infallible—if you type "air" instead of "err," Word probably won't catch it. However, combined with a good proofreading, these tools can be very helpful.

Checking Spelling as You Go

By default, Word identifies problems right in your document as you type. Spelling errors have a red wavy line underneath them, whereas grammatical errors are indicated with a green wavy line.

1. Right-click on an identified **word.** The shortcut menu will appear with suggested corrections.

2. Click on the **correct spelling** or **grammatical suggestion**. The erroneous word will be replaced with your selection.

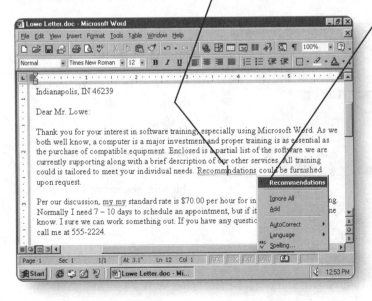

TIP

Do *not*, repeat *DO NOT*, rely on the spell check and grammar features to catch all errors. They are far from perfect and can miss many items. They can also flag errors when your text is really OK, and can suggest wrong things to do to fix both real problems and false error reports. You alone are the only one who knows what your document is intended to say. Proofread it yourself!

NOTE

Sometimes, Word cannot give a suggested grammatical suggestion. In those cases, you'll need to correct the error yourself.

Running a Spelling and Grammar Check

Word is set up to run both a spelling and grammar check at the same time.

1. Click on **Tools**. The Tools menu will appear.

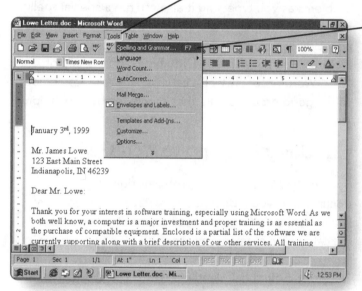

2. Click on **Spelling and Grammar**. The Spelling and Grammar dialog box will open.

The first error encountered, whether spelling or grammar, will be displayed. If the error is in spelling, it is identified in the Not in Dictionary: text box. In the Suggestions: text box, there are possible correct spellings for the word. In this case, the correct spelling is already highlighted.

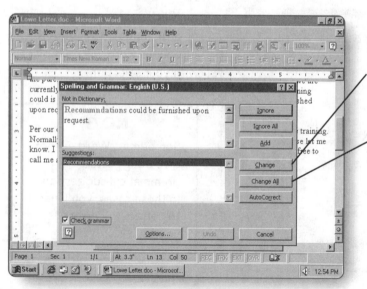

3. Click on **one** of the **following options**:

- **Change.** This will only change this incident of the spelling mistake.

- **Change All.** Use this if you think you could have made the mistake more than once.

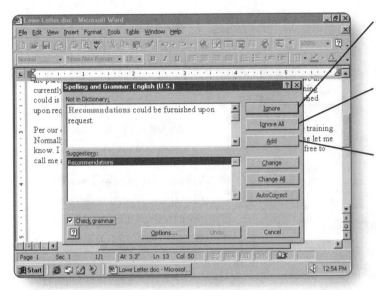

- **Ignore.** If you don't wish to correct this instance of the spelling, use this option.

- **Ignore All.** Click this option if you don't want to correct any instances of the spelling.

- **Add.** You can add a word, such as a proper name or legal term, to Word's built-in dictionary so that it won't be flagged as an error in the future.

After you choose one of these actions, the check will proceed to the next possible error.

If Word finds a grammatical error, it will display it in the top text box, with a suggested revision or explanation of the error in the Suggestions: text box.

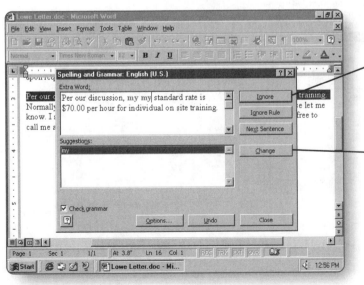

4. Click on **one** of the **following**:

- **Ignore.** If you don't wish to change this instance of the grammatical problem, use this option.

- **Change.** The suggested change will be made to this occurrence.

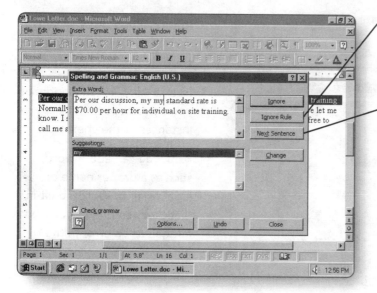

- **Ignore Rule.** Clicking this option will ignore all instances of the grammatical problem.

- **Next Sentence.** This option moves on to the next sentence.

When all mistakes have been identified, Word will notify you that the spelling and grammar check is complete.

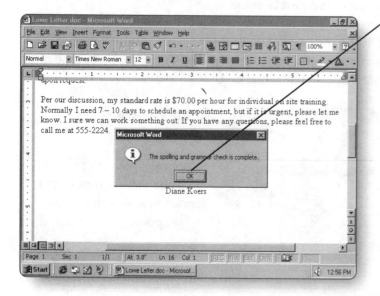

5. Click on **OK**. The message box will close.

Finding That Elusive Word with the Thesaurus

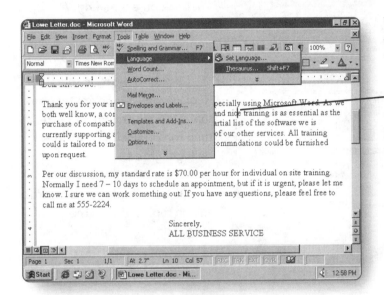

When you just can't remember the word you need, the Thesaurus is invaluable.

1. **Click** in the **word** that you want to replace. The word will be highlighted.

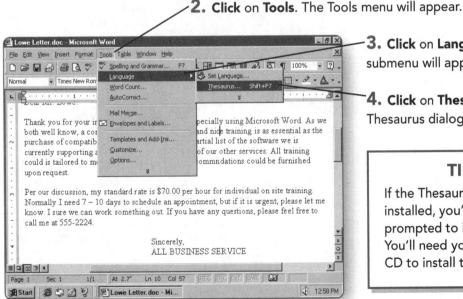

2. **Click** on **Tools**. The Tools menu will appear.

3. **Click** on **Language**. A submenu will appear.

4. **Click** on **Thesaurus**. The Thesaurus dialog box will open.

TIP

If the Thesaurus is not installed, you'll be prompted to install it. You'll need your Word CD to install the feature.

Many words have multiple meanings. Word frequently lists many of the possible meanings of your word.

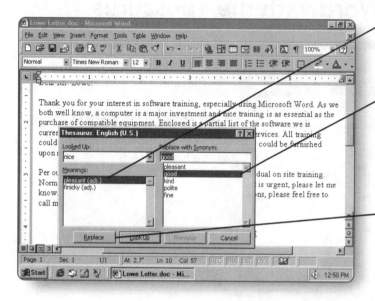

5. **Click** on a **meaning**. A selection of synonyms will appear on the right.

6. **Click** on a **word** in the Replace with Synonym: text box that fits your document better than the original. The word will be highlighted.

7. **Click** on **Replace**. The word will be replaced with the suggestion.

8

Working with Longer Documents

Much of the time that you spend word processing is spent making documents look a certain way. When working with longer documents, you'll find some of the Word features to be wonderful time-savers for you. In this chapter, you'll learn how to:

- Set document margins
- Set paper size and orientation
- Manage page breaks
- Work with headers and footers
- Display non-printing characters

Setting Page Options

Options that you can modify include the margins, the orientation (direction) the paper prints, and the size of the paper.

Changing Margins

Margins are the amount of space between the edges of the paper and where the text actually begins to appear. Word allows you to set margins for any of the four sides of the document and also allows you to mix and match margins for different pages.

The default margins are 1" on the top and bottom and 1.25" for the left and right margins.

1. **Click** on **File**. The File menu will appear.

2. **Click** on **Page Setup**. The Page Setup dialog box will open.

3. If necessary, **click** on the **Margins tab**. The Margins tab will be displayed.

4. Click on the **up or down arrows** (◆) to the right of the Top:, Bottom:, Left: and Right: list boxes to increase or decrease the top, bottom, left, or right margin settings.

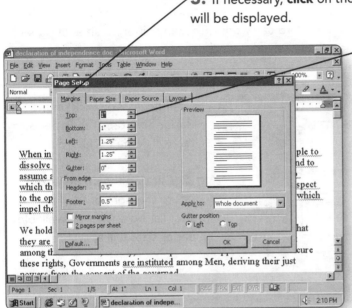

Setting Paper Orientation

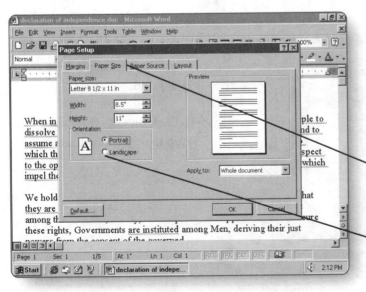

Use the Page Setup dialog box to change your document to Landscape, which will print along the long edge of the paper. The default setting is Portrait, which will print along the short edge of the paper.

1. Click on the **Paper Size tab**. The Paper Size tab will come to the front.

2. Click on **Landscape**. The option will be selected.

Selecting a Paper Size

Although Word can work with many different sizes of paper, the available selections will depend on the type of printer you use.

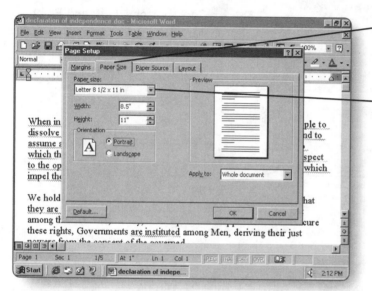

1. If necessary, **click** on the **Paper Size tab**. The Paper Size tab will come to the front.

2. Click on the **down arrow** (▼) to the right of the Paper size: list box. A list of available paper sizes will appear.

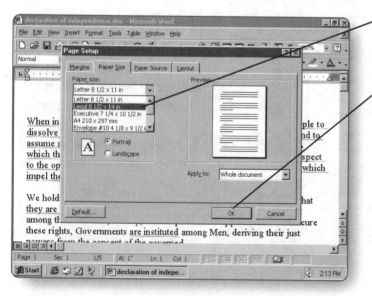

3. Click on a **paper size**. The selected paper size will be highlighted.

4. Click on **OK**. The Page Setup dialog box will close.

Inserting a Page Break Manually

Word automatically inserts a page break when text fills the page. If you want the page break to be in a different place, you can override the automatic page break by creating your own.

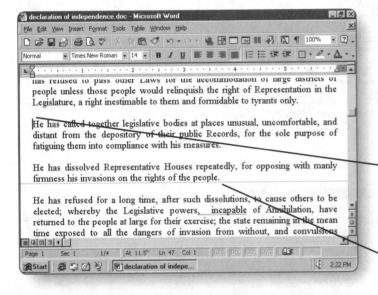

Inserting a Page Break

You can break the page at a shorter position than Word may have chosen, but you cannot make a page longer.

1. Click the **mouse** in front of the text where you want the new page to begin. The blinking insertion point will appear.

Notice the normal page break location Word would be applying.

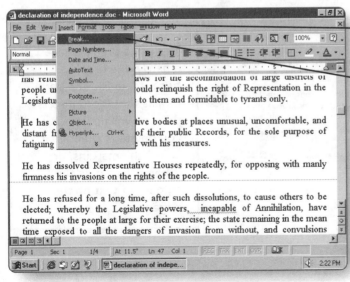

2. Click on **Insert**. The Insert menu will appear.

3. Click on **Break**. The Break dialog box will open.

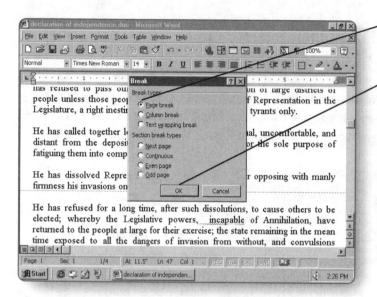

4. **Click** on **Page break**. The option will be selected.

5. **Click** on **OK**. The page break will be inserted.

TIP

A faster way to insert a page break is to follow step 1 and then press Ctrl+Enter.

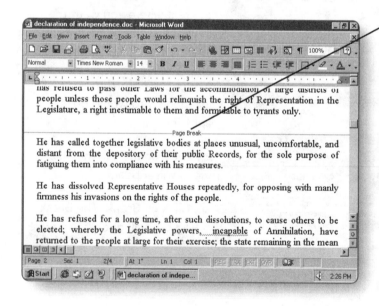

Depending on the document view you are using, you may see the words "Page Break" along with a dotted line where the new page begins.

NOTE

This page break is called a *hard page break* because, unlike the page breaks that Word inserts, this one will not move if you delete text above it, adjust the margins, or otherwise change the amount of text on the page.

Deleting a Page Break

Word's automatic page breaks cannot be deleted, but the hard page breaks that you have inserted manually can be deleted at any time.

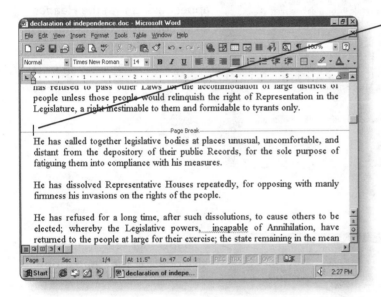

1. **Click** the **mouse pointer** on the page break indication. The blinking insertion point will appear.

2. **Press** the **Delete key**. The page break will be deleted.

Working with Headers and Footers

Headers and footers are features used for placing information at the top or bottom of every page of a document. You can place any information in headers and footers: the author of the document, the date of last revision, or a company logo. It's a good idea to add headers and footers with dates and page numbers.

Creating a Header or Footer

As you'd expect, a header prints at the top of every page, and a footer prints at the bottom.

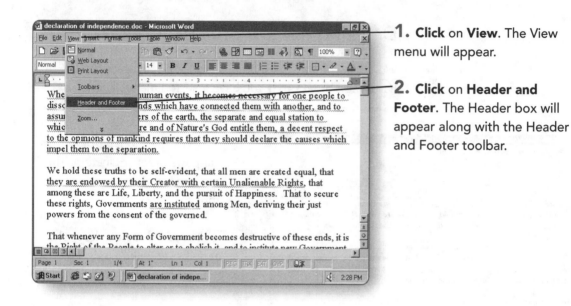

1. Click on **View**. The View menu will appear.

2. Click on **Header and Footer**. The Header box will appear along with the Header and Footer toolbar.

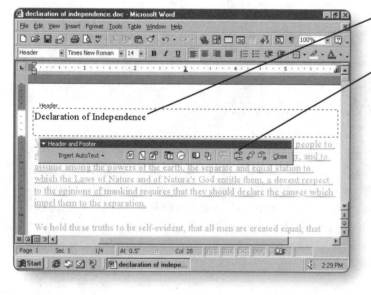

3. Type your **text**. Your text will appear in the Header box.

4. Click on the **Switch Between Header and Footer button.** The Footer box will appear.

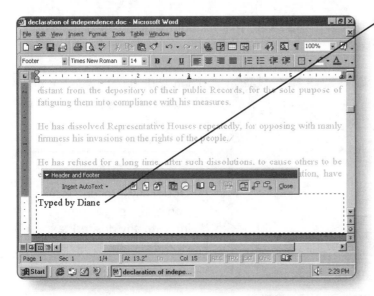

5. **Type** your **text**. The text will appear in the Footer text.

Adding Date, Time, or Page Numbering

When either the header or footer box is open, you can add a field for the date and/or time. Word inserts the current date and time in that field based on the computer's clock and calendar settings when you print the document.

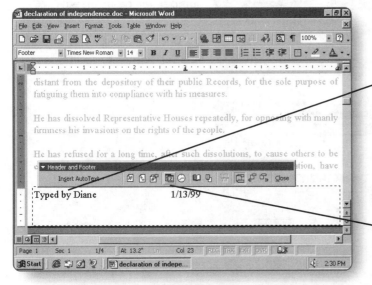

The Insert Page Number feature places the correct page number on each page.

1. **Type** some **text**. The text will appear along the left margin.

2. **Press** the **Tab key**. The insertion point will jump to the center of the page.

3. **Click** on the **Insert Date button**. The current date will be inserted.

4. Press the **Tab key**. This will right align the next text you insert.

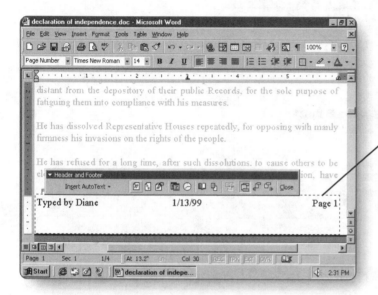

When adding page numbering Word uses a code, so don't type in a number.

TIP

Optionally, precede insertion of the page numbering with any desired text such as "Page."

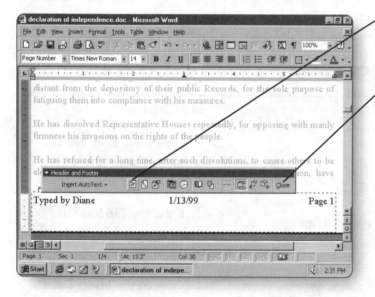

5. Click on the **Insert Page Number button**. The page number will be inserted.

6. Click on **Close**. The Header/Footer bar will close.

Displaying Non-Printing Characters

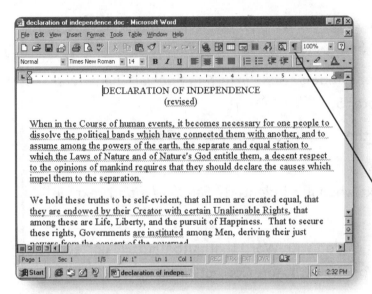

To assist you in editing a document, Word can display some hidden symbols it used to indicate spaces, tabs, and hard returns created when you press the Enter key. These symbols do not print, but can be displayed on your screen.

1. Click on the **Show/Hide ¶ button**. The hidden characters will be displayed.

Spaces are indicated with a dot.

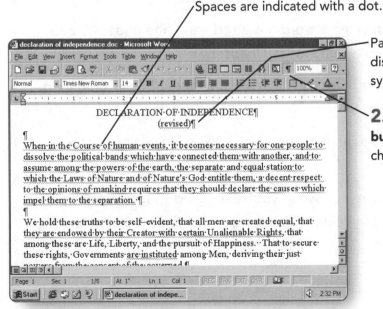

Paragraph hard returns are displayed with the paragraph symbol ¶.

2. Click on the **Show/Hide ¶ button**. The displayed special characters will be hidden.

Part II Review Questions

1. What must you do to text in order to move, copy, delete or change the formatting of it? *See "Selecting Text" in Chapter 5*

2. What are examples of symbols? *See "Inserting Special Characters or Symbols" in Chapter 5*

3. How do you change the font of your text? *See "Changing the Font" in Chapter 6*

4. What happens to text when it is indented? *See "Indenting Text" in Chapter 6*

5. What is the feature included with Word that automatically corrects your typing? *See "Working with AutoCorrect" in Chapter 7*

6. What feature does Word provide that locates text and changes it to different text? *See "Using Replace" in Chapter 7*

7. What does it mean when a word has a red wavy line under it? *See "Checking Spelling As You Go" in Chapter 7*

8. What are the default margins in a Word document? *See "Changing Margins" in Chapter 8*

9. How do you create a manual page break? *See "Inserting a Page Break" in Chapter 8*

10. How can Word inform you when you've entered spaces, tabs, or pressed the Enter key? *See "Displaying Non-Printing Characters" in Chapter 8*

PART III

Using Excel

9

Creating a Simple Spreadsheet

Office has a full-featured spreadsheet program called Excel that you can use to make calculations, create charts, and even sort data! In this chapter, you'll learn how to:

- Create a new spreadsheet
- Explore and move around in the spreadsheet screen
- Enter and edit labels and values
- Undo Mistakes

Exploring the Spreadsheet Screen

In Chapter 1, "Welcome to Office 2000," you learned several ways to launch an Office application. You can use any of those methods to open Excel.

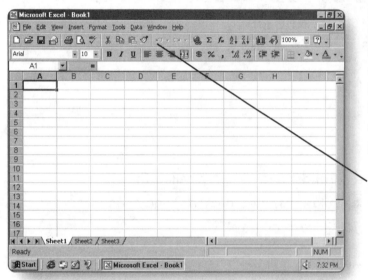

Many items that you see when you open a new spreadsheet are standard to most Windows 95 or Windows 98 programs. However, the following list illustrates a few elements that are specific to a spreadsheet program. These include:

● **Toolbar.** Toolbars with a series of commonly-used Excel features. You can customize the toolbar.

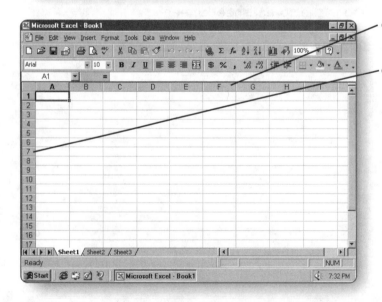

● **Column Headings.** Each spreadsheet has 256 columns.

● **Row Headings.** Each spreadsheet has 65,536 rows.

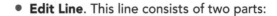

- **Edit Line**. This line consists of two parts:
  - **Selection Indicator**. This area shows the address or name of the current selection.
  - **Contents box**. This area displays the entry you are typing or editing, or the contents of the current cell.

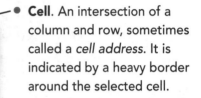

- **Cell**. An intersection of a column and row, sometimes called a *cell address*. It is indicated by a heavy border around the selected cell.

- **Status Bar**. Gives you information about the current selection and what Excel is doing.

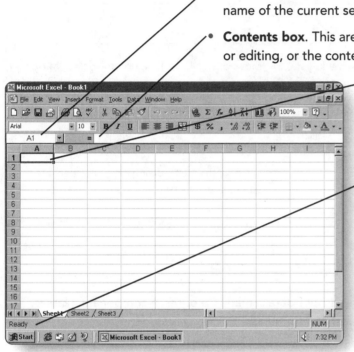

Moving Around the Spreadsheet Screen

You can use your mouse or keyboard to move around in a spreadsheet. Due to the large size of an Excel worksheet, you'll need ways to move around quickly.

1. Drag the **vertical scroll bar** until the row you are looking for is visible.

2. Drag the **horizontal scroll bar** until the column you are looking for is visible.

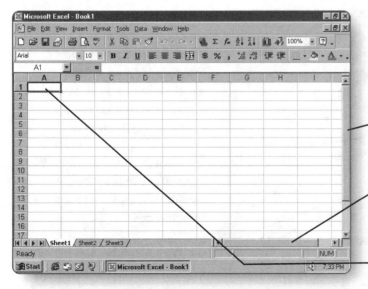

3. Click on the **desired cell**. It will become the current cell.

The following table describes keyboard methods for moving around in your spreadsheet:

Keystroke	Result
Arrow keys	Move one cell at a time up, down, left, or right
Page Down	Moves one screen down
Page Up	Moves one screen up
Home	Moves to column A of the current row
Ctrl+Home	Moves to cell A1
F5	Displays the GoTo dialog box, which enables you to specify a cell address

Entering Data

Spreadsheet data is made up of three components: labels, values, and formulas.

Entering Labels

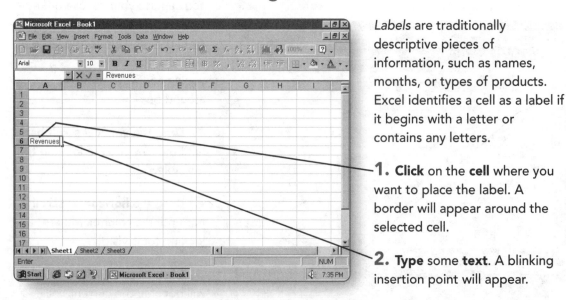

Labels are traditionally descriptive pieces of information, such as names, months, or types of products. Excel identifies a cell as a label if it begins with a letter or contains any letters.

1. Click on the **cell** where you want to place the label. A border will appear around the selected cell.

2. Type some **text**. A blinking insertion point will appear.

TIP

If you make a mistake and you have not yet pressed Enter, press the Backspace key to delete characters and type a correction, or press the Escape key to cancel the typing.

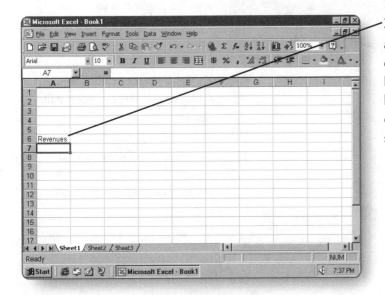

3. Press the **Enter key** to accept the label. The text will be entered and will align along the left edge of the cell. The cell below the one where you just entered data will then be selected.

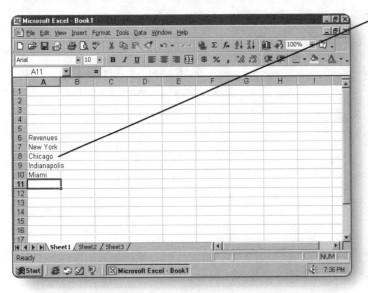

4. Repeat steps 1–3 for each label you want to enter.

NOTE

Optionally, you could press an arrow key instead of the Enter key. This will accept the cell you were typing in and move to the next cell in the direction of the arrow key.

Entering Values

Values are the raw numbers that you track in a spreadsheet. There is no need to enter commas or dollar signs. You'll let Excel do that for you later.

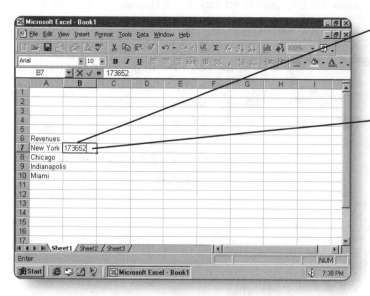

1. Click on the **cell** where you want to place the value. A border will appear around the selected cell.

2. Type the numerical **value**. A blinking insertion point will appear.

3. Press the **Enter key** to accept the value. The number will be entered into the cell.

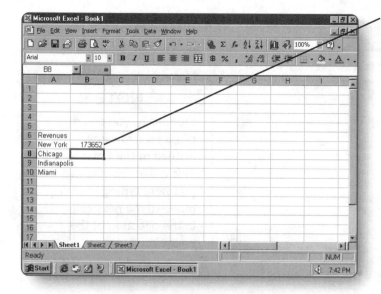

Notice how values are aligned along the right edge of the cell.

4. Repeat steps 1–3 for each value you want to enter.

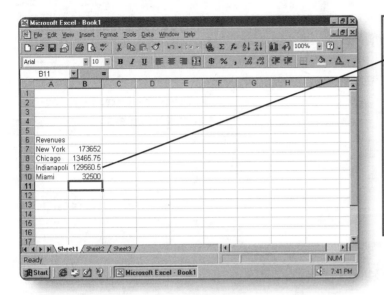

NOTE

If you entered a number such as 39.95, that is exactly what will be displayed in the cell; however, if you entered 39.50, the spreadsheet will display 39.5 (without the trailing zero). Don't worry, nothing is lost. You will change the appearance later.

TIP

To enter a value as a label, type an apostrophe (') character before the number, such as '1999. The apostrophe character tells Excel to treat the information as a label.

Editing Data

You can edit your data in a variety of ways. You may need to change the contents of a cell, or you may want to move the data to another part of the spreadsheet.

Replacing the Contents of a Cell

You can make changes to the contents of a cell in two ways. One is by typing over the contents of a cell.

1. Click on a **cell**. The cell and its contents will be selected.

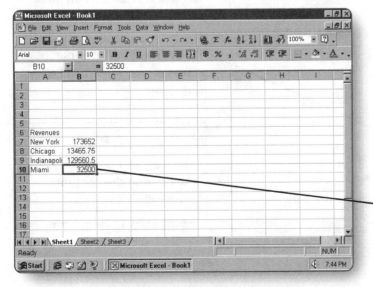

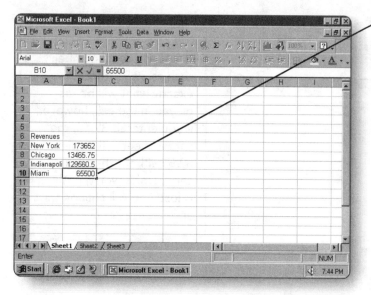

2. Type a new **label** or **value**. The new data will appear in the cell.

3. Press the **Enter key**. The text will be entered in the selected cell.

Editing the Contents of a Cell

The other method to make changes to the contents of a cell is by using the Edit feature.

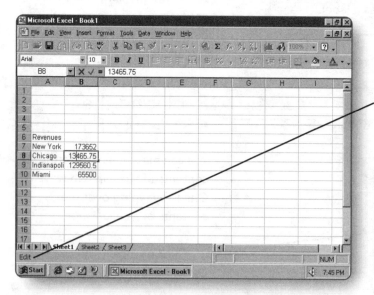

1. Double-click on the **cell** to be edited. The insertion point will blink within the cell.

Notice how the status bar indicates that you are in Edit mode.

TIP

You can also press the F2 key to edit the contents of a cell.

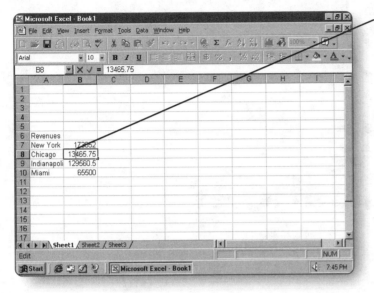

2. Press the **left arrow key**. The insertion point will be relocated within the current cell.

3. Type the **changes**. The changes will appear in the current cell.

4. Press the **Enter key**. The changes will be entered into the current cell.

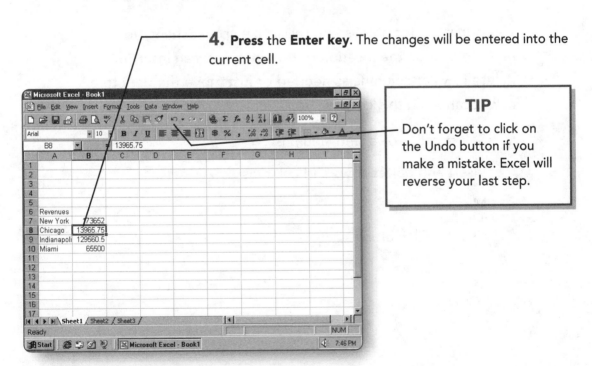

TIP

Don't forget to click on the Undo button if you make a mistake. Excel will reverse your last step.

10

Editing a Spreadsheet

Frequently after data is entered into a spreadsheet, you'll need to change the location of the data. You can insert or delete rows or columns as needed or just move the data to a new location. In this chapter, you'll learn how to:

- Select cells, rows, and columns
- Insert and delete rows and columns
- Move data
- Use the Fill feature

Learning Selection Techniques

To move, copy, delete, or change the formatting of data in the spreadsheet, first select the cells to be modified. When cells are selected, they appear darker on screen—just the reverse of unselected text. However, if a block of cells is selected, the first cell will not have the darker shading around it.

The following table describes some of the different selection techniques.

To Select	Do This
❶ A cell	Click on the desired cell.
❷ A row	Click on the row number on the left side of the screen.
❸ A column	Click on the column letter at the top of the screen.
❹ A sequential block of cells	Click on the first cell and drag to highlight the rest of the cells.
❺ A nonsequential block of cells	Click on the first cell, then hold down the Ctrl key and click on any additional cells.

TIP

Make sure the mouse pointer is a white cross before attempting to select cells.

TIP

To deselect a block of cells, click the mouse in any other cell.

Inserting Rows and Columns

Occasionally you need a column or a row to be inserted into the middle of information that you have already entered. Inserting a row or column moves existing data to make room for blank rows or columns.

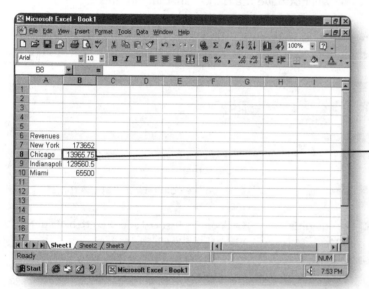

Inserting Columns

Insert a column anywhere you need it. Excel will move the existing columns to make room for the new one.

1. Click anywhere in the Column where you want to insert the new column. A cell in that column will be selected.

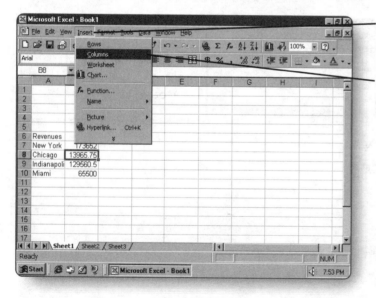

2. Click on **Insert.** The Insert menu will appear.

3. Click on **Columns.** A new column will be inserted.

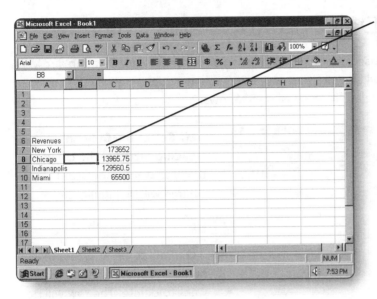

In this example, the information in the existing column B was moved to column C.

Inserting Rows

Insert a row anywhere you need it. Excel will move the existing rows down to make room for the new one.

1. Click in the Row below where you want to insert the new row. A cell in the row will be selected.

2. Click on **Insert.** The Insert menu will appear.

3. Click on **Rows.** A new row will be inserted.

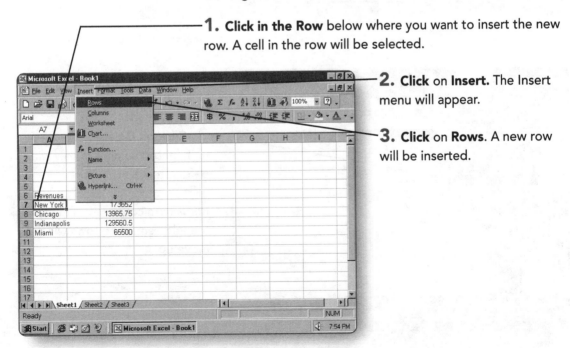

Deleting Rows and Columns

Use caution when deleting a row or column. Deleting a row will delete it across all 256 columns; deleting a column will delete it down all 65,536 rows.

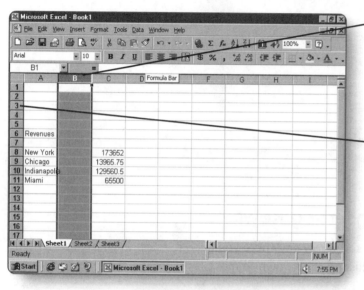

1a. Select the **Column Heading letter** of the column that you want to delete. The column will be highlighted.

OR

1b. Select the **Row Heading number** of the row that you want to delete. The row will be highlighted.

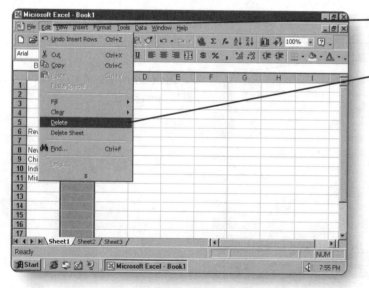

2. Click on **Edit**. The Edit menu will appear.

3. Click on **Delete**. The highlighted column or row will be deleted.

Remaining columns will move to the left; remaining rows will move up.

Moving Data Around

If you're not happy with the placement of data, you don't have to delete it and retype it. Excel makes it easy for you to move it around.

Copying and Pasting Cells

The Windows Clipboard is extremely helpful if you want to transfer information from one place to another. To copy information, Excel uses the Copy and Paste features.

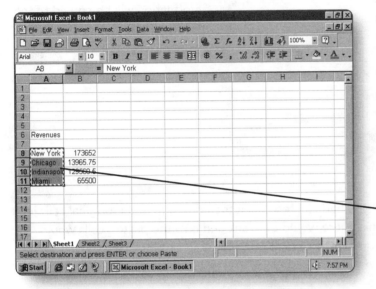

1. Select some **cells** to be duplicated. The cells will be highlighted.

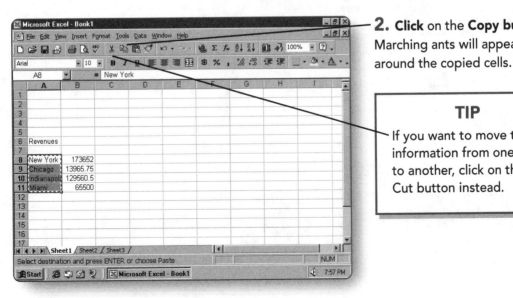

2. Click on the **Copy button**. Marching ants will appear around the copied cells.

TIP

If you want to move the information from one cell to another, click on the Cut button instead.

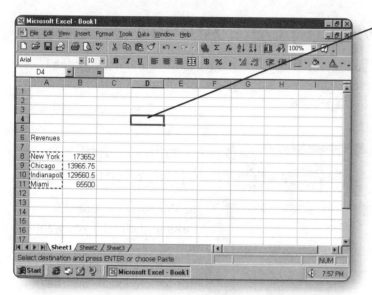

3. Click on the **beginning cell** where you want to place the duplicated information. The cell will be highlighted.

4. Press the **Enter key**. The information will be copied to the new location.

If you had elected to cut the information, the original cells in this figure would be blank and only the pasted cells would contain the data.

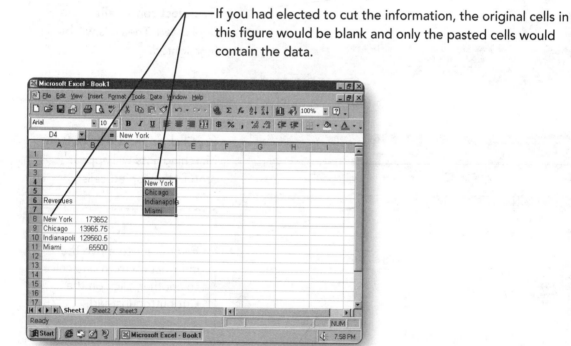

Using Drag-and-Drop to Move Cells

Another method that you can use to move information from one location to another is the drag-and-drop method.

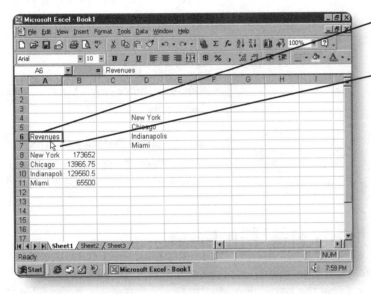

1. Select some **cells** to move. The cells will be highlighted.

2. Position the **mouse pointer** around one of the outside edges of the selection. The mouse pointer will become a small white arrow.

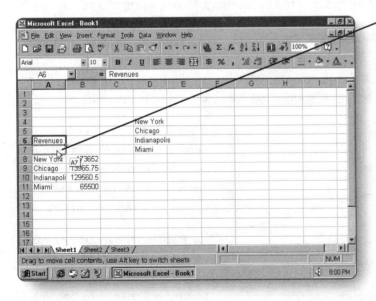

3. Keeping the mouse pointed around the outside edge, **press** and **hold** the **mouse button** and **drag** the **cells** to a new location. The second box represents where the moved cells will be located.

4. Release the **mouse button**. The cells will be moved.

Clearing Cell Contents

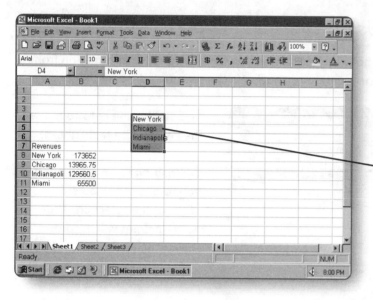

If you have data in cells that you no longer want, you can easily delete the data.

1. Select some **cells** to be cleared. The cells will be highlighted.

2. Press the **Delete key**. The contents of the cells will be removed.

Using the Fill Feature

Excel has a great built-in, time saving feature called *Fill*. If you give Excel the beginning Month, Day, or numbers, it can fill in the rest of the pattern for you. For example, if you type January, Excel fills in February, March, April, and so on.

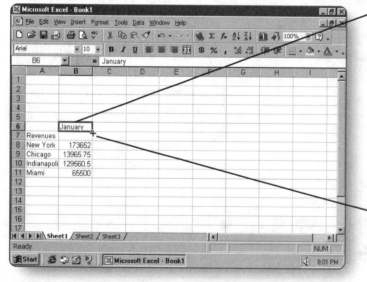

1. Type the **beginning Month, Day, or Number** in the beginning cell. The text will be displayed in the cell.

If you want Excel to fill in numbers, you must first give it a pattern. For example, enter the value of "1" in the first cell, then enter "2" in the second cell.

2. Position the **mouse pointer** on the lower-right corner of the beginning cell. The mouse pointer will change to become a small black cross.

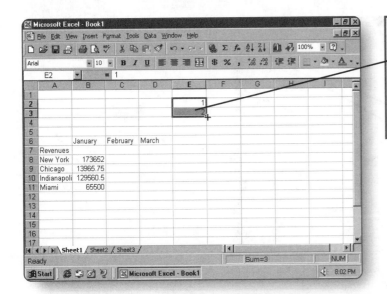

TIP

For numbers, select both the first and second cells before proceeding to step 3.

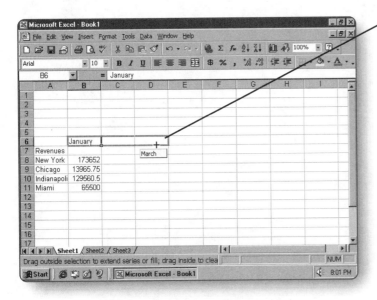

3. **Press** and **hold** the **mouse button** and **drag** to select the next cells to be filled in. The cells will have a gray border surrounding them.

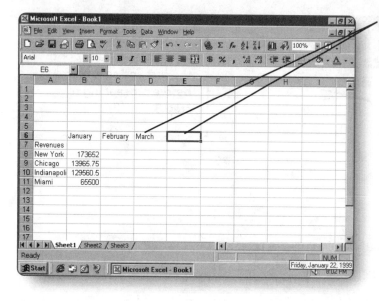

4. Release the **mouse button**. The pattern will be repeated.

11

Working with Functions and Formulas

Formulas in an Excel spreadsheet will do the calculations for you. For example, by referencing cell addresses in a formula, if the data changes, so will the formula answer. In this chapter, you'll learn how to:

- Create simple and compound formulas
- Copy formulas
- Create an absolute reference
- Use functions

Creating Formulas

All formulas must begin with the equal (=) sign, regardless of whether the formula consists of adding, subtracting, multiplying, or dividing.

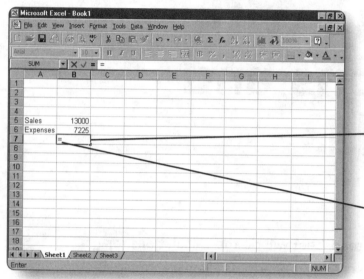

Creating a Simple Formula

An example of a simple formula might be =B5–B6.

1. Click on the **cell** in which you want to place the formula answer. The cell will be selected.

2. Type an **equal sign (=)** to begin the formula. The symbol will display in the cell.

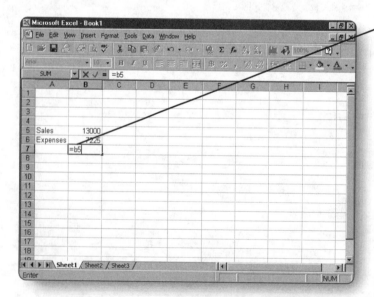

3. Type the **cell address** of the first cell to be included in the formula. This is called the cell *reference*.

NOTE

Spreadsheet formulas are not case sensitive. For example, B5 is the same as b5.

A formula needs an *operator* to suggest the next action to be performed.

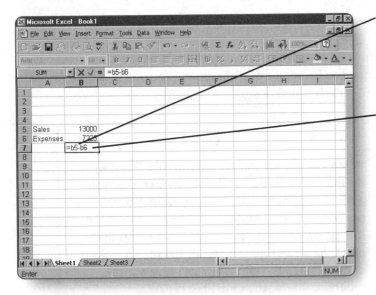

4. Type the **operator**: plus (+), minus (−), multiply (*), or divide (/). The operator will display in the formula.

5. Type the **reference** to the second cell of the formula. The reference will display in the cell.

6. Press the **Enter key**. The result of the calculation will appear in the cell.

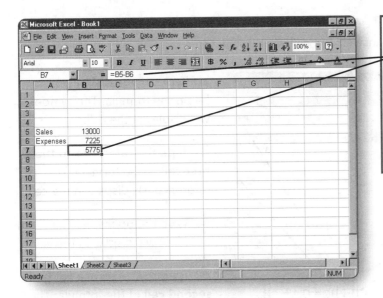

NOTE

Notice how the result appears in the cell, but the actual formula, =B5−B6, appears in the Contents box of the Edit line.

Creating a Compound Formula

You use compound formulas when you need more than one operator. Examples of a compound formula might be =B7+B8+B9+B10 or =B11–B19*A23.

NOTE

When you have a compound formula, Excel will do the multiplication and division first, then the addition and subtraction. If you want a certain portion of the formula to be calculated first, put it in parentheses. Excel will do whatever is in the parentheses before the rest of the formula. Such a formula as =B11–B19*A23 will give a totally different answer than =(B11–B19)*A23.

---

1. **Click** on the **cell** in which you want to place the formula answer. The cell will be selected.

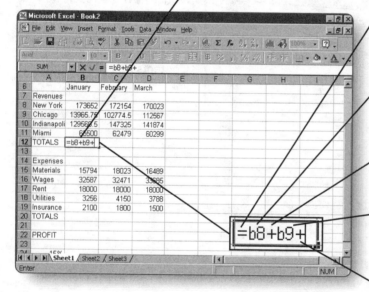

2. **Type** an **equal sign (=)** to begin the formula. The symbol will display in the cell.

3. **Type** the **reference to the first cell** of the formula. The reference will display in the cell.

4. **Type** the **operator**. The operator will display in the cell.

5. **Type** the **reference to the second cell** of the formula. The reference will display in the cell.

6. **Type** the **next operator**. The operator will display in the cell.

7. Type the **reference to the third cell** of the formula. The reference will display in the cell.

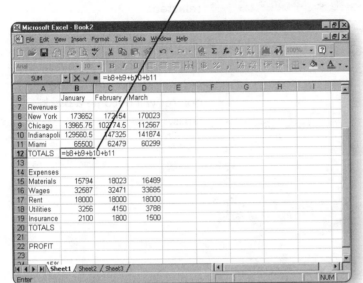

8. Repeat steps 6 and **7** until the formula is complete, adding parentheses wherever necessary.

9. Press the **Enter key** to accept the formula. The calculation answer will be displayed in the cell and the formula will be displayed in the content bar.

Try changing one of the values you originally typed in the spreadsheet and watch the answer to the formula change.

Copying Formulas

Now that you've created a formula, there's no reason to type it over and over for subsequent cells. Let Excel copy the formula for you!

Copying Using the Fill Feature

If you're going to copy a formula to a surrounding cell, you can use the Fill method.

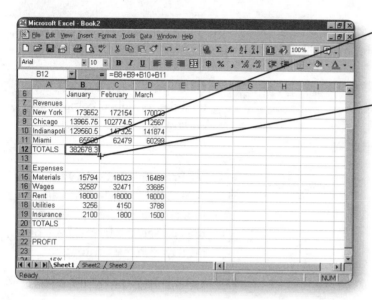

1. Click on the **cell** that has the formula. The cell will be selected.

2. Position the **mouse pointer** on the lower-right corner of the beginning cell. The mouse pointer will become a black cross.

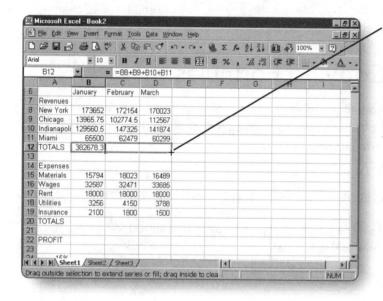

3. Press and **hold** the **mouse button** and **drag** to select the next cells to be filled in. The cells will be selected.

4. Release the **mouse button**. The formula will be copied.

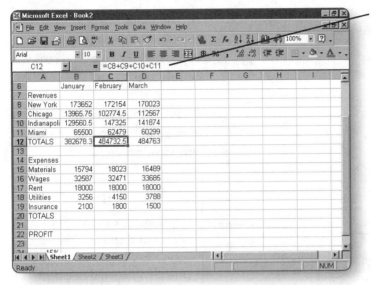

When Excel copies a formula, the references change as the formula is copied. If the original formula was =B11–B19 and you copied it to the next cell to the right, the formula would read =C11–C19. Then, if you copied it to the next cell to the right, it would be =D11–D19, and so on.

Copying with Copy and Paste

If the cells are not sequential, you can use Copy and Paste. Fill and Copy and Paste were discussed in Chapter 10, "Editing a Spreadsheet."

1. Select the **cell** with the formula that you want to duplicate. The cell will be selected.

2. Click on the **Copy button**. Marching ants will appear around the copied cells.

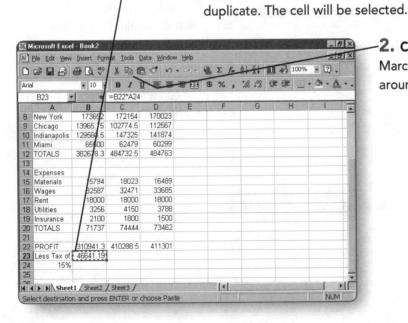

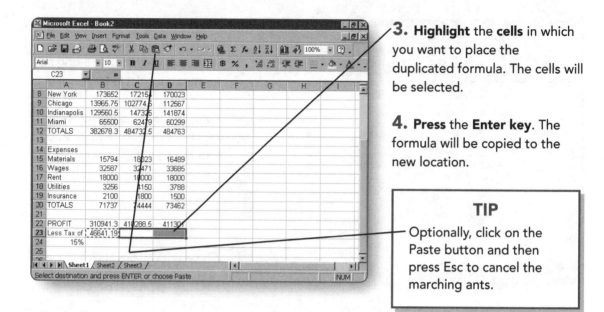

3. Highlight the **cells** in which you want to place the duplicated formula. The cells will be selected.

4. Press the **Enter key**. The formula will be copied to the new location.

TIP

Optionally, click on the Paste button and then press Esc to cancel the marching ants.

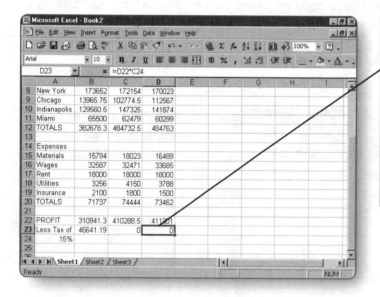

NOTE

If you are following the examples in the book, don't be alarmed by the answers you see in the exercise. You'll discover why the answers are incorrect in the next section.

Creating an Absolute Reference in a Formula

Occasionally when you copy a formula, you do not want one of the cell references to change. That's when you need to create an absolute reference. To indicate an absolute reference, use the dollar sign ($).

It's called an *absolute reference* because when you copy it, it absolutely and positively stays that cell reference and never changes. An example of a formula with an absolute reference might be =B22*B24. The reference to cell B24 will not change when copied.

For this exercise, you'll need to delete the original formulas and start again.

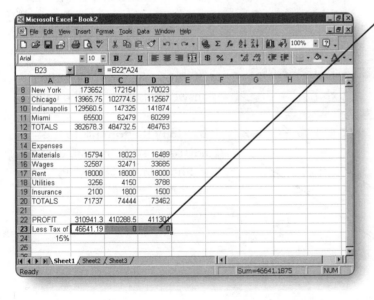

1. Highlight the **cells** in which the original formulas exist. The cells will be selected.

2. Press the **Delete key**. The information in these cells will be deleted.

3. Click on the **cell** in which you want to place the formula answer. The cell will be selected.

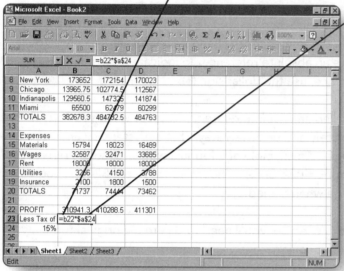

4. Type the **formula** again, except this time, if any references are to be an absolute reference, add dollar signs ($) in front of both the column reference and the row reference.

NOTE

Compound formulas can also have absolute references.

5. Press the **Enter key.** The answer will display in the cell.

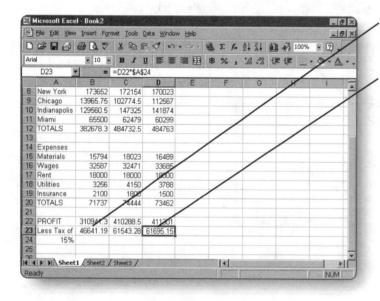

6. Copy the **formula** to the adjacent cells using one of the methods in the preceding section.

Using Functions

Sometimes, formulas can be quite complex and time consuming to build. Excel has hundreds of different functions to assist you with your calculations. All Excel functions begin with the equal (=) sign and have the basis (arguments) for the formula in parentheses.

Using the SUM Function

The SUM function totals a range of values. The syntax for this function is =SUM(*range of values to total*). An example might be =SUM(B8:D8).

NOTE

There are two ways to reference a range of values. If the cells to be included are sequential, they are separated by a colon (:). If the range is nonsequential, the cells are separated by a comma (,). For example, the range (B8:D8) would include cells B8, C8, and D8; the range (B8:D8,F4) would include cells B8, C8, D8, and F4.

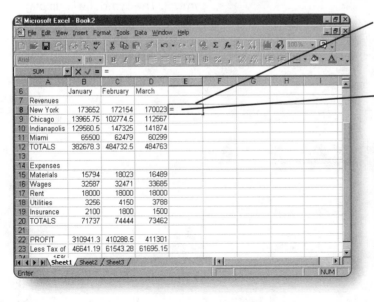

1. Click on the **cell** in which you want to place the sum of values. The cell will be selected.

2. Type the **equal (=) sign**. The symbol will display in the cell.

NOTE

Remember that functions are complex formulas and all formulas must begin with the equal (=) sign.

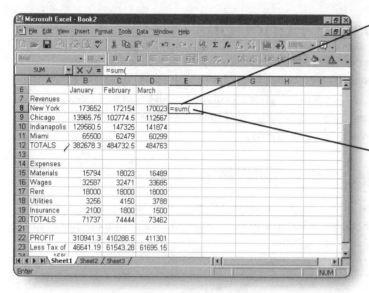

3. Type the function name **SUM.** The characters will display in the cell. Function names are not case sensitive, therefore typing "SUM" is the same as typing "sum."

4. Type the **open parentheses** symbol. The symbol will display in the cell.

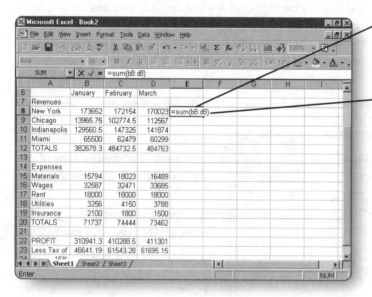

5. Type the **range** to be totaled. The range will display in the cell.

6. Type the **close parentheses** symbol. The symbol will display in the cell.

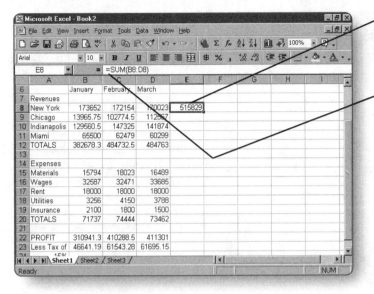

7. Press the **Enter key**. The total of the range will be displayed in the selected cell.

Again, while the result displays in the selected cell, the formula is displayed in the contents box.

Using the AutoSum Button

Excel includes the SUM function as a button on the toolbar. This makes creating a simple addition formula a mouse click away!

1. Click on the **cell** below or to the right of the values to be totaled. The cell will be selected.

2. Click on the **AutoSum button**. The cells to be totaled are highlighted.

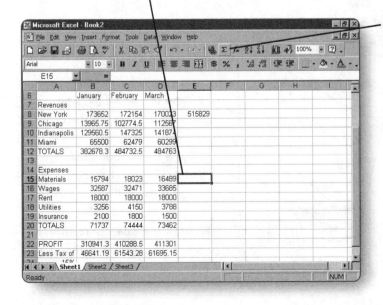

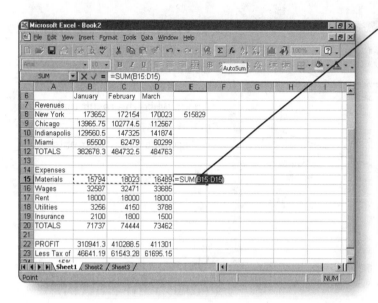

3. Press the **Enter key**. Excel will enter the sum of the values above it or to the left of it.

NOTE

Excel will sum the values above it first. If no values are above it, Excel will look for values in the cells to the left.

Using the AVERAGE Function

The AVERAGE function finds an average of a range of values. The syntax for this function is =AVERAGE(*range of values to average*). An example might be =AVERAGE(B7:D7).

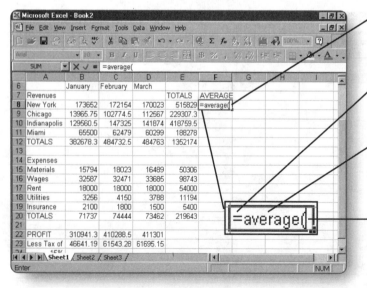

1. Click on the **cell** in which you want to place the average. The cell will be selected.

2. Type the **equal (=)** sign. The symbol will display in the cell.

3. Type the function name **AVERAGE**. The characters will display in the cell.

4. Type the **open parentheses** symbol. The symbol will display in the cell.

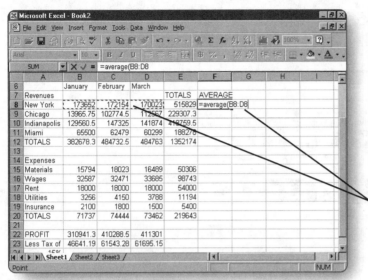

TIP

Instead of typing the range as noted in step 4, you can highlight the range with the mouse. Excel will fill in the cell references for you.

5. Type or **highlight** the **range** to be averaged. The range will display in the cell.

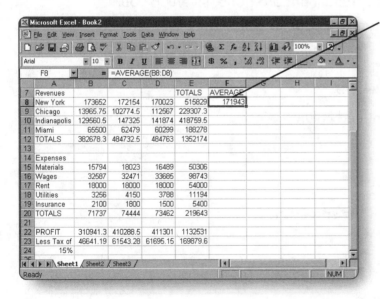

6. Press the **Enter key**. Excel will place the closing parentheses and average the values in the selected range.

12

Formatting Worksheets

The days of the dull spreadsheet are gone. Liven up your spreadsheet by changing its appearance. In this chapter, you'll learn how to:

- Set number formatting
- Change alignment and column width
- Select fonts
- Add borders to cells
- Adjust the view of the spreadsheet

Formatting Numbers

By default, values are displayed as general numbers. Values can be displayed as currency, percentages, fractions, dates, and many other formats. Three popular number styles are accounting, commas, and percentages. Accounting and comma formats automatically apply two decimal points, whereas the percentage format doesn't apply any decimal points. The accounting style also applies a dollar sign to the number. Excel includes buttons on the toolbar for these formats.

1. Select some **cells** to be formatted. The cells will be highlighted.

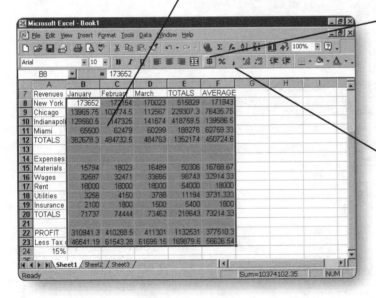

2a. Click on the **Currency button**. The cells will be formatted to accounting style with two decimal places.

OR

2b. Click on the **Comma style button**. The numbers will have two decimal points and if the number is greater than one thousand, it will also have a comma between the thousands.

NOTE

There's a fooler here. The tooltip calls this button the "currency style," however it actually applies an accounting style. The difference is the placement of the dollar sign. In currency style, the dollar sign is right next to the numbers, whereas in accounting, the dollar sign is on the left edge of the cell.

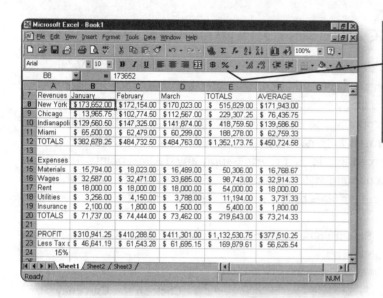

TIP

Click on the Percentage button to format numbers to a percentage style with no decimal places.

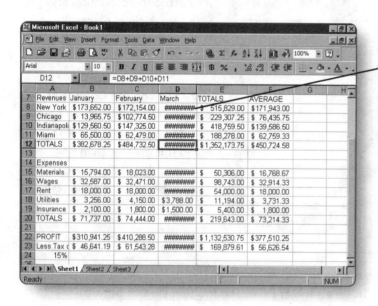

NOTE

Don't be alarmed if any of the cells display a series of number signs (######) or in scientific format (1E+08) instead of your values. This is due to the column width being too small. You will learn how to change this later in this chapter.

Changing the Decimal Point Places

The number of decimal places assigned to a style may not be exactly what you want. Excel includes two buttons on the toolbar to give you control over the number of decimal places. Each cell can have from 0 to 15 decimal places.

1. Select some **cells** to have the decimal place changed. The cells will be highlighted.

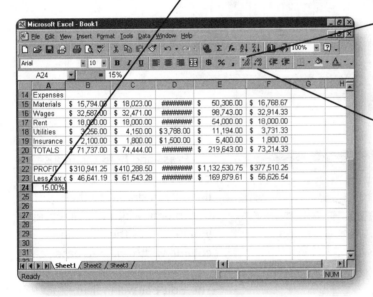

2a. Click on the **Increase decimal button**. An additional decimal place will be assigned.

OR

2b. Click on the **Decrease decimal button**. The number of decimal places will be decreased.

Each additional click on these buttons will increase or decrease the decimal place one position.

Adjusting Column Widths

The default width of a column is 8.43 characters, but each individual column can be from one to 240 characters wide.

A line located at the right edge of each column heading divides the columns. You will use this line to change the column width.

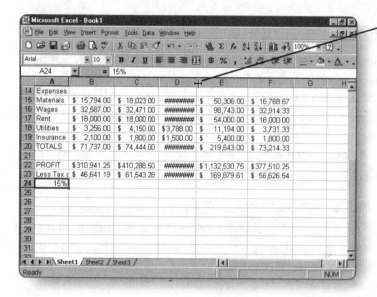

1. Position the **mouse pointer** on the right column line for the column that you want to change. The mouse pointer will become a black, double-headed arrow.

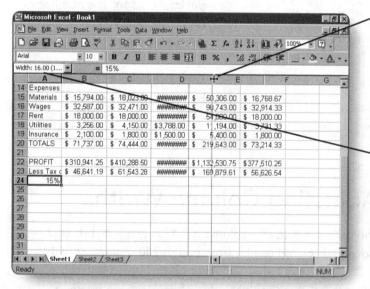

2. Press and **hold** the mouse button and **drag** the **column line**. If you drag it to the right, the column width will increase; if you drag it to the left, the column width will decrease.

The Edit bar will indicate the width as you drag the column line.

TIP

Double-click on the column line to have Excel automatically adjust the column to fit all entries in that column.

3. Release the **mouse button**. The column width will be changed.

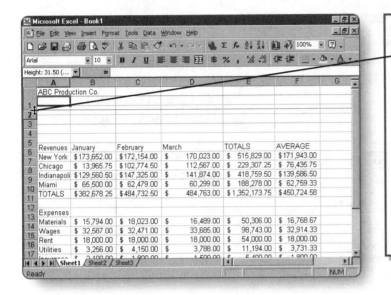

TIP

Row Height can be adjusted in a similar manner. Position the mouse pointer on the bottom edge of the row heading. Again, the mouse will change to a black, double-headed arrow. Drag the line down to increase row height or up to decrease row height.

Setting Cell Alignment

Labels are left aligned and values are right aligned by default; however, you can change the alignment of either one to be left, right, centered, or full justified. Also by default, both are vertically aligned to the bottom of the cell.

Wrapping text in cells is useful when text is too long to fit in one cell and you don't want it to overlap to the next cell.

Adjusting Cell Alignment

Adjust cells individually or adjust a block of cells.

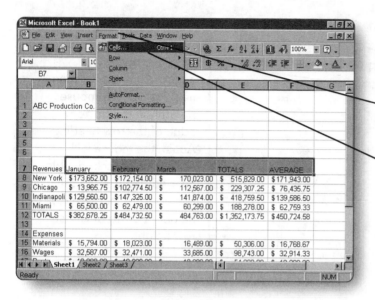

1. Select the **cells** to be formatted. The cells will be highlighted.

2. Click on **Format**. The Format menu will appear.

3. Click on **Cells**. The Format Cells dialog box will open.

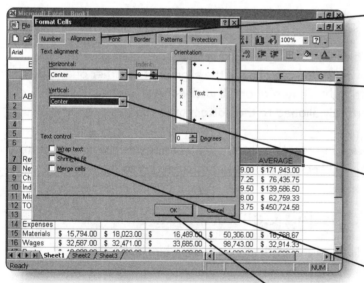

4. If necessary, **click** on the **Alignment tab**. The Alignment tab will come to the front.

5. Click on an **option** under the Horizontal: list box. The horizontal alignment of the text in the cell will change.

6. Click on an **option** under the Vertical: list box. The vertical alignment of the text in the cell will change.

7. Click in a **check box** under Text control to make the option active. A check mark will appear in the selection box.

8. Click on **OK**. The selections will be applied to the highlighted cells.

TIP

The Wrap text feature treats each cell like a miniature word processor, with text wrapping around in the cell.

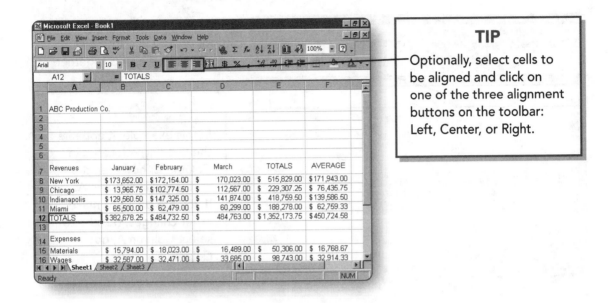

Centering Headings

Text also can be centered across a group of columns to create attractive headings.

1. Type the **heading text** in the first column of the worksheet body. This is usually column A.

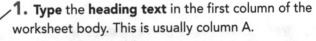

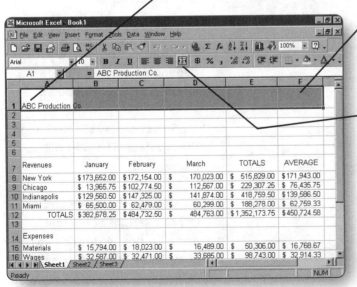

2. Select the **heading cell** and the **cells** to be included in the heading. The cells will be highlighted.

3. Click on the **Merge Cells button**. The title will be centered.

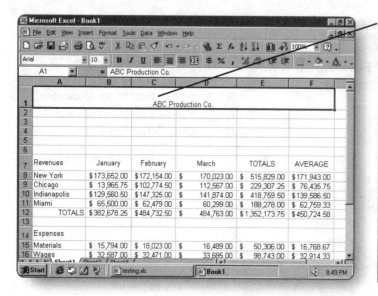

Notice the gridlines have disappeared and the cells appear to be joined together.

NOTE

In this example, it appears the heading is located in Column C; however, the text is still in Column A. If you are going to make other changes, be sure to select Column A, not Column C.

Formatting with Fonts

The default font in a spreadsheet is Arial 10 points, but either the typeface or size can easily be changed.

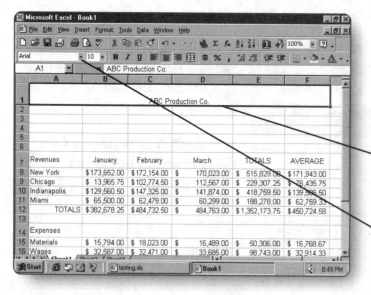

Selecting a Font Typeface

Your font choices will vary depending on the software installed on your computer.

1. Select some **cells** to change the typeface. The cells will be highlighted.

2. Click on the **down arrow** (▾) to the right of the font name list box. A drop-down list of available fonts will appear.

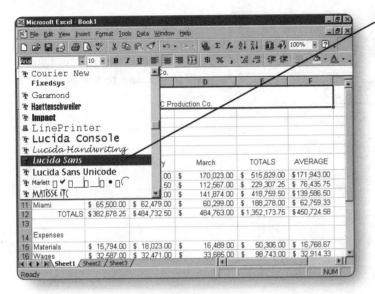

3. Click on the **font** of your choice. The selection list will close and the new font will be applied to the selected cells. Your font selections may vary from the ones shown here.

Selecting a Font Size

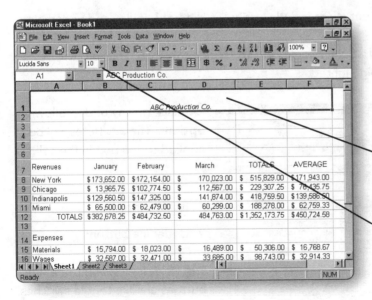

The default font size in an Excel spreadsheet is 10 points. There are approximately 72 points in an inch, so a 10-point font is slightly less than one-seventh of an inch tall.

1. Select some **cells** to change the font size. The cells will be highlighted.

2. Click on the **down arrow** to the right of the font size list box. A drop-down list of available font sizes will appear.

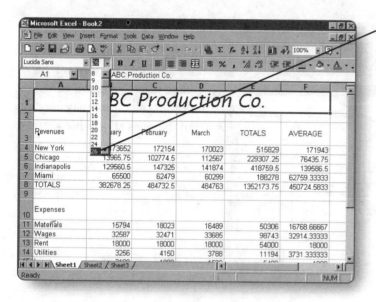

3. Click on the **font size** of your choice. The selection list will close and the new font size will be applied to the selected cells.

Selecting a Font Style

Font styles include attributes like **bold**, *italics,* and underlining.

1. Select some **cells** to change the style. The cells will be highlighted.

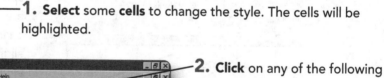

2. Click on any of the following **options**: The attributes will be applied to the text in the cell.

- Bold button
- Italics button
- Underline button

The Bold, Italics, and Underline buttons are like toggle switches. Click on them a second time to turn off the attribute.

TIP

Shortcut keys include Ctrl+B for Bold, Ctrl+I for Italics, and Ctrl+U for Underline.

NOTE

Underlining is not the same as a cell border. Cell borders are discussed in the next section.

Adding Borders

You can add borders or lines to cells to emphasize important data. Borders are different from the gridlines that separate cells in the sheet. You can change the style and color of borders.

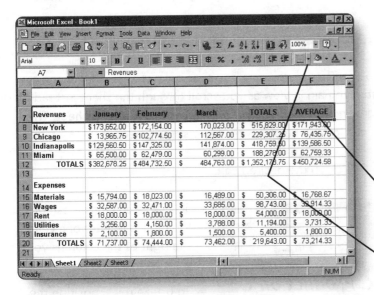

1. Select the **cells** to have borders or lines. The cells will be highlighted.

2. Click on the **down arrow** (▼) next to the Borders button. A selection of border styles will display.

3. Choose a **border line style**. The selected cells will display the border.

Changing the Spreadsheet Display

Excel includes several options to modify the display of your spreadsheet. Most display options do not affect how the spreadsheet prints, only the way you see it on the monitor.

Freezing Spreadsheet Titles

You can freeze columns, rows, or both so that column and row titles remain in view as you scroll through the sheet instead of scrolling off the screen with the rest of the spreadsheet. This is particularly helpful with larger spreadsheets.

1. **Click** on the desired **cell**:

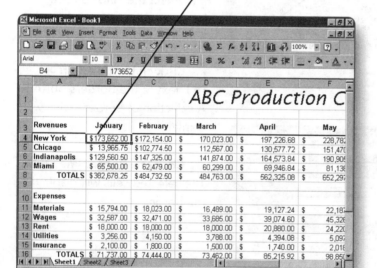

- To freeze columns, position the mouse pointer one cell to the right of the columns you want to freeze.

- To freeze rows, position the cell pointer one cell below the rows you want to freeze.

- To freeze both columns and rows, position the cell pointer in the cell below the rows and to the right of the columns you want to freeze.

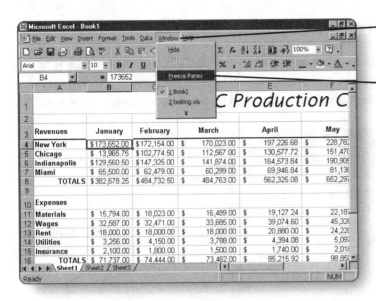

2. Click on **Window**. The Window menu will appear.

3. Click on **Freeze Panes**. Lines will appear on the document indicating the frozen areas.

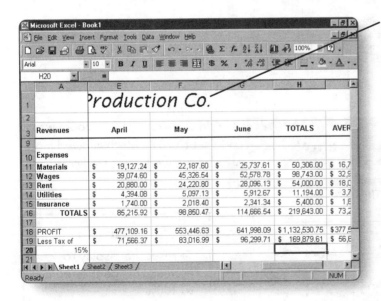

As you scroll downward or across in your document, the frozen part stays stationary on the screen while the rest of the text moves.

TIP

Repeat steps 2 and 3 to unfreeze the windows.

Using Zoom

Zoom enlarges or shrinks the display of your spreadsheet to allow you to see more or less of it. Zooming in or out does not affect printing. The normal display of your spreadsheet is 100%.

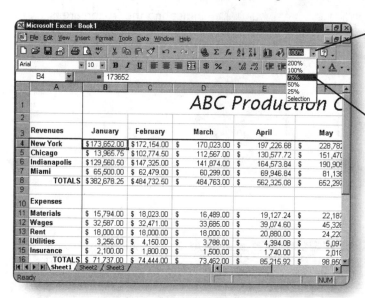

1. Click on the **down arrow** (▼) to the right of the Zoom button. A list of choices will display.

2. Click on a **magnification** (%) choice. The higher the number, the larger the cells will appear on screen. The display of your screen will adjust according to your selection.

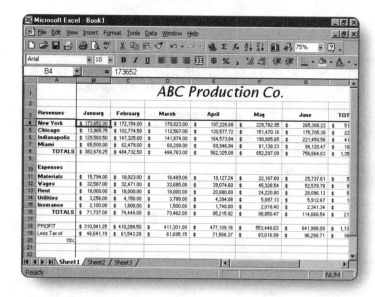

In this example, the zoom was set to 75%, which allowed more of the worksheet to display on the screen.

TIP

To reset the display to normal, change the zoom to 100%

Viewing Formulas

When you create formulas, the result of the formula is displayed in the spreadsheet, not the formula itself. Having the formula displayed is a wonderful tool for troubleshooting formula errors in your spreadsheet.

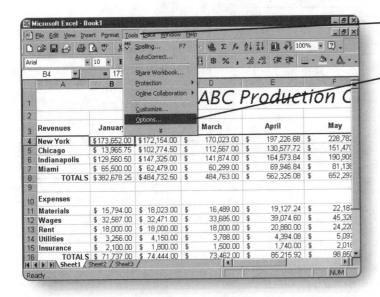

1. Click on **Tools**. The Tools menu will appear.

2. Click on **Options**. The Options dialog box will open.

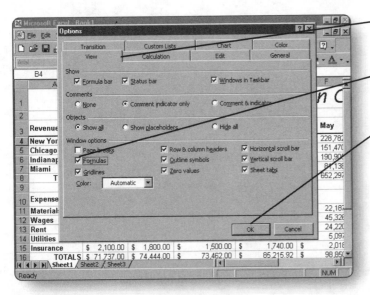

3. Click on the **View tab**. The View tab will come to the front.

4. Click on **Formulas**. A check mark will display in the option.

5. Click on **OK**. The dialog box will close.

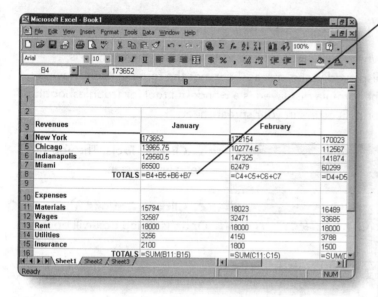

The spreadsheet formulas will be displayed in each cell instead of the result of the formula.

6. **Repeat** these **steps** to turn off display of the formulas.

> ### NOTE
>
> If you print the spreadsheet while the formulas are displayed, the formulas will print, but not the formula results.

13

Completing Your Spreadsheet

Now that you have created your spreadsheet with all its text, values, and formulas, you'll want to prepare it for final output. You should proofread it for errors and specify what area you want to print. In this chapter, you'll learn how to:

- Save, close, and open a spreadsheet
- Use Print Preview
- Print a spreadsheet

Preparing to Print

Before you print your spreadsheet, you may want to tell Excel what size paper you'd like to use, how large the margins should be, and whether to print the gridlines or not. These options and others are selected from the Page Setup feature of Excel.

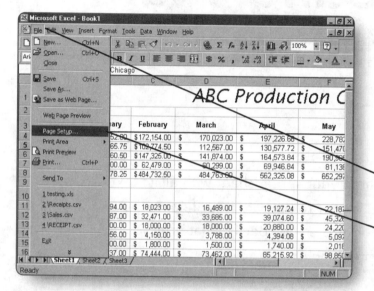

Setting up Margins

By default, the top and bottom margins are set at 1 inch and the left and right margins are set at .75 inch. You can change these margins.

1. Click on **File**. The File menu will appear.

2. Click on **Page Setup**. The Page Setup dialog box will open.

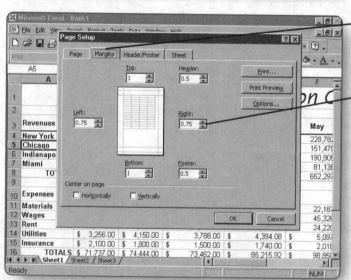

3. If necessary, **click** on the **Margins tab**. The Margins tab will come to the front.

4. Click on the **up or down arrow** (◆) on each margin that you want to change. A sample is displayed in the sample box.

Setting Page Orientation and Size

If your spreadsheet uses quite a few columns, you may want to change the orientation or paper size. The default size is 8½ by 11 inch paper in portrait orientation—the short side at the top. Changing to landscape orientation will print with the long edge of the paper at the top.

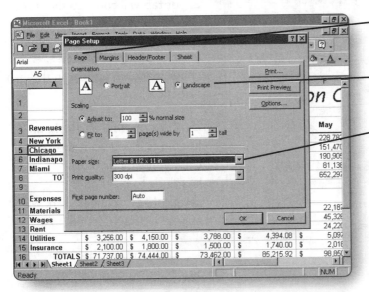

1. Click on the **Page tab**. The Page tab will come to the front.

2. Click on an **Orientation**. The option will be selected.

3. Click on the **down arrow** (▼) at the right of the Paper Size: list box. The list of available paper size options will appear.

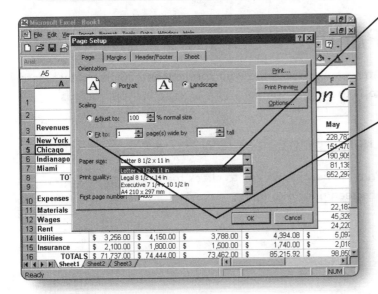

4. Click on a **paper size**. The paper size will be selected.

TIP

If you want to reduce the spreadsheet data when you print so that it fits on a specified number of pages, click on the Page tab and click the Fit to: option button and enter the desired number of pages wide and pages tall.

Setting Other Printing Options

You may want to consider other options for your worksheet, such as whether to print the gridlines or the row and column headings.

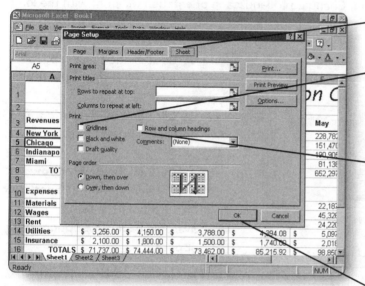

1. **Click** on the **Sheet tab**. The Sheet tab will come to the front.

2. **Click** on **Gridlines** if you want to print the gridlines. A check mark will appear in the selection box.

3. **Click** on **Row and column headings** if you want the column headings or row headings to print on the spreadsheet. A check mark will appear in the selection box.

4. **Click** on **OK**. The Page Setup dialog box will close.

Printing a Spreadsheet

After you have created your spreadsheet, you can print a hard copy to send to someone else or keep for your records.

Using Print Preview

Print Preview allows you to check the overall spreadsheet onscreen prior to printing.

1. Click on the **Print Preview button**. The document will be sized so that an entire page is visible on the screen.

Don't strain your eyes trying to read the text in the Preview windows. You are looking at the overall perspective here, not necessarily the individual cells. The document is not editable on this screen.

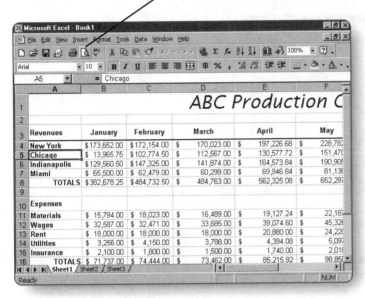

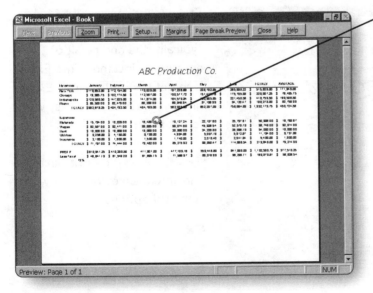

2. Position the **mouse pointer** over the document. The mouse pointer will turn into a magnifying glass.

3. Click on the **document**. The text will become larger onscreen.

4. Click on the **document** again. The text will become smaller onscreen.

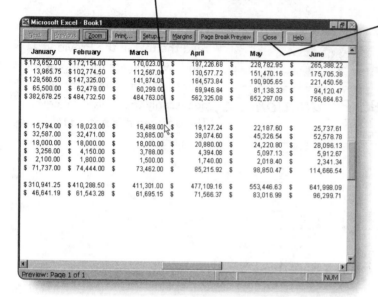

5. Click on **Close**. The spreadsheet will be returned to the normal view.

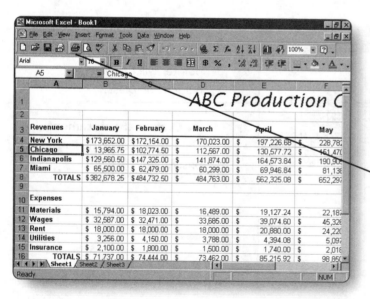

Printing Your Work

Typically, the end result of entering a document into Excel is to get text onto paper. Excel gives you a quick and easy way to get that result.

1a. Click on the **Print button**. The spreadsheet will print with standard options.

OR

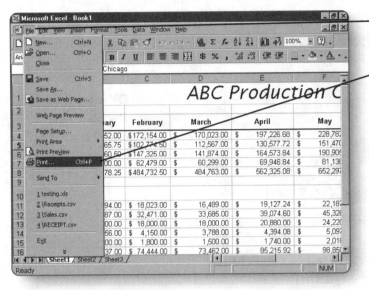

1b. **Click** on **File**. The File menu will appear.

2. **Click** on **Print**. The Print dialog box will open.

Many options are available from the Print dialog box including:

- **Printer name**. If you are connected to more than one printer, you can choose the name of the printer to use for this print job. Click on the down arrow at the right of the Name: list box and make a selection.

- **Print range**. Choose which pages of your document to print with the Print range option boxes.

- **Number of copies**. Choose the number of copies to be printed by clicking on the up or down arrow (◆) in the Number of copies: list box.

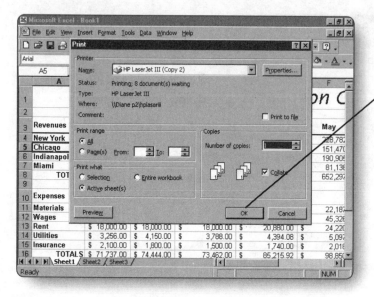

3. Click on any desired **options.** The options will be activated.

4. Click on **OK** after you have made your selections. The document will be sent to the printer.

14

Creating Charts

A chart is an effective way to illustrate the data in your spreadsheet. It can make relationships between numbers easier to see because it turns numbers into shapes and the shapes can then be compared to one another. In this chapter, you'll learn how to:

- Create a chart
- Modify a chart
- Delete a chart

Creating a Chart

Creating a chart is a simple process using the Excel Chart Wizard. You first decide what you want to chart and how you want it to look.

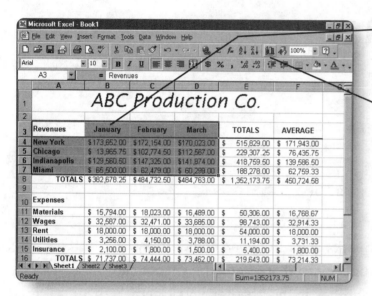

1. **Select** the **range** that you want to chart. The range will be highlighted.

2. **Click** on the **Chart Wizard button**. Step 1 of the Chart wizard will display onscreen.

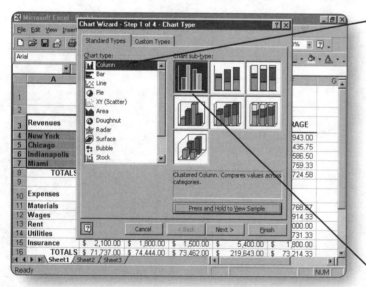

3. **Click** on a **Chart type**. A selection of chart subtypes will be displayed.

NOTE

Traditionally, bar charts compare item to item, pie charts compare parts of a whole item, and line charts show a trend over a period of time.

4. **Click** on a **Chart subtype**. The option will be selected.

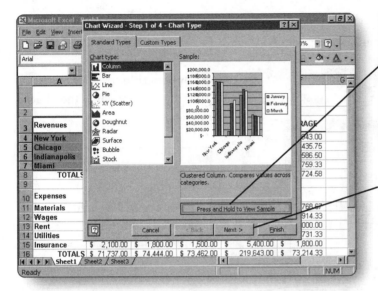

5. **Click** on **Next**. Step 2 of the Chart Wizard will display.

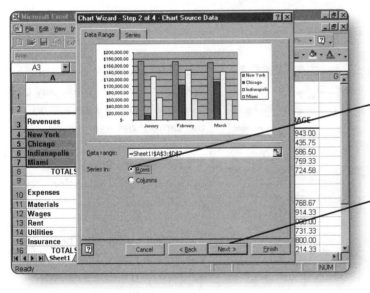

Excel will next try to determine the direction of the data; whether the values to be plotted are in rows or columns.

6. **Click** on the **option** to display the data series in rows or columns. The option will be selected.

7. **Click** on **Next**. Step 3 of the Chart Wizard will display.

8. **Click** in the **Chart title: text box**. A blinking insertion point will appear.

9. **Type** a **title** for your chart. The title will appear in the chart preview.

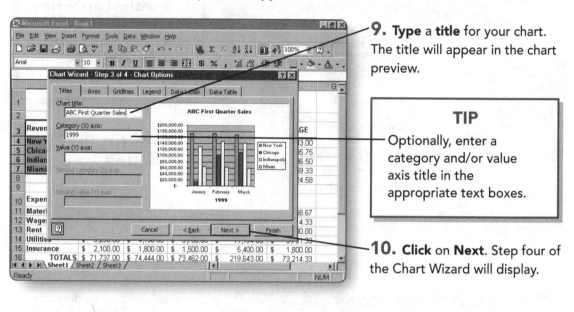

TIP

Optionally, enter a category and/or value axis title in the appropriate text boxes.

---

10. **Click** on **Next**. Step four of the Chart Wizard will display.

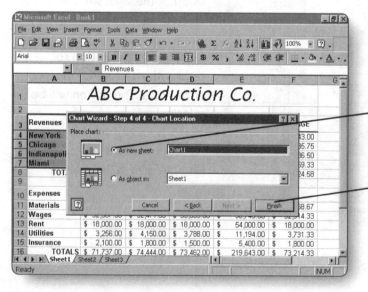

You must now choose whether you want the chart to display on its own sheet or to appear on the same sheet as the data.

11. **Click** on a **Place chart option button**. The option will be selected.

12. **Click** on **Finish**. The Wizard will close. The chart will be displayed either as a new sheet or below the existing data.

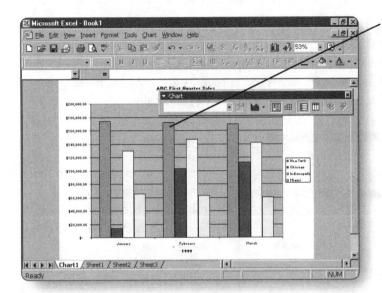

The data from the selected cells of the spreadsheet is plotted out in a chart. If the data in the spreadsheet changes, the chart will also change.

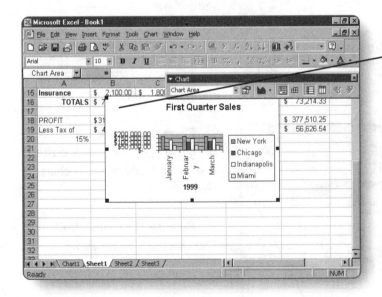

NOTE
When a chart is located on the same page as the data, the chart is selected when eight black handles appear around the outer edge of a chart. Click outside of the chart to deselect it, or click on the chart to select it.

Modifying a Chart

Creating a chart is so simple that it probably made you want to enhance the chart to improve its appearance. Items you can change include the size, style, and color.

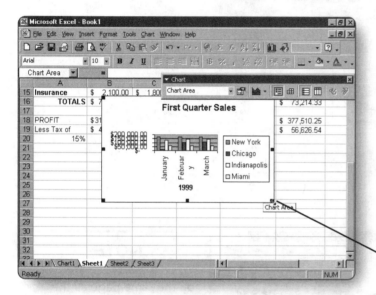

Resizing a Chart

When a chart is inserted on the spreadsheet page, it will probably be too small to read the data correctly. Use your mouse to resize it.

1. If necessary, **click** on the **chart** to select it. The chart will have eight small handles around it.

2. Position the **mouse pointer** over one of the handles. The mouse pointer will change to a double-headed arrow.

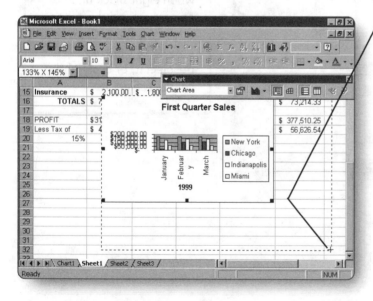

3. Press the **mouse button** and drag the black **handle**. A dotted line will indicate the new chart size.

4. Release the **mouse button**. The chart will be resized.

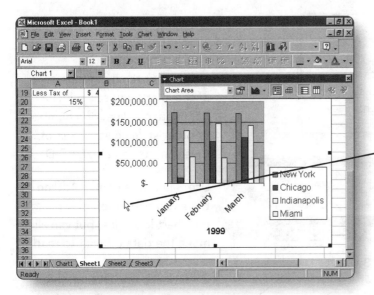

Moving a Chart

When a chart is inserted on the spreadsheet page, you can easily move it to any location on the page.

1. Position the **mouse pointer** anywhere over a blank area of the chart. The mouse pointer will be a left-pointing, white arrow.

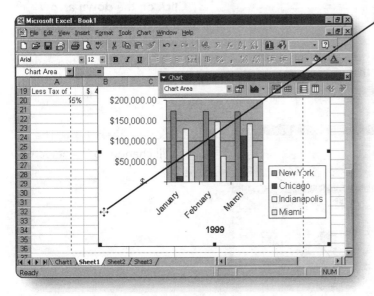

2. Press the **mouse button** and **drag** the **chart** to the new location. The mouse will turn into a four-headed arrow and a dotted line box will indicate the new position.

3. Release the **mouse button**. The chart will be moved.

NOTE

If your chart is on its own page, you don't need to click on the chart to select it. Just having the chart displayed makes it eligible for modification.

Changing a Chart Style

If you want to change the style of the chart, you can select a bar, area, pie, line, or a number of other style charts. Most of these charts can also be 3-D.

Use 3-D charts lightly. Adding the extra dimension may make the chart look nice, but can also make the data difficult to read.

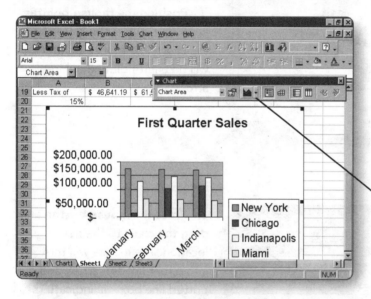

1. If necessary, **click** on the **chart**. The chart will be selected.

2. Click on the **down arrow** (▼) to the right of the Chart Type button on the Chart Toolbar. A list of chart types will display.

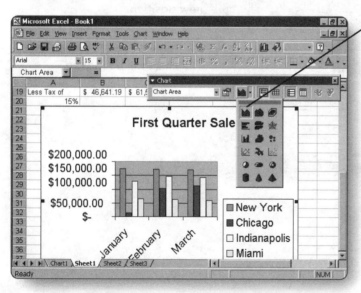

3. Click on a **chart type**. The chart will change to the selected type.

Changing the Series Appearance

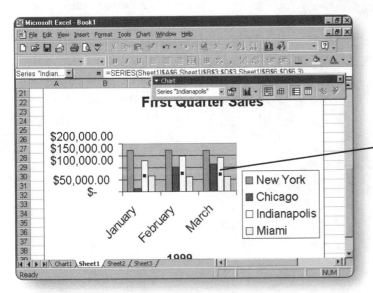

If you do not like the default colors assigned to a chart, you can change them for any series.

1. If necessary, **click** on the **chart**. The chart will be selected.

2. Double-click on any colored **bar, line, or series** item. A small black square will appear in all items in the selected series and the Format Data Series dialog box will open.

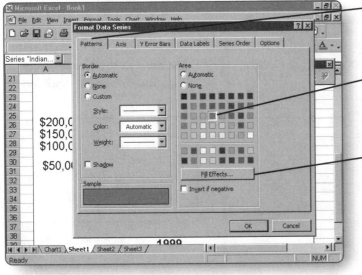

3. If necessary, **click** on **Patterns**. The Patterns tab will come to the front.

4. Click on a **color** for the selected series. The color will be highlighted.

5. Click on **Fill Effects**. The Fill Effects dialog box will open.

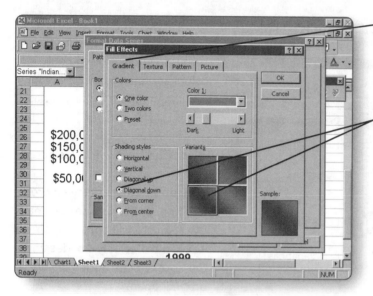

6. Click on either the **Gradient, Texture, or Pattern tabs**. The tab will come to the front with its available options.

7. Click on any desired **pattern options** for the selected series. The pattern will be highlighted.

8. Click on **OK**. The Fill Effects dialog box will close.

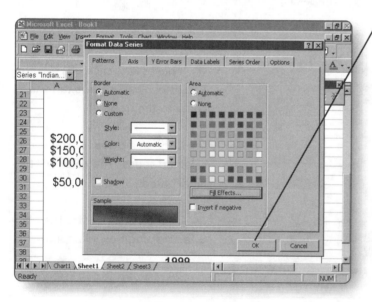

9. Click on **OK**. The Format Data Series dialog box will close and the series will change to the selected options.

10. Repeat the above **steps** for each series to be modified.

TIP

Double-click on any section of the chart to edit options for that section.

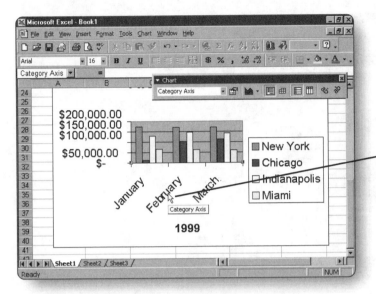

Modifying Chart Text

Any text font, size, color, or border can be modified by double-clicking on the text.

1. Double-click on the **text** to be modified. The Format dialog box for that section will open.

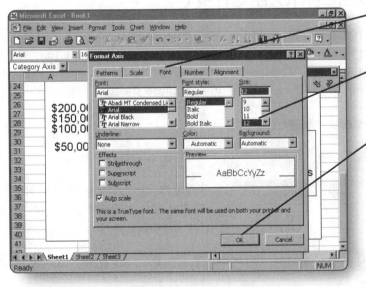

2. Click on the **Font tab**. The Font tab will come to the front.

3. Click on any desired **font changes**. The options will be selected.

4. Click on **OK**. The dialog box will close and the font changes will appear.

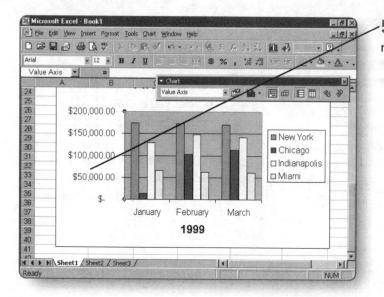

5. Repeat for any **text** to be modified.

Deleting a Chart

If you no longer want the chart created from your spreadsheet, you can delete it. The method you'll use to delete the chart depends on whether the chart is on the same sheet as the data or if it's on a separate sheet.

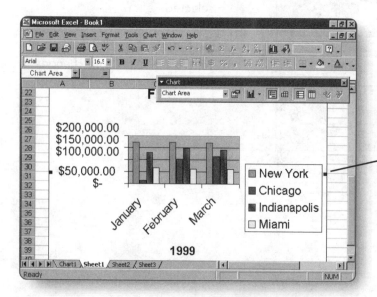

Deleting a Chart on a Data Sheet

If the chart is on the same sheet as the data, you'll delete it with the Delete key.

1. Click on the **chart**. The chart will be selected.

2. Press the **Delete key**. The chart will be deleted.

Deleting a Chart on Its Own Sheet

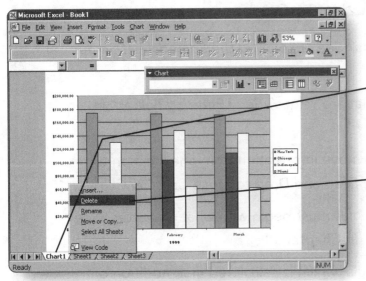

If the chart is on a separate sheet, you'll need to delete the entire sheet to delete the chart.

1. Right-click on a **sheet tab**. This tab is usually marked Chart1, Chart2, and so forth. A shortcut menu will appear.

2. Click on **Delete**. A confirmation message will appear.

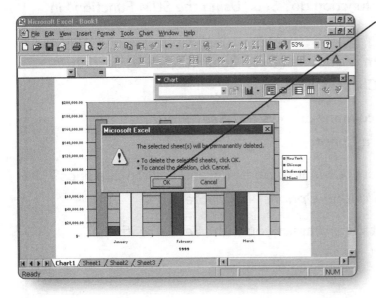

3. Click on **OK**. The sheet will be deleted.

Part III Review Questions

1. What is a cell address? *See "Exploring the Spreadsheet Screen" in Chapter 9*

2. In a spreadsheet, what are values? *See "Entering Values" in Chapter 9*

3. What is a method to move information from one location to another? *See "Using Drag and Drop to Move Cells" in Chapter 10*

4. All spreadsheet formulas must begin with what character? *See "Creating Formulas" in Chapter 11*

5. In a compound formula, which is calculated first: addition or multiplication? *See "Creating a Compound Formula" in Chapter 11*

6. What does the SUM function do? *See "Using the SUM Function" in Chapter 11*

7. What is the maximum width of an Excel column? *See "Adjusting Column Widths" in Chapter 12*

8. What does freezing columns or rows do? *See "Freezing Spreadsheet Titles" in Chapter 12*

9. How do you tell Excel you want to print row and column headings? *See "Setting Other Printing Options" in Chapter 13*

10. What does the Chart Wizard assist you with? *See "Creating a Chart" in Chapter 14*

PART IV

Using PowerPoint

15

Creating and Viewing Presentations

You can use PowerPoint to enhance your presentations. Each PowerPoint presentation file consists of *slides* that contain information that you want to convey to an audience. Think of PowerPoint slides as pages of your presentation. Don't confuse PowerPoint presentation slides with 35 mm slides, which are only one of the ways you can store (and present) your presentation. You can also store your PowerPoint presentation slides on overhead transparencies, or you can simply print them on paper and give them to your audience. And, if you prefer, you can create a computer slide show in PowerPoint as well. In this chapter, you'll learn how to:

- Create a presentation using a template
- Change views

Creating a Presentation

PowerPoint creates each presentation file based on a *template*. A template contains predefined information, such as text and colors.

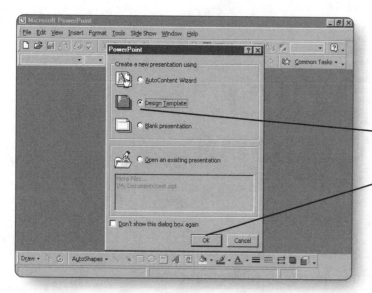

1. Start PowerPoint. The PowerPoint dialog box will open, and you will choose a method to start working in PowerPoint.

2. Click on **Design Template**. The option will be selected.

3. Click on **OK**. The New Presentation dialog box will open.

Some templates contain more information that may help you, such as sample text.

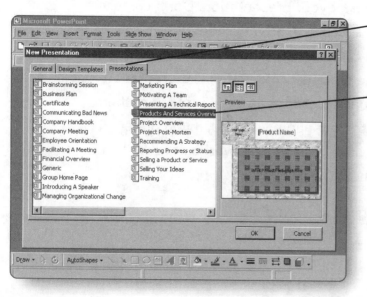

4. Click on the **Presentations tab**. The tab will come to the front.

5. Click on a **template** on which to base your presentation. You will see a preview of the template on the right side of the dialog box. Choose a template that most closely represents the concept you're trying to communicate. In Chapter 16, "Editing a Presentation," you'll learn how to edit the text to match your needs.

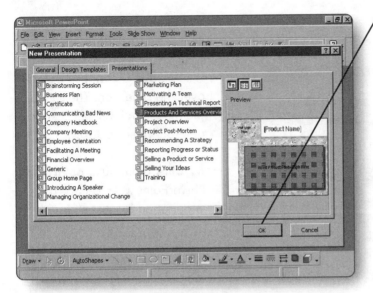

6. Click on **OK**. PowerPoint will display your new presentation in Tri-Pane view.

> **TIP**
>
> Save this presentation using the procedures you learned in Chapter 3, "Finding Common Ways to Work in Documents."

Switching Views

You can display your presentation in one of several views in PowerPoint. In the following task, you will explore each of the views in PowerPoint and see how to move from slide to slide in each view.

Using Normal Tri-Pane View

Normal view is really a combination of several views. With Normal view you can see your individual slides as well as speaker notes and an outline all at the same time.

Viewing the Outline

In the Outline pane, your presentation appears like an outline that you would use when organizing your thoughts. Use the Outline view to help you organize your presentation's information. In the Outline pane, you can see all the information on each slide; the title of each slide appears as a heading, and the information on the slide appears below.

A number and an icon will appear to the left of each slide. You can click on the icon to select that slide.

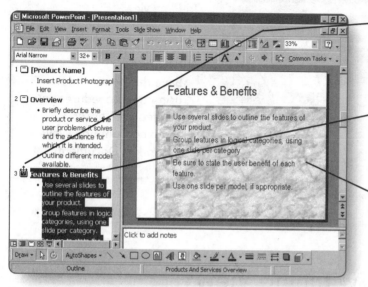

1. Position the **mouse pointer** over the slide icon. The shape of the mouse pointer will change to a four-headed arrow.

2. Click the **mouse pointer**. PowerPoint will select all the information for that slide.

The slide will display in the slide pane.

Viewing Slides

The Slide pane shows you a close-up image of your slide the way it will appear when you print it.

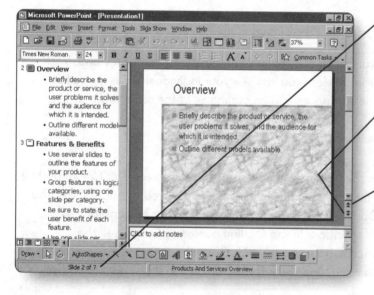

The status bar tells you the number of slides in your presentation and which slide you are viewing.

1. Click on the **Next Slide button**. The next slide in the presentation will appear.

2. Click on the **Previous Slide button**. The previous slide will appear.

Viewing Speaker Notes

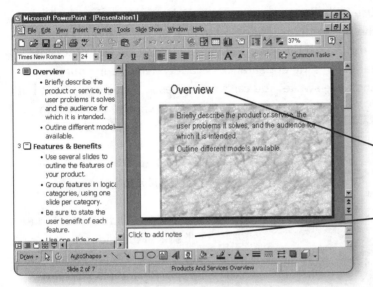

You can create speaker notes —
notes to remind yourself of what
you want to say when a slide
appears. In Chapter 16, "Editing
a Presentation," you'll learn how
to print these notes.

1. Display the **slide** to have a
note attached. The slide will
display in the Slide pane.

2. Click in the **Notes pane**. The
blinking insertion point will
appear.

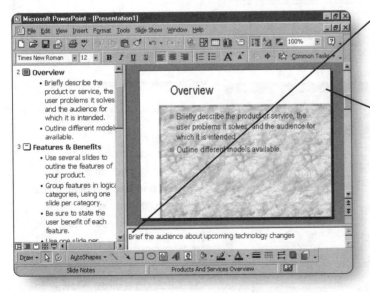

3. Type the **text** that you want
to store as a note for the
selected slide. The text will
display in the Notes pane.

4. Click on the **slide**.
PowerPoint will accept the
changes to the notes box.

Using Slide Sorter View

Use Slide Sorter view to see a miniature view of each slide in the presentation. Slide Sorter view provides an easy way to view the overall effects of your presentation and check for variety in slide appearance —variety helps keep your audience awake. You can't edit slides in Slide Sorter view, but you can change the order in which the slides appear.

1. Click on **View**. The View menu will appear.

2. Click on **Slide Sorter**. You will see all the slides in your presentation. A dark border will appear around the selected slide.

TIP

Optionally, click on the Slide Sorter view button.

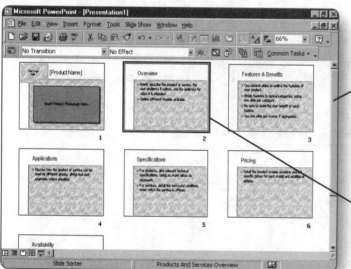

TIP

If you can't see all the slides in your presentation, use the vertical scroll bar to scroll down and view additional slides.

3. Click on a **slide**. PowerPoint will select the slide, and a black border will appear around the slide.

Viewing a Slide Show

Use Slide Show view to display your presentation onscreen. In Chapter 17, "Working With Presentation Special Effects," you'll learn how to make a livelier on-screen presentation.

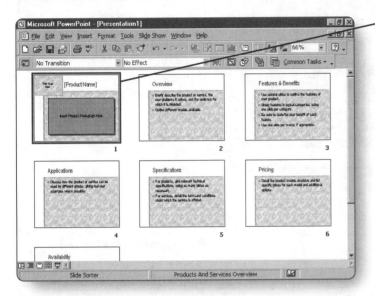

1. Click on the **first slide** of the presentation. If you are still in Slide Sorter view, the slide will have a border around the slide.

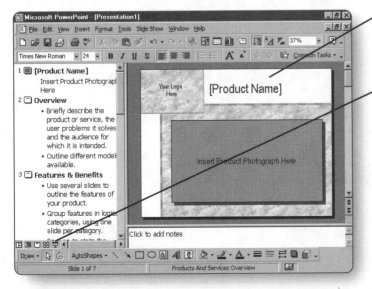

If you are in Normal view, the first slide will display in the Slide pane.

2. Click on the **Slide Show button**. All screen elements will disappear, and the image of the first slide will fill your screen.

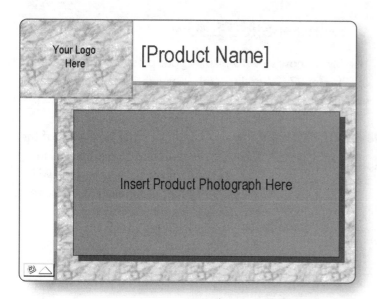

3. **Click** the **mouse button** or **press** the **right arrow key**. The slide show will advance to the next slide.

TIP

Press the left arrow key to return to the previous slide.

Overview

■ Briefly describe the product or service, the user problems it solves, and the audience for which it is intended.
■ Outline different models available.

4. **Continue clicking** the **mouse button** or **pressing** the **right arrow key**. Each subsequent slide will display.

TIP

Press the Esc key to end the slide show at any time.

16

Editing a Presentation

Although PowerPoint templates provide some rather impressive slides, you'll need to make modifications to any presentation you create. In this chapter, you'll learn how to:

- Add, edit, and delete slides
- Rearrange the order of slides
- Change a presentation's background appearance
- Change a slide's layout
- Print a presentation

Adding, Deleting, and Rearranging Slides

Each page in your presentation is called a slide, and all the slides are saved in a single file. You can have as many slides in your presentation as you need.

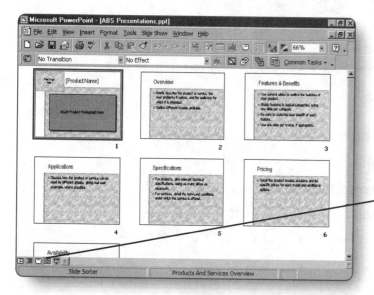

Adding Slides

You can add a slide to a presentation at any time. When you add a slide, you'll need to decide on a *layout*. Layouts take care of alignment and placement of text and objects on a page.

1. **Click** on the **Slide Sorter view button**. The slides will appear in the slide sorter.

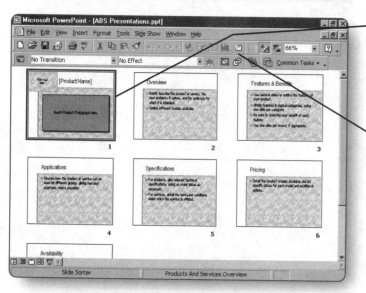

2. **Click** on a **slide**. The selected slide will have a black border around it. PowerPoint will add slides immediately after the selected slide.

3. **Click** on the **New Slide button**. The New Slide dialog box will open with the Bulleted List slide layout suggested.

You'll need to choose the layout which best matches the type of information you want to put on the new slide.

4. Click on an **AutoLayout**. The selected layout will have a box around it.

A description of the selected layout will display.

5. Click on **OK**. PowerPoint will add a blank slide formatted with the layout you selected.

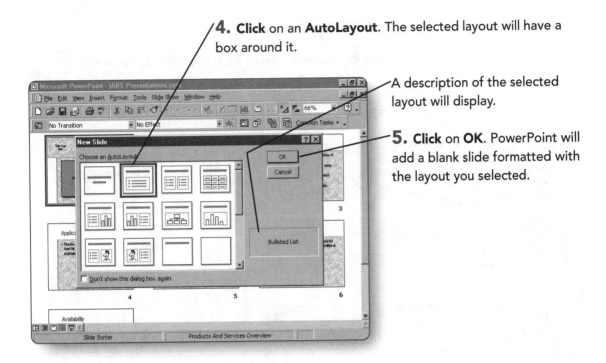

The new slide is automatically selected. The background is the same as the other slides. The slide appears blank but actually has text instruction blocks on it.

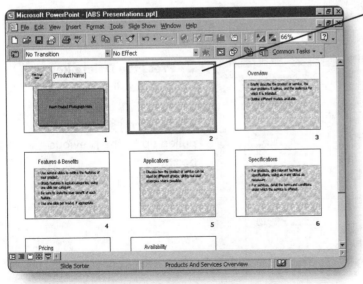

Deleting Slides

Deleting a slide is easiest from the Slide Sorter view.

1. If necessary, **click** on the **Slide Sorter view button**. All the slides in your presentation will appear.

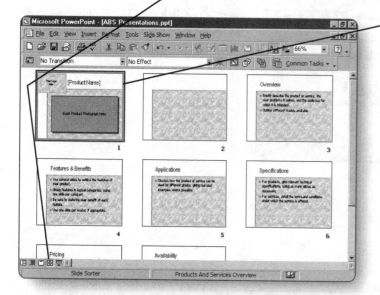

2. Click on a **slide** to delete. The slide will be selected.

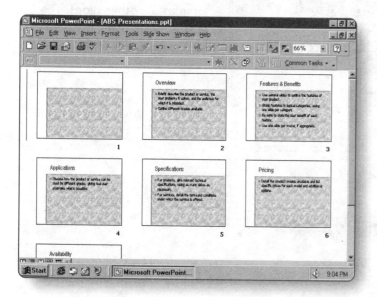

3. Press the **Delete key** to remove the slide.

All remaining slides will be pulled up to the previous position.

Rearranging Slides

You might decide that you'd rather display slides in an order other than the one you originally created. Use the Slide Sorter view to rearrange slides.

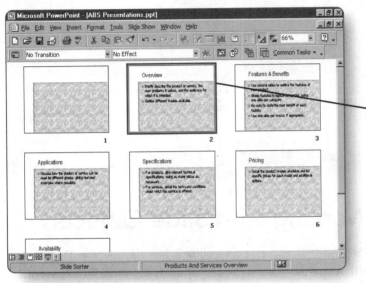

1. If necessary, **click** on the **Slide Sorter view button**. All the slides in your presentation will appear.

2. Click on the **slide** you intend to move. The slide will be selected.

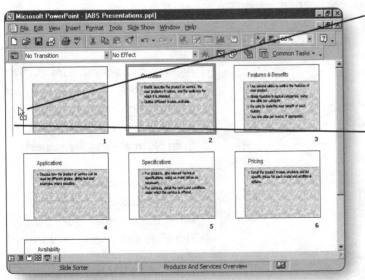

3. Drag the **selected slide** to its new location. As you drag, the mouse pointer shape will change to an arrow with a box at the bottom of it.

You will see a large dark vertical line as you drag. This bar represents the location where the new slide will appear when you drop the slide.

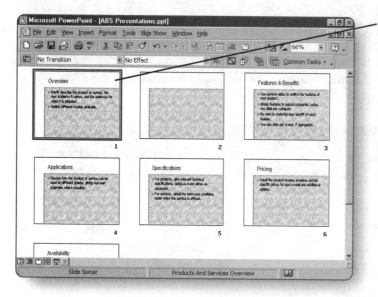

4. **Release** the **mouse button**. The slide will appear in its new position.

Working with Slide Objects

The text that appears on a slide is handled differently than with a standard word processor such as Word. Text is stored in objects called Text blocks.

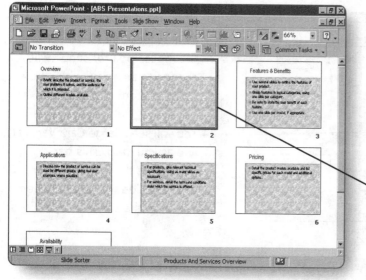

Adding Text to a New Slide

All new slides contain instruction blocks to help you organize your presentation. Instruction blocks do not print. You'll find working from Normal view the easiest.

1. If you are in Slide Sorter view, **double-click** on the new **slide** (the one that looks blank). The slide will display in Normal view.

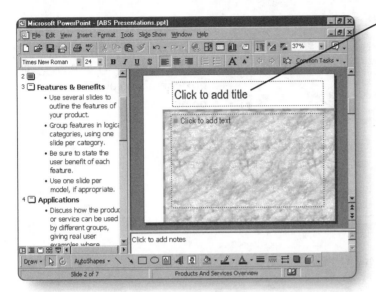

2. Click on **Click to add title**. The words will disappear and be replaced by a text object box containing an insertion point.

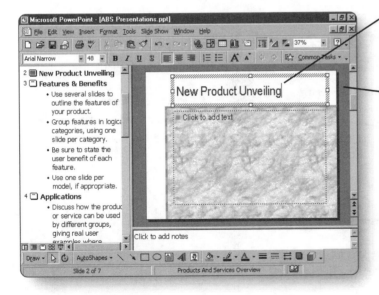

3. Type a **title** for the slide. The text will appear in the text object box.

4. Click on the **gray area** onscreen. Both the insertion point and the handles that surrounded the text object box will disappear.

If your new slide is in a bullet layout, you can add bulleted text in a manner similar to a title.

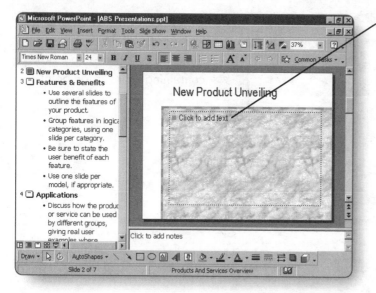

5. Click on **Click to add text**. Those words will disappear and will be replaced by a text object box containing an insertion point.

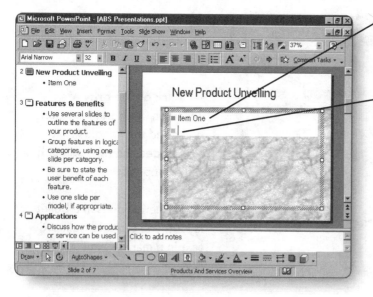

6. Type some **text**. The text will appear on the line with a bullet point in front.

7. Press the **Enter key**. PowerPoint will start a new line preceded by a bullet.

8. Type more **text.** The text will appear on the screen.

9. Press the **Enter key**. An additional bullet will appear.

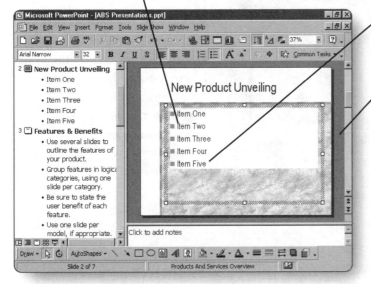

10. Type text for each bullet you need until you finish typing the last bullet.

11. Click on the **gray area** onscreen. The insertion point and the handles that surrounded the text object box will disappear and you will see the bullets you typed onscreen.

NOTE

Clicking on the gray area indicates that you are done typing and ready to take some other action.

Editing Text Objects

When you start a presentation with a design template, PowerPoint inserts some text to guide you through your presentation content. You can edit the text that appears on your slides in a variety of ways.

Changing Text

You'll want to change sample text that appears automatically on slides.

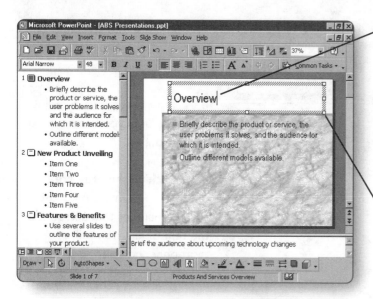

1. Display a **slide** that contains sample text to be changed. The slide will display.

2. Click on the **sample text** that appears on the slide. PowerPoint will display the text in a text object box.

Text object boxes appear surrounded by a border that contains small white squares called *handles*.

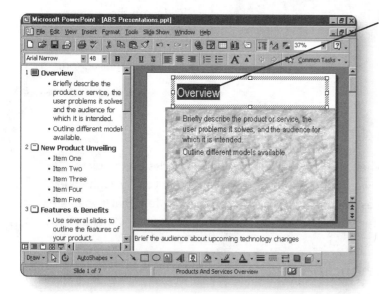

3. Select all the **text** in the box. Use the same technique to select text that you use when selecting text in Word. The selected text will be highlighted.

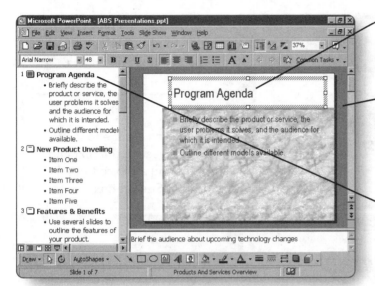

4. Type text to replace the sample text. The new text will appear in the text object box.

5. Click on the **gray area** onscreen. Your text changes will be accepted.

TIP

If you're more comfortable working in a word processing environment, click on the Outline and make your changes to text in that view.

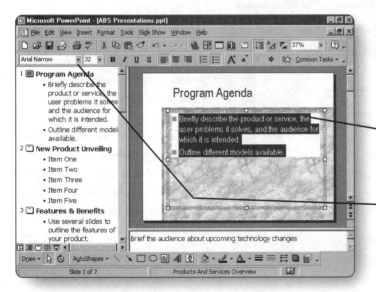

Changing the Font

You might want to change the font type or size of text in a slide.

1. Select the **text** you want to change. The text will be highlighted.

2. Click on the **down arrow** (▼) next to the Font list box. A list of available fonts will appear.

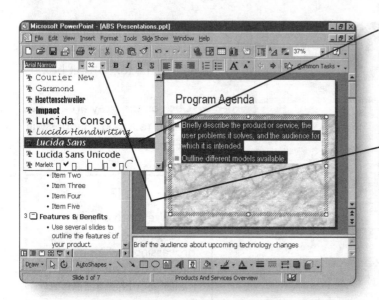

3. Click on the **font** that you want to use. The font of the selected text will change.

TIP

You can change font size by selecting the text and making a choice from the Font Size list box.

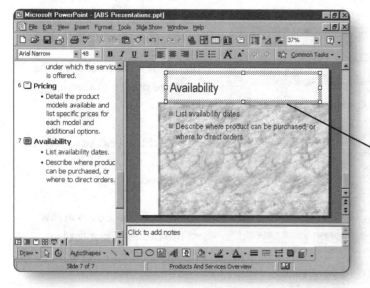

Deleting a Text Object

You might find that you need to delete a text object on a slide without deleting the slide.

1. Click on the **text object** that you want to delete. The selected object will have eight small handles surrounding it and the border will have a striped appearance to it.

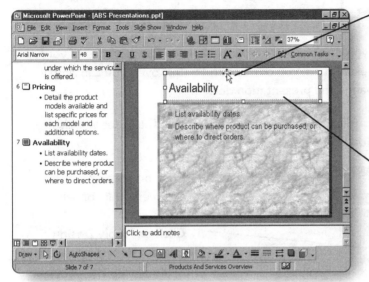

As the mouse pointer passes over the border, you will see a four-headed arrow.

2. **Click** on the **border** of the text object. The border will change from stripes to dots.

3. **Press** the **Delete key**. The existing text will disappear and the Instruction block will reappear.

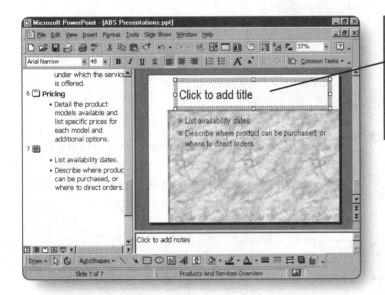

NOTE

Remember that instruction blocks do not print or display when using the Slide Show.

Changing Presentation Designs

If you don't really like the background appearance of your presentation, you don't need to start over; you can simply change the presentation design.

1. Click on the **Slide Sorter button**. The slides will display in Slide Sorter view.

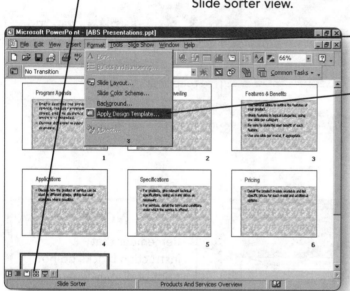

2. Click on **Format**. The Format menu will appear.

3. Click on **Apply Design Template**. The Apply Design Template dialog box will open.

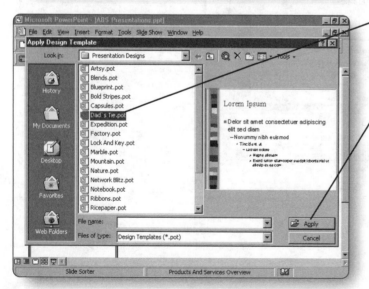

4. Click on a **design** in the list on the left side of the dialog box. A sample of the design will appear to the right.

5. Click on **Apply**. PowerPoint will redisplay the presentation using the design you chose.

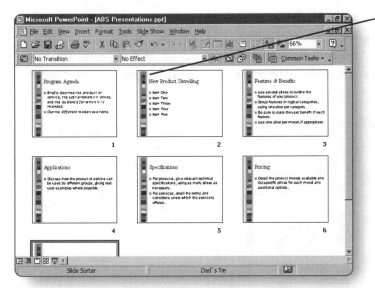

All slides will adopt the new design.

Changing Slide Layouts

You might find that you need to change the layout of a slide. For example, you may need to change a bullet layout to a table layout or a double column layout. The layout can be modified from either Normal or Slide Sorter view.

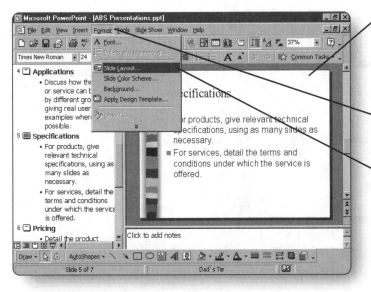

1. Click on the **slide** with the layout you want to change. The slide will be selected or displayed.

2. Click on **Format**. The Format menu will appear.

3. Click on **Slide Layout**. The Slide Layout dialog box will open.

On the left side of the dialog box, you will see visual representations of possible slide layout styles. In the lower-right corner, you will see a description of the selected layout that you can use to make sure you select the correct slide layout.

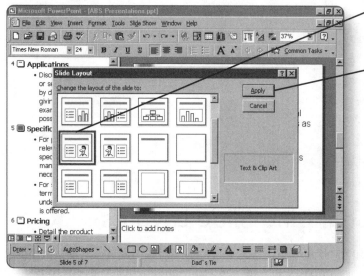

4. **Click** on a **layout**. The layout will be selected.

5. **Click** on **Apply**. The layout of the selected slide will change to the layout you chose.

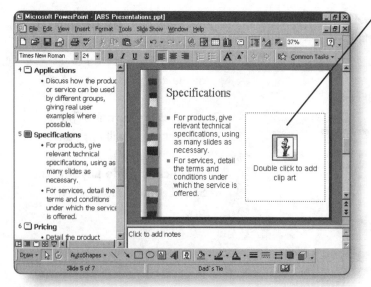

The existing objects on the slide are rearranged and, depending on the layout and the current view, new placeholders may appear.

Printing in PowerPoint

You can print a presentation and any notes that you created for slides.

Printing a Presentation

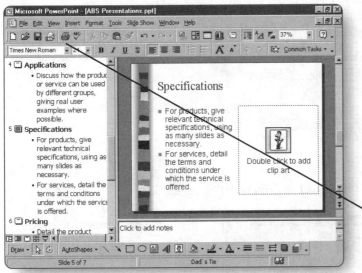

You can print your presentation on paper or on overhead transparencies (which you can use to display the presentation on an overhead projector). The steps you follow to print are the same, regardless of the medium to which you choose to print; just place the correct medium in your printer.

1a. Click on the **Print button**. One copy of each slide in your presentation will print to the default printer.

OR

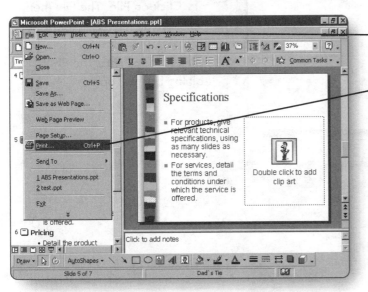

1b. Click on **File**. The File menu will appear.

2. Click on **Print**. The Print dialog box will open.

From the Print dialog box, you can specify a different printer, a specific slide to print, or the number of copies to print.

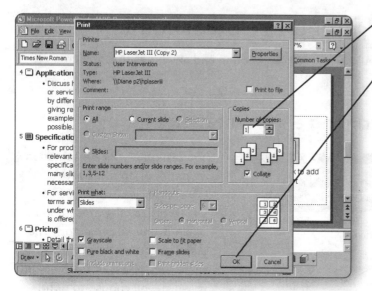

3. Choose any desired **options**. The options will be selected.

4. Click on **OK**. The presentation will print with your options.

Printing Speaker Notes

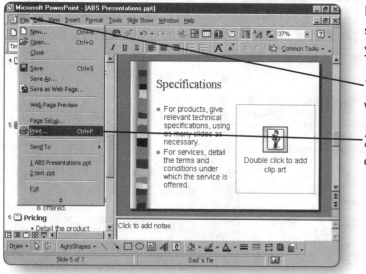

If you created notes for any slides, you can print those for your own use.

1. Click on **File**. The File menu will appear.

2. Click on **Print**. The Print dialog box will open.

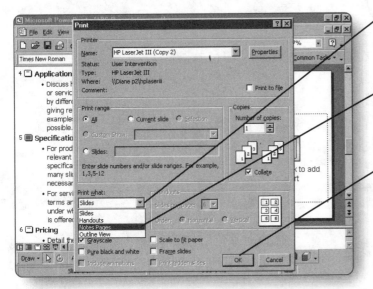

3. Click on the **down arrow** (▼) next to the Print what: list box. A list of choices will appear.

4. Click on **Notes Pages**. The selection will appear in the list box.

5. Click on **OK**. All your slides with any notes you created for those slides will print.

17

Working with Presentation Special Effects

Adding special effects to a presentation is perhaps the most fun part of creating a presentation. Special effects can enhance the effectiveness of your presentation, if you use them in moderation. In this chapter, you'll learn how to:

- Add tables or charts to a slide
- Work with clip art
- Create a summary slide
- Add transitions between slides
- Animate slides

Adding Tables

When you add a table to a slide in PowerPoint, you actually insert a Microsoft Word table.

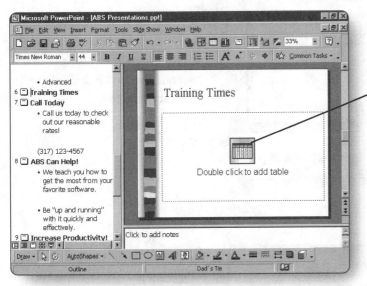

1. Display the **slide** to which you will add a table. The slide will be displayed.

2. Double-click on the **button** in the center of the slide. The Insert Word Table dialog box will open, suggesting a table of two columns and two rows.

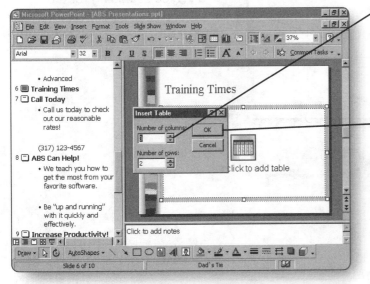

3. Click on the **up or down arrows** (⬥) if you need to change the number of columns or rows. The new quantity will display in the box.

4. Click on **OK**. After a few moments, a table will appear on your slide.

The table may look very large onscreen; don't worry, PowerPoint will adjust the size when you finish entering the table information.

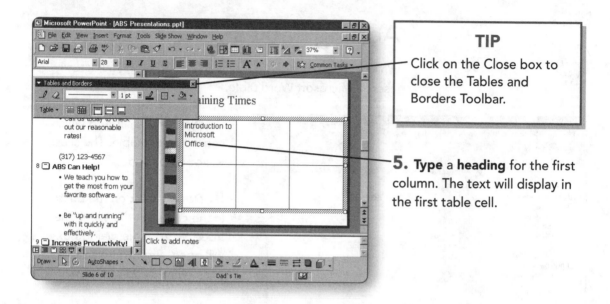

TIP
Click on the Close box to close the Tables and Borders Toolbar.

5. **Type** a **heading** for the first column. The text will display in the first table cell.

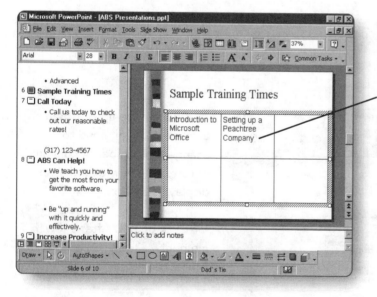

6. **Press** the **Tab key**. The blinking insertion point will move to the next cell.

7. **Type** a **heading** for the second column. The text will display in the second table cell.

8. Press the **Tab key.** The insertion point will move to the next cell.

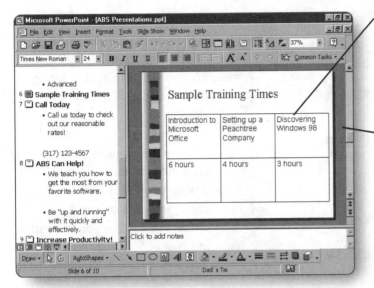

9. Type some **text** for the rest of the cells in the table, pressing the Tab key to move from cell to cell. The text will display in the table cells.

10. Click on the **gray area** outside the slide. If necessary, PowerPoint will adjust the size of the table so that it fits on the slide.

TIP

To edit the data in the table, click in the cell to be modified and type a change.

Inserting Charts

You can insert charts in PowerPoint in two ways: you can create the chart in PowerPoint or you can copy a chart you created in Excel.

Creating a Chart in PowerPoint

You can add a slide that contains a chart created by PowerPoint.

1. Display the **slide** to contain the chart. A prompt in the middle of the slide will display telling you how to add a chart.

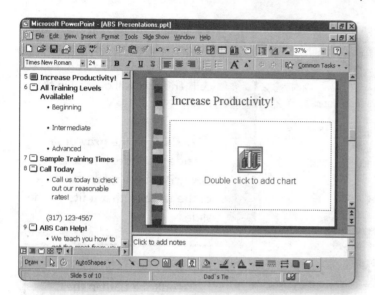

2. Double-click on the **button** in the center of the slide. A sample chart and a Datasheet window will display containing the data used in the sample chart.

You'll make changes in the Datasheet window to make changes to the chart. Make changes to the cells of a datasheet just like you learned in Chapter 9, "Creating a Simple Spreadsheet."

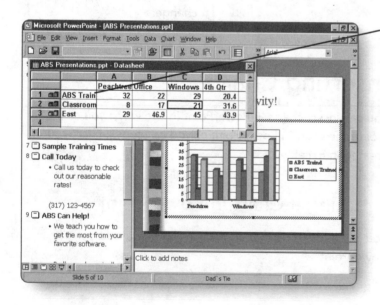

3. Change the **text** and **values** in the cells of the datasheet as needed. Your text and values will display.

You may need to delete any extra sample column or row data.

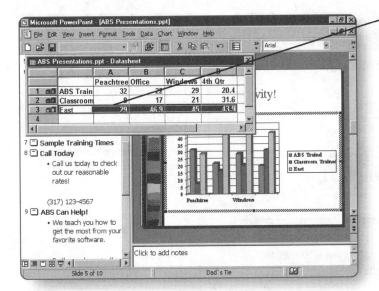

4. Press and **drag** the **mouse** across any unwanted data. The data will be highlighted.

5. Press the **Delete key**. All the data in the column will disappear, and the chart will adjust itself to display only data for the remaining columns.

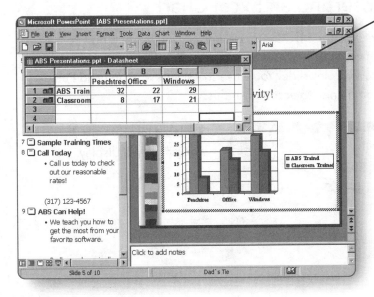

6. Click on the **gray area** outside the slide. The changes to the chart will be accepted and the Datasheet window will close.

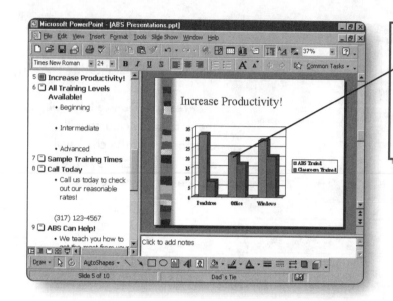

TIP

If you need to modify any information on the chart, double-click on the chart to reopen the Datasheet window.

Inserting an Excel Chart

In Chapter 14, "Creating Charts," you learned how to create charts in Excel. You can insert an Excel chart into a PowerPoint slide. You'll use the Windows Copy and Paste commands to accomplish this.

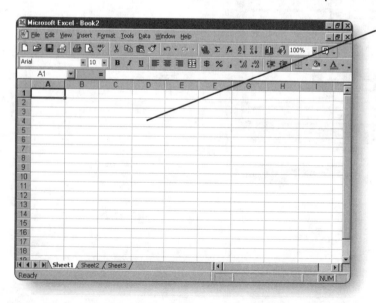

1. Start Excel. A blank worksheet will display.

2. Open the **worksheet** containing the chart that you want to place in PowerPoint. The chart will display on the screen.

3. Click on the **edge** of the chart. The chart will be selected.

4. Click on the **Copy button**. "Marching Ants" will appear and Excel will copy the chart to the Windows Clipboard.

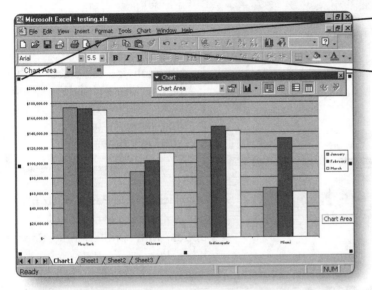

5. Click on the **PowerPoint button**. Your presentation will display.

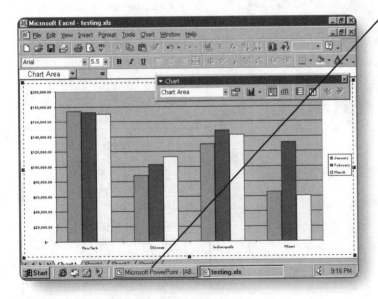

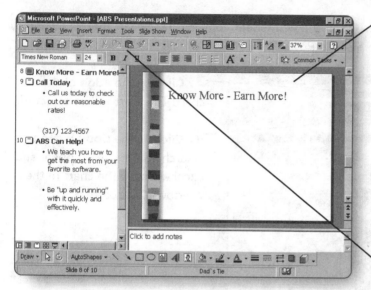

6. **Display** the **slide** to contain a chart. The slide will display on the screen.

TIP

Although you can place the chart on any slide layout, the best type of slide layout to use is a Title Only slide.

7. **Click** on the **Paste button**. A copy of the Excel chart will appear with handles, indicating it is selected.

The chart probably will be hard to read because it is too small. You'll need to resize it.

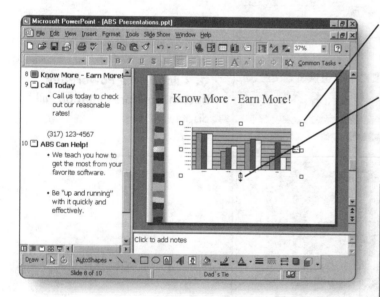

8. **Position** the **mouse** over one of the handles. The mouse pointer will turn into a double-headed arrow.

TIP

Dragging on a corner handle allows you to resize the chart in both directions (length and width) simultaneously and maintain the chart's proportions.

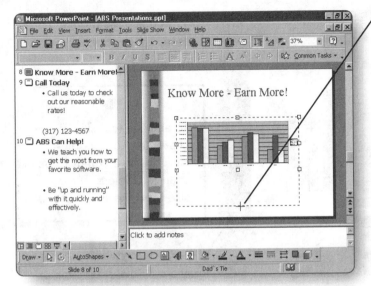

9. Drag a **chart handle** outward. The mouse pointer will change to a cross and a dotted line will indicate the new chart size.

10. Release the **mouse button**. The chart will be resized.

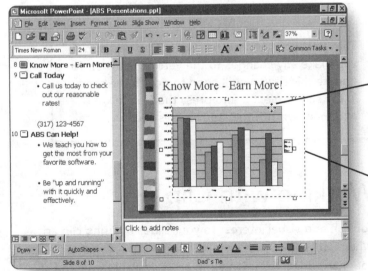

You may also want to move the chart to a different position on the page.

11. Move the **mouse pointer** over the chart. The mouse pointer will change to a four-headed arrow.

12. Drag the **chart** to a different location on the slide. A dotted box indicates the new position.

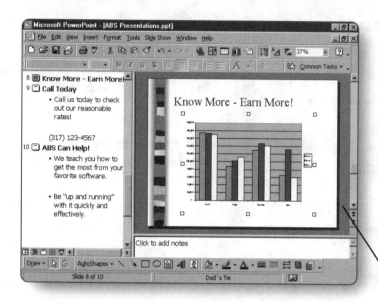

13. **Release** the **mouse button**. The chart will be moved.

TIP

To edit the text size of any chart element, double-click on the element to be changed. Select a new size from the size button.

14. **Click anywhere** on the gray area. PowerPoint will cancel the selection.

NOTE

The chart you just inserted will not be updated if you make any changes to the version in Excel. To update this slide, you'll need to delete the chart in the slide (select it and press the Delete key) and then perform the steps in this section again.

Working with Clip Art

You can add visual interest to your slides by using clip art. When Office 2000 was installed, some clip art was copied to your hard drive. Additional clip art is available from the Microsoft web site.

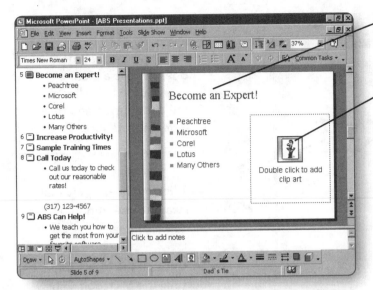

1. Display the **slide** to which you want to add clip art. The slide will be displayed.

2. Double-click on the **button** with the words Double click to add clip art. The Microsoft Clip Gallery will open.

TIP

If your slide does not have the words Double-click to add clip art, choose Insert, then Picture, then Clip art.

Included with Microsoft Office are 51 different categories of artwork.

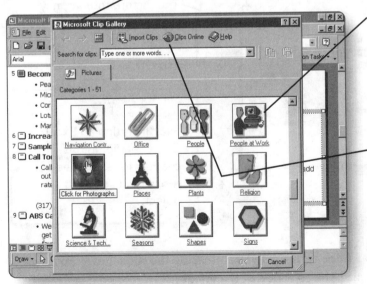

3. Click on the **category** that you want to use. Available clip art in the selected category will display.

TIP

Download additional clip art, pictures, and sound clips from Microsoft by clicking on the Clips Online button and following the displayed instructions.

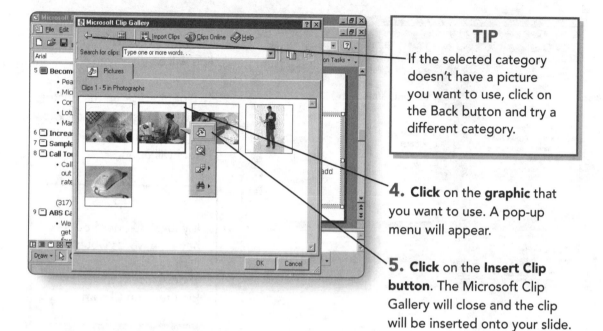

TIP

If the selected category doesn't have a picture you want to use, click on the Back button and try a different category.

4. Click on the **graphic** that you want to use. A pop-up menu will appear.

5. Click on the **Insert Clip button**. The Microsoft Clip Gallery will close and the clip will be inserted onto your slide.

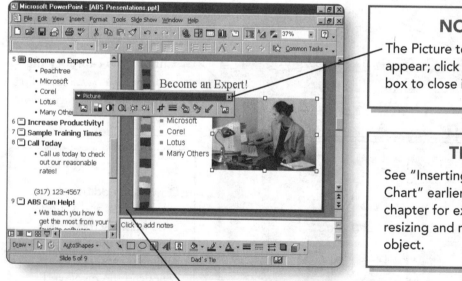

NOTE

The Picture toolbar may appear; click on the Close box to close it.

TIP

See "Inserting an Excel Chart" earlier in this chapter for examples of resizing and moving an object.

6. Click on the **gray area** outside the slide. PowerPoint will cancel the selection of the image.

Adding Transitions

Transitions are special effects you can use if you're creating a presentation you intend to show as a slide show on a computer. Transitions make the change between slides appear smoother by fading, wiping, or dissolving slides.

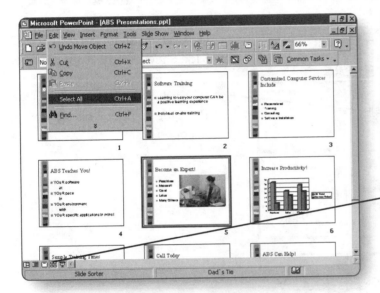

TIP

Use only one type of transition, or possibly two, for each presentation. If you use more, the audience will be distracted from your presentation.

1. Click on the **Slide Sorter View button**. PowerPoint will switch to Slide Sorter view.

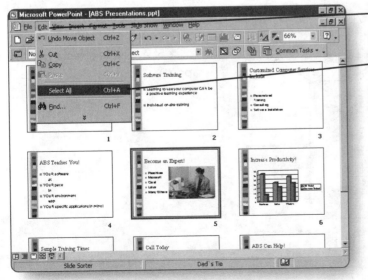

2. Click on **Edit**. The Edit menu will appear.

3. Click on **Select All**. PowerPoint will select all slides in the presentation.

NOTE

The transition you choose will apply to all slides in the presentation. If you want the transition to apply only to certain slides, select just those slides by holding down the Ctrl key while clicking on each slide.

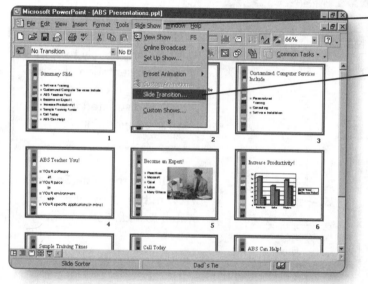

4. **Click** on **Slide Show**. The Slide Show menu will appear.

5. **Click** on **Slide Transition**. The Slide Transition dialog box will open.

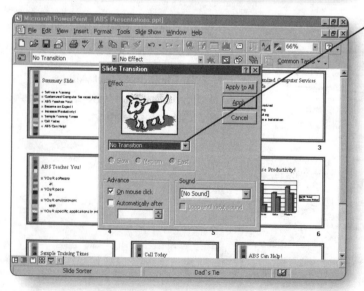

6. **Click** on the **down arrow** (▼) below the effect picture. A list of available effects will appear.

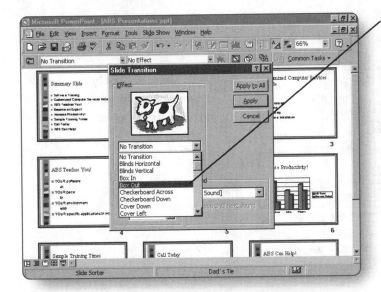

7. Click on an **effect.** The effect will be selected.

TIP

You'll need to experiment with the effects to find the best one for your presentation. An effect such as Dissolve works well if you have design elements in the background of each slide. Dissolve keeps the backgrounds steady while dissolving only text.

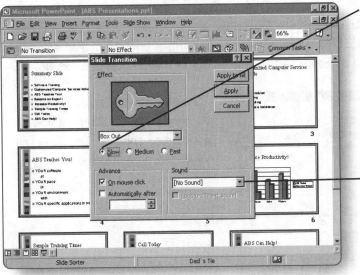

8. Click on a **speed** (Slow, Medium, or Fast). The effect picture will demonstrate how the effect works.

You can also apply sounds to play as each slide transitions to the next one.

9. Click on the **down arrow** (▼) at the right of Sound. A list of available sounds will display.

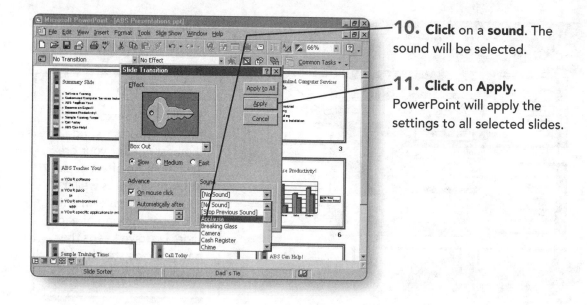

10. **Click** on a **sound**. The sound will be selected.

11. **Click** on **Apply**. PowerPoint will apply the settings to all selected slides.

Animating Slides

Animations are transitions you apply to elements on a slide, not to the entire slide. For example, you can use an animation to make a chart fade in or out or a slide title to trickle in.

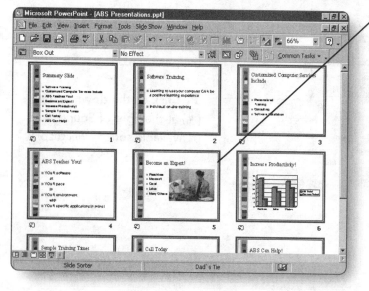

1. **Double-click** on the **slide** containing the element you want to animate. The slide will display in Normal view.

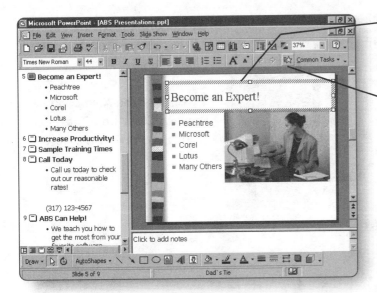

2. Click on the **object** that you want to animate. Handles will surround the object.

3. Click on the **Animation Effects button**. The Animation Effects toolbar will display.

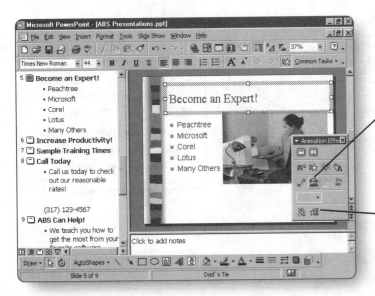

4. Click on the **effect** that you want to use. PowerPoint will apply the effect to the selected object.

5. Click on **Animation Preview**. A small sample slide will display with the animation effects for the current slide.

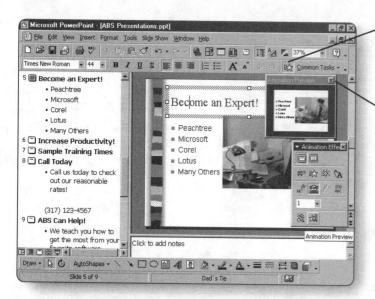

6. **Click** on the **Animation Effects button**. The Animation Effects toolbar will close.

7. **Click** on the **Animation Preview Close box**. The Animation Preview will close.

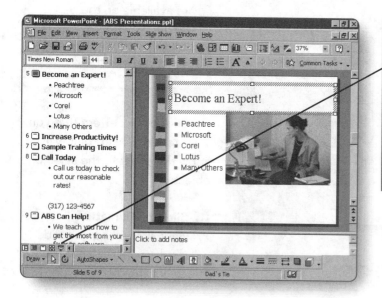

TIP

Test all your special effects by displaying a slide show. Click on the Slide Show View button. Click the mouse to advance through each slide; press the Esc key to end the show.

Part IV Review Questions

1. What three elements are displayed in Normal view? *See "Using Normal Tri-Pane View" in Chapter 15*

2. Why might you want speaker notes? *See "Viewing Speaker Notes" in Chapter 15*

3. What key can be pressed at any time to end a slide show? *See "Viewing a Slide Show" in Chapter 15*

4. What is each page of a presentation called? *See "Adding, Deleting, and Rearranging Slides" in Chapter 16*

5. What do Layouts do? *See "Adding, Deleting, and Rearranging Slides" in Chapter 16*

6. What are instruction blocks and do they print? *See "Adding Text to a New Slide" in Chapter 16*

7. What steps must you take to print Speaker Notes? *See "Printing Speaker Notes" in Chapter 16*

8. If you've created a chart from an Excel worksheet, do you need to recreate it to display it in a PowerPoint presentation? *See "Inserting Charts" in Chapter 17*

9. What is on a summary slide? *See "Creating a Summary Slide" in Chapter 17*

10. What are transitions? *See "Adding Transitions" in Chapter 17*

PART V

Using Outlook

18

Getting Started with Outlook

Outlook is the information organizer of Office 2000—you can send and receive e-mail, store names and addresses, maintain a calendar, keep track of things you need to do, review a history of the things you've done, and keep notes. Microsoft has designed Outlook so that you can use it as an information center; you can even use Outlook to open Office documents. You should start by understanding the Outlook window. In this chapter, you'll learn how to:

- Understand the Outlook window
- Add and display folders
- Add a shortcut to the Outlook bar
- Reorder shortcuts on the Outlook bar
- Move a shortcut to a different group

Understanding the Outlook Window

In Outlook, you store information in folders. You open a folder in Outlook by clicking on a shortcut for the folder that appears in the Outlook bar. On the Outlook bar, shortcuts are organized into groups.

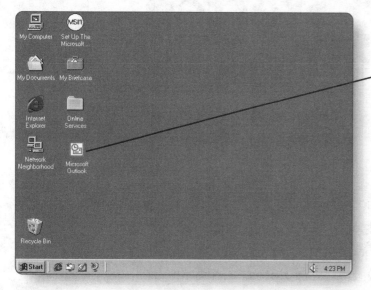

1. Double-click on the **Outlook icon** to start Outlook. The Outlook window will open.

TIP
You might be asked to choose a Profile; accept whatever profile is suggested by clicking on OK.

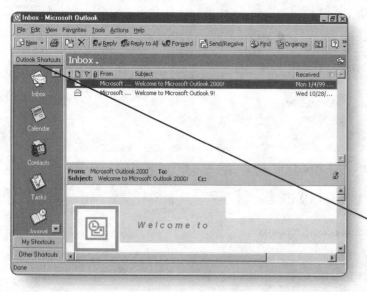

Along the left side of the screen, you will see the Outlook bar that contains shortcuts to folders. The shortcuts you see initially are to folders that are created by default in Outlook. You can add shortcuts to the Outlook bar to organize information in Outlook in a way that suits your work style.

Notice on the Outlook Bar that Outlook organizes shortcuts into groups. The default group that appears is the Outlook Shortcut group.

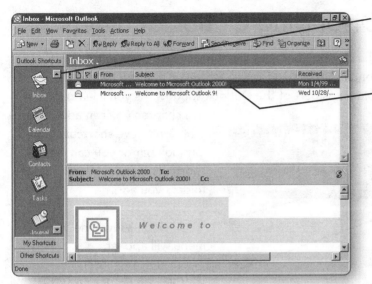

Use the arrows to scroll through the shortcuts on the Outlook bar.

The right side of the window shows the contents of the folder that is currently selected on the left side of the window. When you first start Outlook, you will see the contents of the Inbox that stores e-mail.

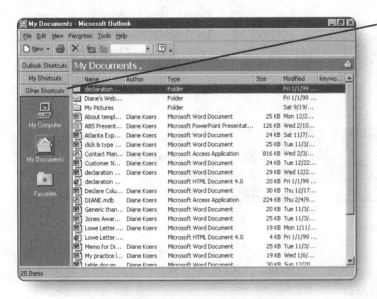

You can also click on the Other Shortcuts group, which contains shortcuts that allow you to open folders on your computer or on any attached network drive.

Displaying Outlook Folders

The Outlook bar contains shortcuts to folders; it doesn't contain the actual folders. However, you can display the folders as part of the Outlook window. As you'll learn later in this chapter, you can add folders that don't have shortcuts in the Outlook bar or you can create shortcuts in the Outlook bar for folders you add.

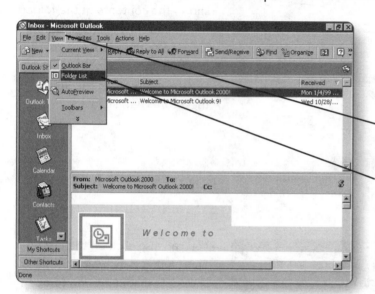

1. Click on **View**. The View menu will appear.

2. Click on **Folder List**. The Folder List will appear.

Initially, the folders in the Folder List match the shortcuts that appear in the Outlook bar.

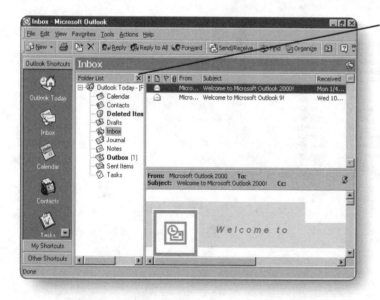

3. Click on the **Folder List Close box**. The Folder list will close.

Adding a Folder in Outlook

To further organize your work in Outlook, you may need additional folders.

1. Click on **File**. The File menu will appear.

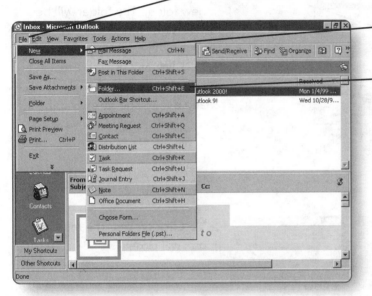

2. Click on **New**. A cascading menu will appear.

3. Click on **Folder**. The Create New Folder dialog box will open.

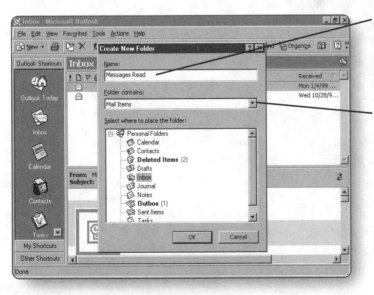

4. Type the **folder name** in the Name: text box. The folder name will display in the text box.

5. Click on the **down arrow** (▼) of the Folder contains: list box. A list of items you can track in Outlook will appear.

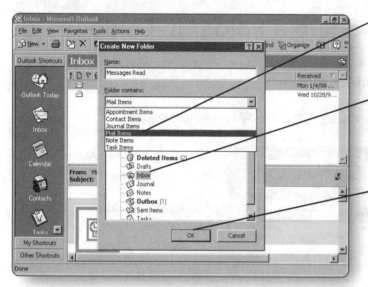

6. **Click** on the **type of information** the new folder will contain.

7. **Click** on the **folder** inside which you want to place the new folder. The folder will be selected.

8. **Click** on **OK**. The Create New Folder dialog box will close and a message box will appear.

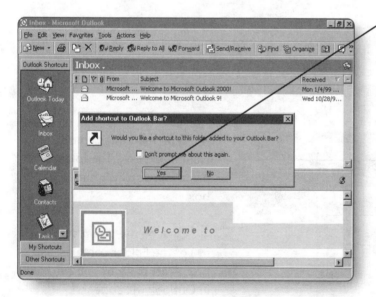

9. **Click** on **Yes**. The message box will close.

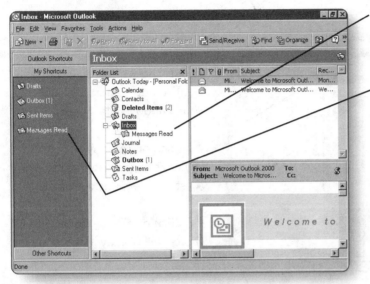

The new folder will appear in the Folder List under the folder you selected.

The shortcut is also added to the My Shortcuts group.

TIP

You might want to add folders to Outlook to help you organize the e-mail you receive.

Adding a Shortcut to the Outlook Bar

You can use Outlook as an information center from which you open documents. The default Outlook bar already contains a shortcut to the My Documents and Favorites folders. You can add an Outlook bar shortcut that will display all the shortcuts that currently appear on your Desktop.

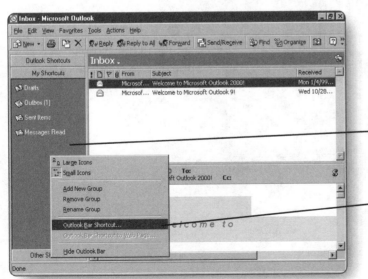

1. Right-click on the **Outlook bar**. A shortcut menu will appear.

2. Click on **Outlook Bar Shortcut**. The Add to Outlook Bar dialog box will open.

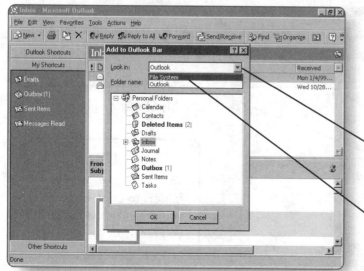

Outlook is assuming that you want to add a shortcut that already exists in the Outlook folders; however, you'll probably want to add a shortcut from your Windows file system.

3. Click on the **down arrow** (▼) next to the Look in: list box. A list of selections will display.

4. Click on **File System**. The choice will display in the Look in: list box.

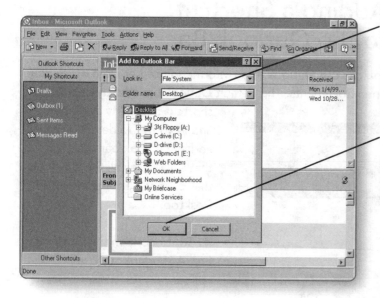

5. Locate and **click** on the **folder** containing the shortcut you want to add to the Outlook bar. The folder name will be selected.

6. Click on **OK**. The folder containing the shortcut will appear at the bottom of the Outlook bar.

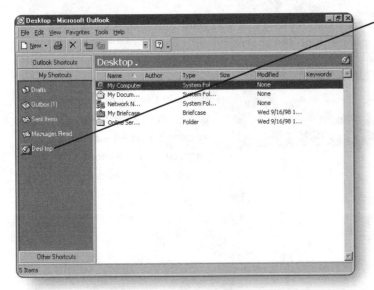

7. Click on the **shortcut** that you just added to the Outlook bar. You will see the shortcuts stored in the folder on the right side of the Outlook window.

TIP

You can add items that appear in the Programs folder on the Windows Start menu using these steps. In step 5, open the Windows\Start menu\Programs folder and find the folder containing the program you want to add to the Outlook bar. All the shortcuts in that folder will be added to the folder that appears on the Outlook bar.

Changing the Order of Outlook Bar Shortcuts

You can move a shortcut up or down on the Outlook bar or move it to a different group.

1. Point at the **shortcut** you want to move. A square will appear around the shortcut icon.

2. Drag the **shortcut** up or down in the list or to a different group. A black marker will appear between existing shortcuts as the mouse pointer moves over an acceptable spot.

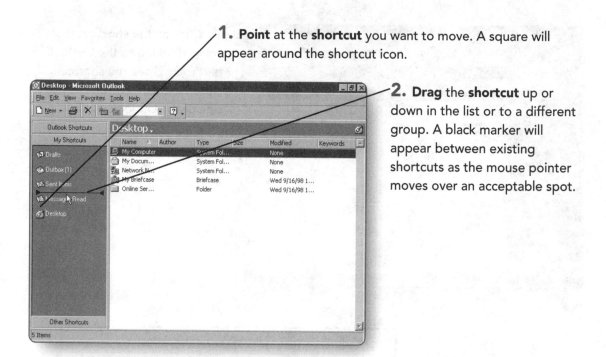

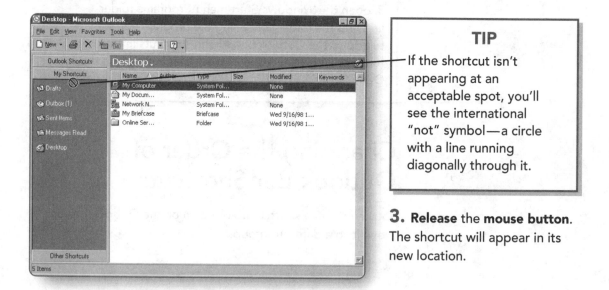

TIP

If the shortcut isn't appearing at an acceptable spot, you'll see the international "not" symbol—a circle with a line running diagonally through it.

3. Release the **mouse button**. The shortcut will appear in its new location.

Deleting a Shortcut

If you've created a shortcut on the Outlook bar and decide you no longer need it there, you can easily delete it. Deleting the icon will only delete the display of the shortcut on the Outlook bar, not the folder itself or its contents.

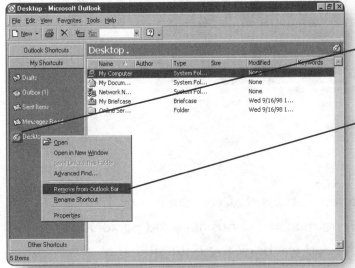

1. Right-click on the Outlook Bar shortcut to be deleted. A shortcut menu will appear.

2. Click on **Remove from Outlook Bar**. A confirmation window will display.

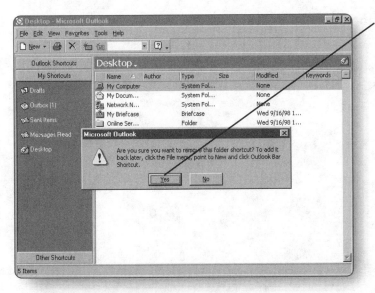

3. Click on **Yes**. The shortcut will be removed.

19

Working with the Address Book

Outlook contains an address book that you can use to maintain a variety of information about business and personal contacts. You can use the address book to print a phone or address list, telephone a contact, or send e-mail to a contact. In this chapter, you'll learn how to:

- Add an address book entry
- Delete a contact
- Print a contact list

Adding an Address Book Entry

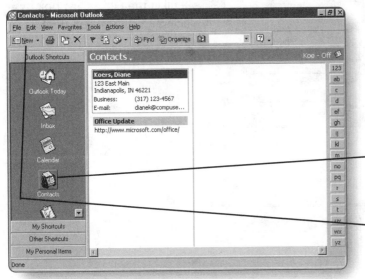

It is easy to add entries to the address book in Outlook. Initially, the contact list will contain only an entry for you and one for Microsoft. Contacts are listed in alphabetical order by last name.

1. **Click** on the **Contacts shortcut**. Your list of entries will appear.

2. **Click** on the **New contact button**. The Contact window will appear.

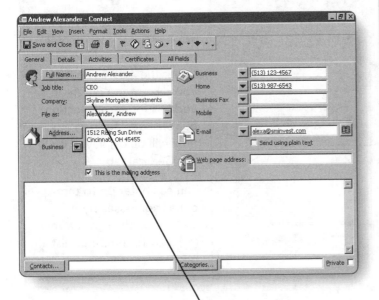

NOTE

The New button in Outlook is context-sensitive. When you're viewing the Inbox, clicking on New will start a new mail message. When you're viewing Contacts, clicking on New will start a new contact.

The first tab to be displayed is the General tab. This is where the contact's primary information, such as name and address, is stored.

3. **Type information** in each box on the General tab. Use the Tab key to move from box to box. The data you type will display in the appropriate boxes.

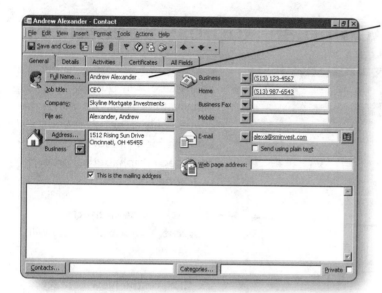

When you enter the full name as first name, last name, Outlook will fill in the File as: list box by placing it as last name, first name.

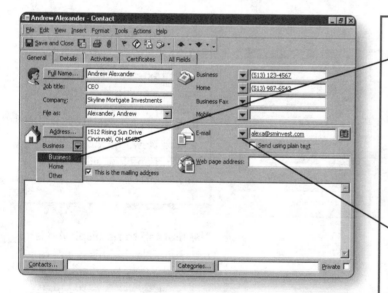

TIP

You can enter up to three addresses for each contact by clicking on a selection under the Address button. You can enter a different address for each selection but only one address at a time will be displayed on the General tab.

You can enter up to three e-mail addresses by clicking on the down arrow (▼) next to the E-mail list box.

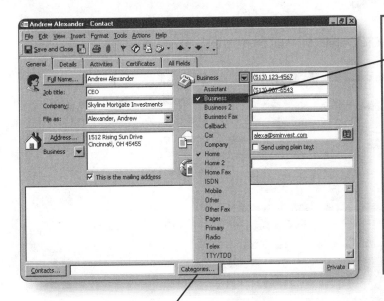

NOTE

To enter several phone numbers for a category, click on the down arrow next to a phone number list box and click on a selection. Up to four telephone numbers can be displayed at the same time on the General tab—one each for Business, Home, Business Fax, and Mobile.

5. Click on the **Categories button**. The Categories dialog box will open.

Categories can be used to divide your contacts into those with similar characteristics. You can then use that information to produce telephone or mailing lists to specific groups.

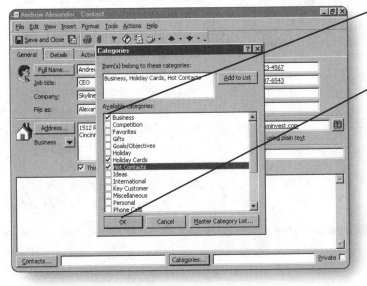

6. Click on **any** of the **available categories**. The options will be selected.

7. Click on **OK**. The Categories dialog box will close.

8. **Click** on the **Details tab**.
The Details tab will come to the front.

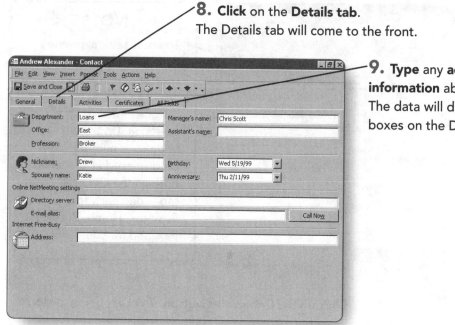

9. **Type** any **additional information** about the contact. The data will display in the boxes on the Details tab.

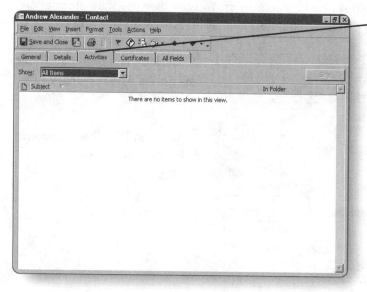

10. **Click** on the **Activities tab**. The Activities tab will come to the front.

Outlook can use the Journal to keep a list of recorded contacts you have made with this person, such as meetings you have scheduled or e-mail you have sent or received. Those journal entries will display in the Activities tab. Because this is a new contact, no journal entries have yet been made.

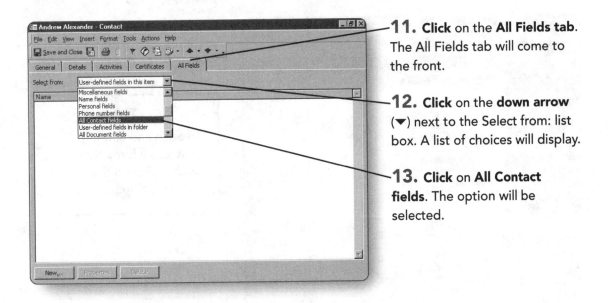

11. **Click** on the **All Fields tab**. The All Fields tab will come to the front.

12. **Click** on the **down arrow** (▼) next to the Select from: list box. A list of choices will display.

13. **Click** on **All Contact fields**. The option will be selected.

You will now see information about the contact in a table format.

14. **Click** on the **Save and Close button**. Outlook will save this entry and close the New Contact box.

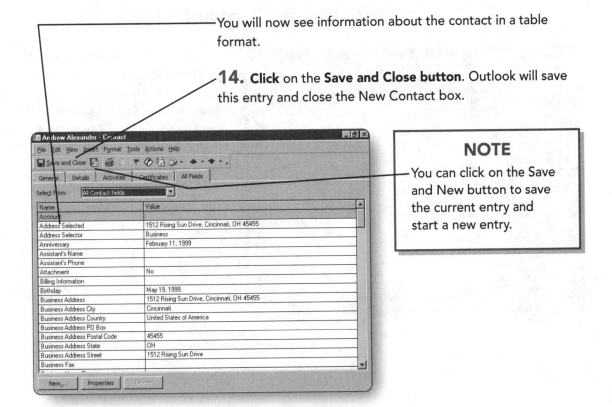

NOTE

You can click on the Save and New button to save the current entry and start a new entry.

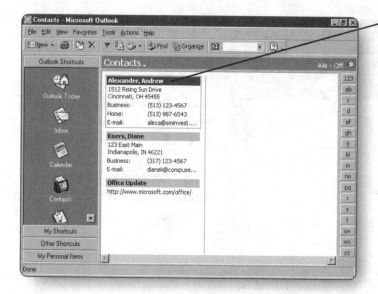

After you enter a new contact, you'll see information about the contact in the Contacts window.

TIP

To open and edit any contact's information, double-click on the contact's name.

Printing a Contact List

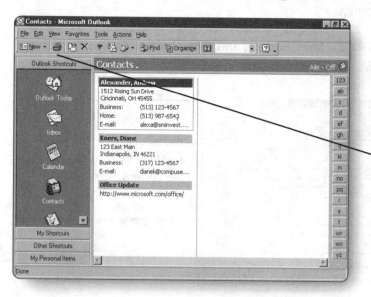

You can print the information you store about your contacts in a variety of formats: Card Style, Small Booklet Style, Medium Booklet Style, Memo Style, and Phone Directory Style.

1. **Click** on the **Print button**. The Print dialog box will open.

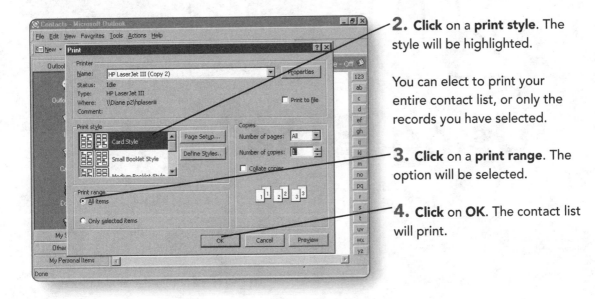

2. Click on a **print style**. The style will be highlighted.

You can elect to print your entire contact list, or only the records you have selected.

3. Click on a **print range**. The option will be selected.

4. Click on **OK**. The contact list will print.

Deleting a Contact

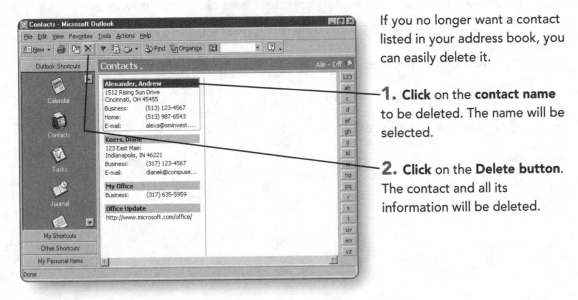

If you no longer want a contact listed in your address book, you can easily delete it.

1. Click on the **contact name** to be deleted. The name will be selected.

2. Click on the **Delete button**. The contact and all its information will be deleted.

20

Using E-mail

Outlook enables you to send and receive e-mail messages. You can also create an e-mail message and check for new mail in Outlook. In this chapter, you'll learn how to:

- Send an e-mail message
- Respond to an e-mail message
- Manage e-mail messages

Configuring Outlook
for Internet E-mail

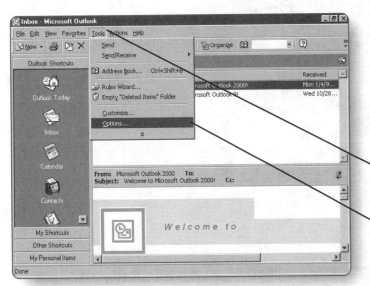

In order to use Outlook's e-mail process, you must have some type of e-mail. That could be an internal company e-mail or one through the Internet. You'll need to advise Outlook how to connect to your e-mail.

1. Click on **Tools**. The Tools menu will appear.

2. Click on **Options**. The Options dialog box will open.

3. Click on the **Mail Delivery tab**. The Mail Delivery tab will come to the front.

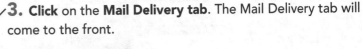

4. Click on the **check box** to send messages immediately when connected. The option will be checked.

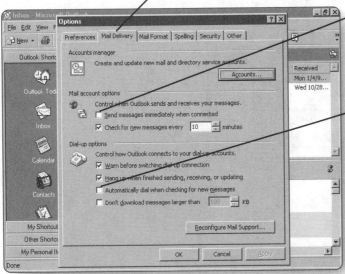

5. Click on the **check box** to automatically dial when checking for new messages. The option will be checked.

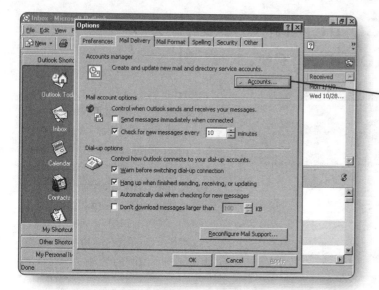

Now you'll need to tell Outlook what Internet account to use for your e-mail.

6. Click on **Accounts**. The Accounts dialog box will open.

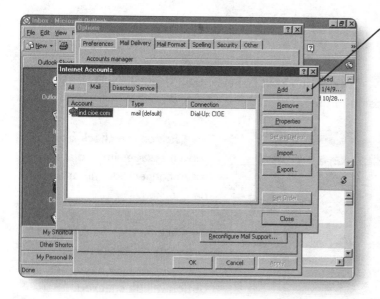

7. Click on **Add**. A menu of choices will display.

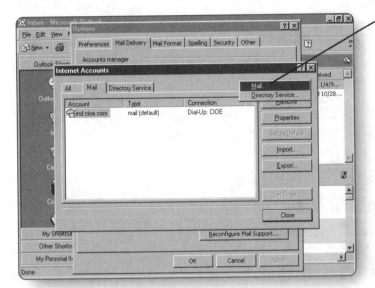

8. **Click** on **Mail**. The Internet Connection Wizard (ICW) will begin.

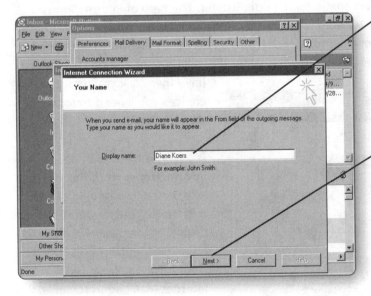

9. **Enter** your **name** as you would like it to appear on the From line of your e-mail messages. Your name will display in the Display name: text box.

10. **Click** on **Next**. The second page of the ICW will display.

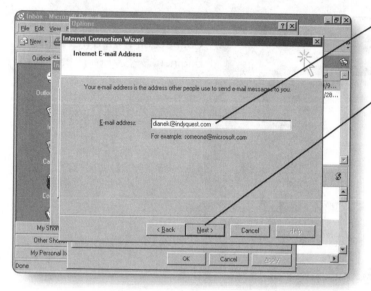

11. Type your **e-mail address**. The address will display in the E-mail address: text box.

12. Click on **Next**. The E-mail Server Names page of the ICW will display.

This next step is a little trickier. The type of information you enter here will depend on the requirements of your Internet Service Provider (ISP). If you don't have written instructions for these steps from your ISP, call them on the phone and have them talk you through the choices you'll need to make for their connection.

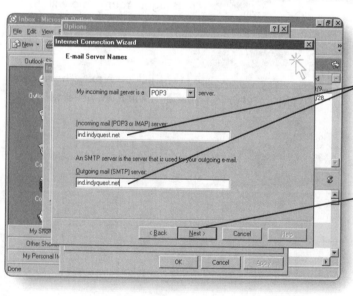

13. Type the required **information** in both the incoming and outgoing server text boxes. The information will display in the designated boxes.

14. Click on **Next**. The Internet Mail Logon screen will display.

15. Type your **account name** as provided by your ISP. This may or may not be the same as your display name. The name will display in the Account name: text box.

16. Press the **Tab key**. The blinking insertion point will move to the Password screen.

17. If you wish to store your password, **type** your **password** in the Password: text box. The password will not display, only a series of asterisks.

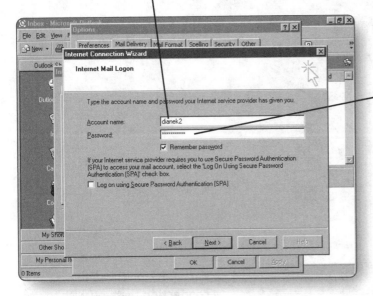

TIP

Password information is optional. If you are the only person with access to your computer, you may wish to store your password so you don't need to type it each time you send or receive e-mail. If you prefer to type it in each time (for security reasons), leave this box blank.

18. Click on **Next**. The Choose Connection Type screen will display.

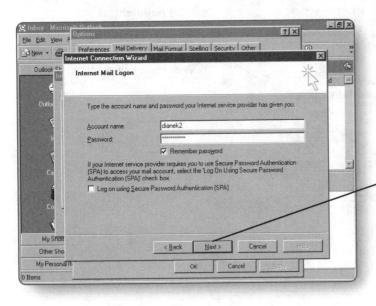

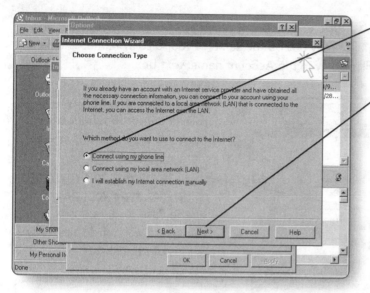

19. **Click** on an **option** to connect to the Internet. The option will be selected.

20. **Click** on **Next**. The Dial-Up Connection screen will display.

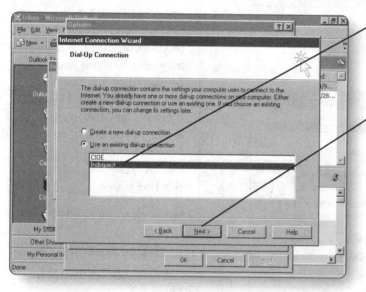

21. **Click** on the **dial-up connection** that you wish to use for Outlook. The dial-up name will be highlighted.

22. **Click** on **Next**. The final ICW screen will display.

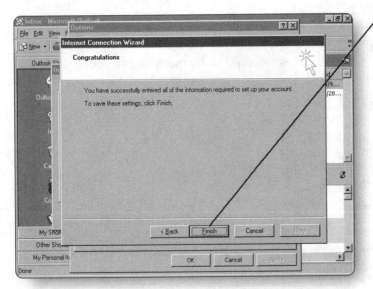

23. **Click** on **Finish**. The connection you selected will display in the Internet Accounts dialog box.

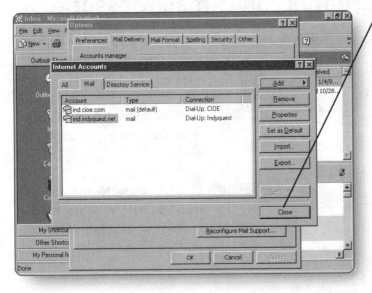

24. **Click** on **Close**. The Internet Accounts dialog box will close and you'll return to the Options dialog box.

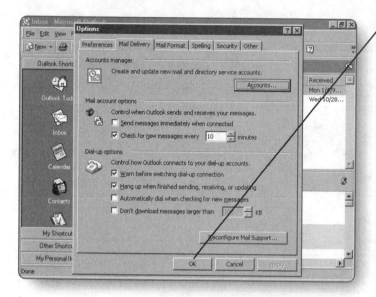

25. Click on **OK**. The Options dialog box will close and you'll be ready to use your Outlook e-mail.

Creating an E-mail Message

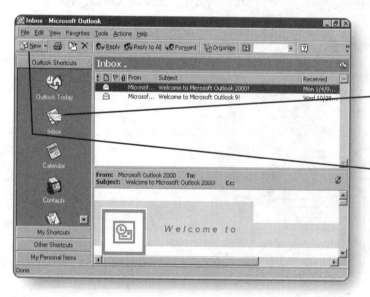

In Outlook, you can access your e-mail software to send e-mail messages.

1. Click on the **Inbox shortcut** in the Outlook bar to display the Inbox.

2. Click on the **New Mail Message button**. A new mail message window will appear.

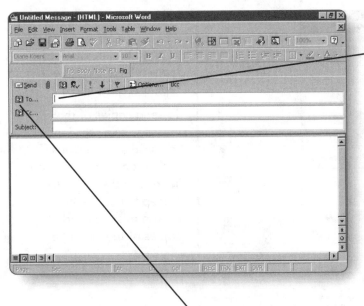

3. Click on the **To: button**. The e-mail addresses you have stored in the Contact list will appear in the Select Names dialog box.

4. Click on the recipient's **name**. The name will be highlighted.

5. Click on the **To button**. The recipient's name will appear in the Message Recipients text box.

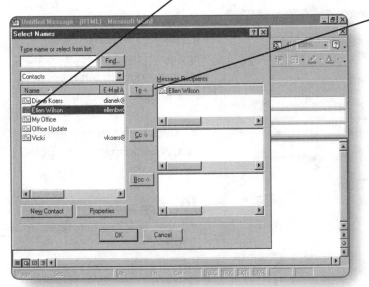

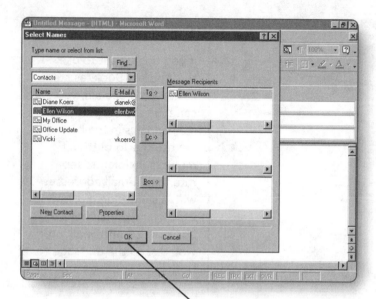

TIP

To send the message to more than one recipient, repeat steps 4 and 5.

To send copies of the message to a recipient, repeat the same steps, but click on the Cc button instead of the To button in step 5. Use the Bcc button to send blind copies of the message.

6. Click on **OK**. The Select Names dialog box will close. The names you selected will appear in the To and Cc text boxes.

7. Click in the **Subject: text box**. The insertion point will move to the subject line.

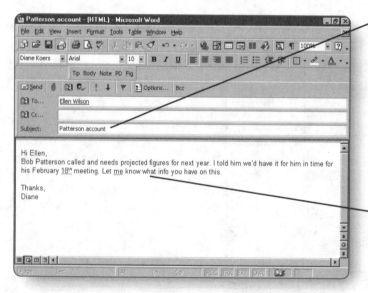

8. Type a **subject** for the message. The subject will appear in the Subject: text box. It's not required, but messages should have a subject.

9. Click in the large **message box**. A blinking insertion point will appear.

10. Type a **message**. The text will appear in the message box.

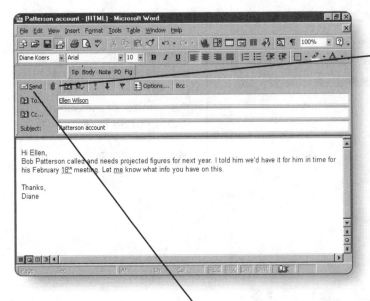

TIP

To send a file, click on the Insert File button (it looks like a paper clip). The Insert File dialog box will open. Navigate to the folder containing the file and choose the file. When you click on OK, you'll see an icon representing the file in your mail message.

11. Click on the **Send button**. The Message window will close and the Inbox window will appear.

Sending Your Message

If you are on a corporate e-mail system, e-mail messages are sent immediately; however if you're connecting via the Internet, Outlook will hold messages in the Outbox until you connect and send your messages.

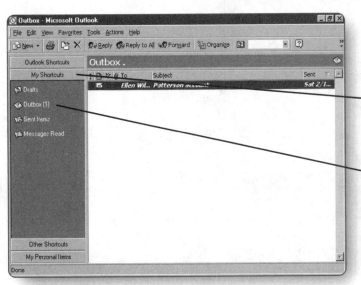

1. Click on the **My Shortcuts group**. A list of shortcuts will display.

2. Click on the **Outbox** shortcut. A list of messages waiting to be sent will display.

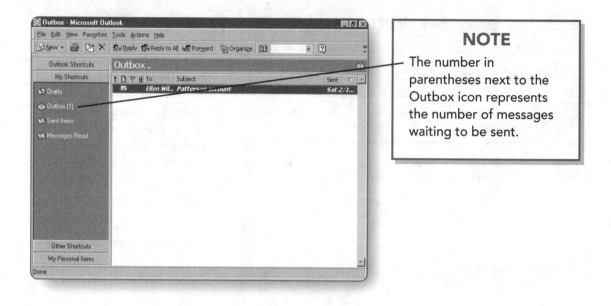

3. Click on **Tools**. The Tools menu will display.

4. Click on **Send**. Your ISP will be dialed and the message will be sent.

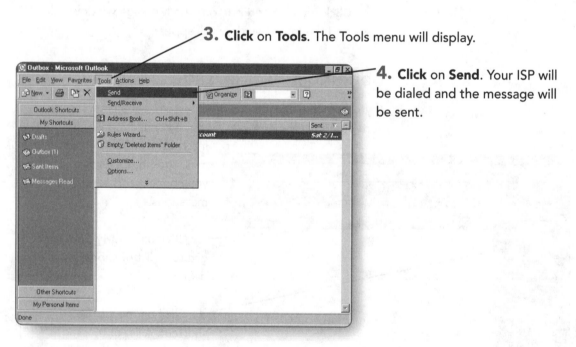

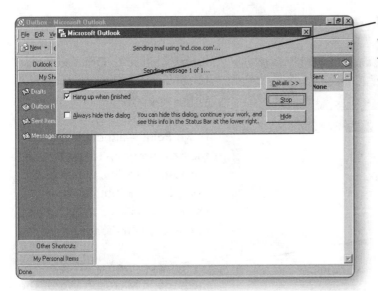

If this box is checked, Outlook will automatically disconnect from your ISP upon completion of sending your message.

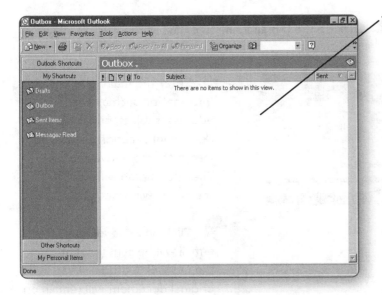

The Outbox is now empty.

Sending a Message via Office Mail

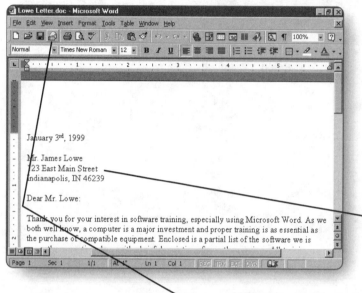

A new feature to Office 2000 is to send mail while using your Office applications such as Word, Excel, or even PowerPoint—although Word is the best program to use for this purpose. In reality, Office is still using Outlook, but you don't have to actually go into Outlook to create the message.

1. **Type** or **open** a **letter or message** in Microsoft Word. The document will display on the screen.

2. **Click** on the **E-mail icon**. An e-mail window will display.

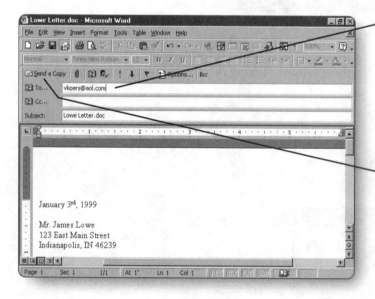

3. **Enter** the **mailing information** such as e-mail address, subject, and other desired information just like you learned in the above section. The information will display in the e-mail window.

4. **Click** on **Send a Copy**. The e-mail will be sent (or sent to the Outlook Outbox). The original document will remain on your screen. Treat this document as any other Word document by choosing to save, edit, print, or close it.

Checking for Messages

You can check for new mail from Outlook; any e-mail you receive will appear in your Outlook Inbox.

1. Click on **Tools**. The Tools menu will appear.

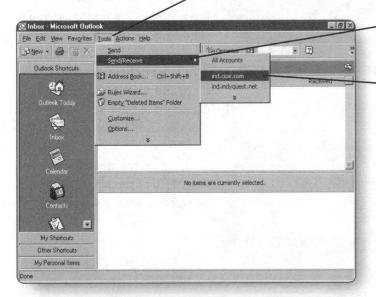

2. Click on **Send/Receive**. A submenu will appear.

3. Click on the **e-mail account** that you want to check. Outlook will check for messages and send any messages waiting to be sent.

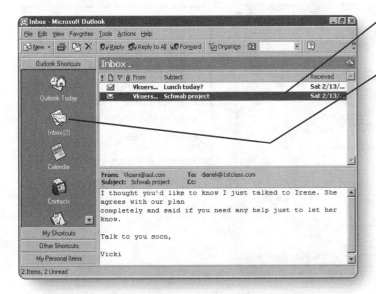

Any new messages you receive will appear in the Outlook Inbox.

The number of unread messages in your Inbox appears in parentheses after the Inbox shortcut.

TIP

If you are always connected to your e-mail system, messages will appear automatically in your Inbox and you won't need to check for messages.

Reading Your Messages

The Inbox window has two panes that you can use to work with messages. The top half of the Inbox lists the messages. The current message is displayed in the bottom half of the window. The first thing you'll want to do is read the message.

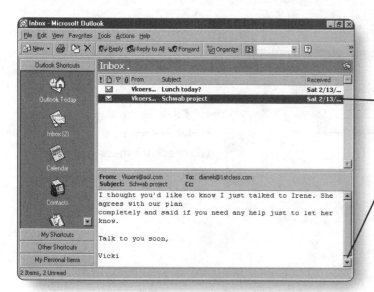

1. Click on the **message** to be read. The message will be displayed in the bottom half of the Inbox window.

2. Click on the **down arrow** (▼). More of the message will be scrolled onto the screen.

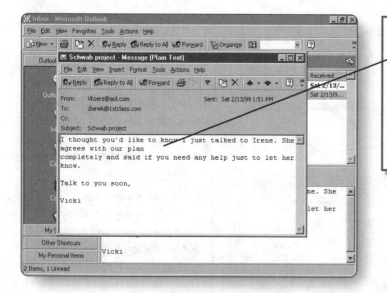

TIP

Optionally, if you double-click on a message, the entire message will display in a separate window. This may make some messages easier to read.

Responding to a Message

You can respond to a message in a number of ways: reply to the message, forward the message, delete the message, or close the message without answering.

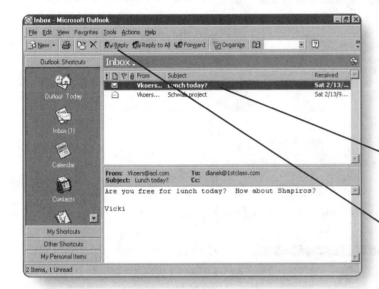

Replying to a Message

Most people consider it a common courtesy to respond to a message they receive.

1. Click on a **message**. The message title will be highlighted.

2. Click on the **Reply button**. A reply message window will open.

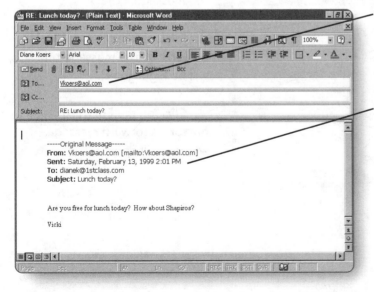

Outlook will fill in the To: text box with the address of the original sender as well as the Subject: text box.

Outlook will copy the original message and allow you space to add reply information at the top of the message.

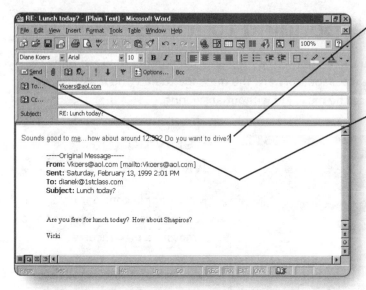

3. **Type** the **reply message**. The text will display in the message window above the original text.

4. **Click** on the **Send button**. The reply message will be sent and the reply window will close.

Forwarding a Message

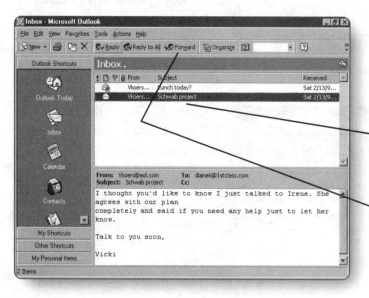

On occasion, information might come to you via e-mail that you want to share with others. In these cases, you can forward the message.

1. **Click** on the **message** to be forwarded. The message title will be highlighted.

2. **Click** on the **Forward button**. A forward message window will open.

Just like in a reply message, Outlook will copy the original message and allow you space to add the forwarding message at the top of the message.

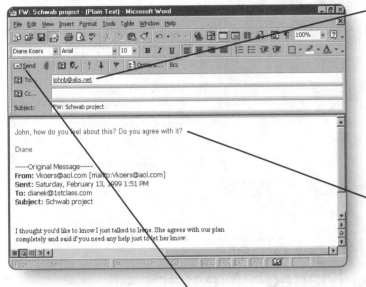

3. Type or **select** from the address book the forwarding recipients **e-mail address**. The recipient's address will display in the To: text box.

4. Click in the **message box**. The blinking insertion point will appear.

5. Type any desired forwarding **message**. The text will display in the message window above the original text.

6. Click on the **Send button**. The forwarded message will be sent and the forward message window will close.

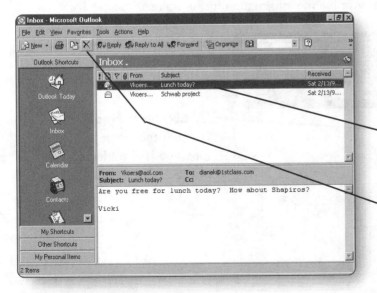

Deleting a Message

Some messages require no response and you might want to delete them.

1. Click on a **message** to be deleted. The message title will be highlighted.

2. Click on the **Delete button**. The message will be deleted from the Inbox.

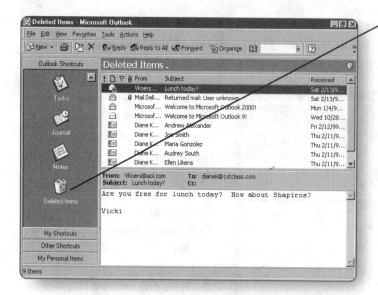

Outlook will move the message from the Inbox to the Deleted Items folder. You can display the contents of that folder and see the deleted message.

TIP

Items remain in the Deleted Items folder until you delete them from that folder.

Using Folders to Manage Messages

In some cases, you might not be ready to respond to a message when you receive it. You might want to answer it later or file the information for future use. You can file messages into different folders; perhaps one you created in Chapter 18, "Getting Started With Outlook."

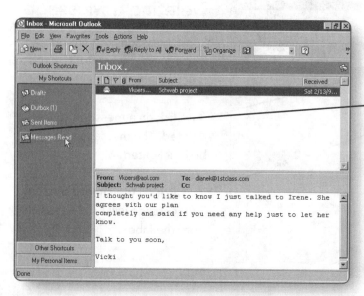

1. Click on the **group** that contains the folder to hold your message. The folder icon will display in the Outlook bar.

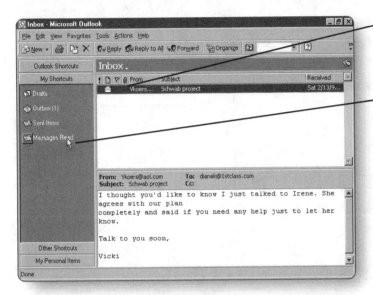

2. **Click** on the **message** to be stored. The message title will be highlighted.

3. **Drag** the **message** to the storage folder. As you are dragging the mouse, the pointer will become an arrow with a small box under it.

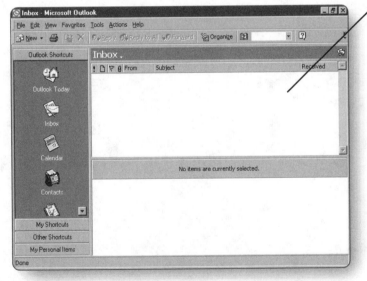

4. **Release** the **mouse button**. The message will be removed from the Inbox and moved to the folder.

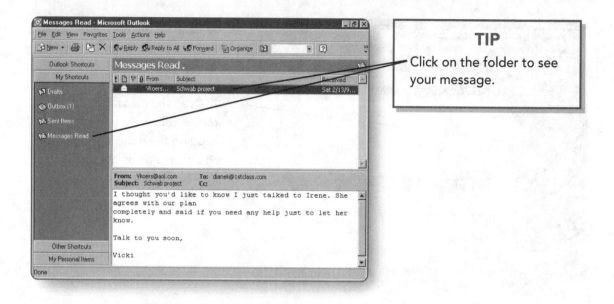

TIP
Click on the folder to see your message.

21

Using the Calendar

You can use the Outlook Calendar to schedule appointments, meetings, and events. You can also use the Outlook Calendar for individual or group scheduling. In this chapter, you'll learn how to:

- Change the Calendar's display
- Schedule an appointment or meeting
- Create a recurring appointment
- Reschedule and delete appointments
- Print the Calendar

Viewing the Calendar

You can view your Calendar from several different perspectives: one day at a time, one week at a time, one month at a time, and in a tabular format. You can switch to these views in different ways.

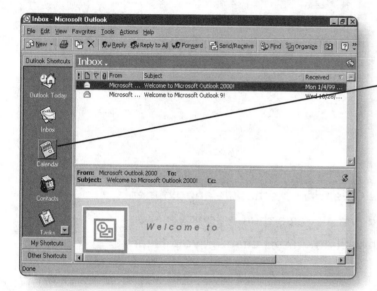

Changing the Calendar's View

1. Click on the **Calendar shortcut** in the Outlook bar. The Calendar will appear in the one-day-at-a-time view.

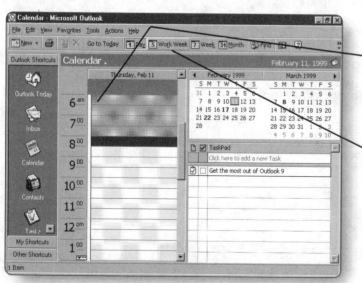

TIP

Times that appear darker are not standard "business hours."

2. Click on the **Work Week button**. The Calendar view will change to display one work week at a time without Saturday and Sunday.

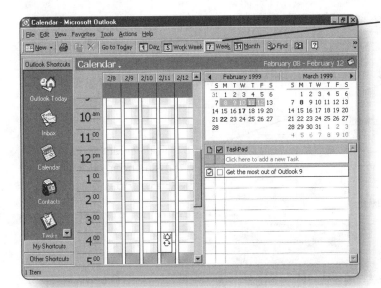

3. Click on the **Week button**. The Calendar view will change to display one week at a time—this time, including the weekend.

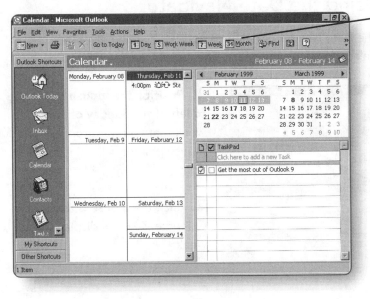

4. Click on the **Month button**. The Calendar view will change to display one month at a time.

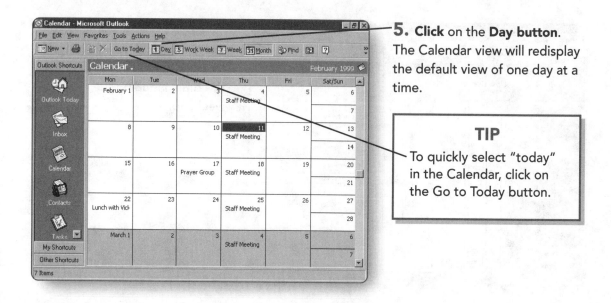

5. **Click** on the **Day button**. The Calendar view will redisplay the default view of one day at a time.

> **TIP**
>
> To quickly select "today" in the Calendar, click on the Go to Today button.

Using the Date Navigator

The Date Navigator helps you quickly switch between Calendar views and select days, weeks, or months to view.

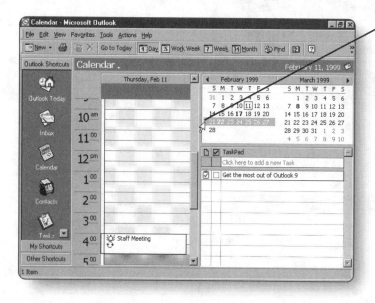

1. **Position** the **mouse pointer** to left of the Sunday of the week that you want to view. The mouse pointer will point to the right.

2. **Click** the **mouse button**. The Calendar view will display that week.

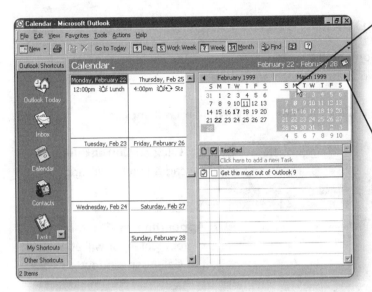

3. Click anywhere on the day of the week headings for the month you want to view. The Calendar view will display that month.

NOTE

If you need to see a different month, click on the left or right arrows that appear next to the month names.

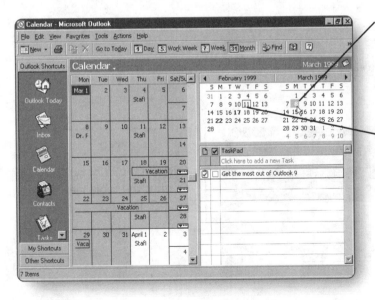

4. Click on the **day** you want to view. The Calendar view will show that day.

TIP

The current day is surrounded by a square so you can easily identify it.

Looking at the Calendar in Table View

Sometimes, seeing a list of appointments on the Calendar works better than any of the views.

1. Click on **View**. The View menu will appear.

2. Click on **Current View**. A cascading menu will appear.

3. Click on **Active Appointments**. The table view of your Calendar will appear in the Calendar window.

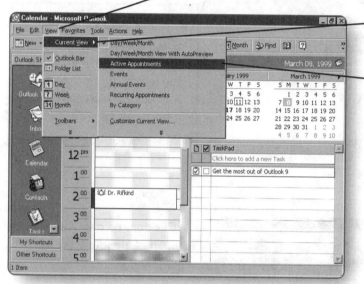

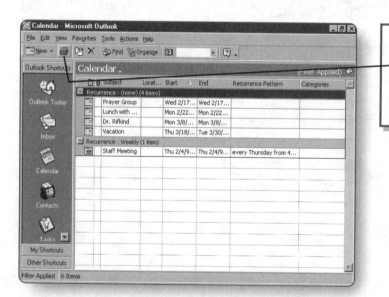

TIP

Click on the Print button to print the table view of your Calendar.

You'll find it just as easy to return to the appointment view.

4. Click on **View**. The View menu will appear.

5. Click on **Current View**. A cascading menu will appear.

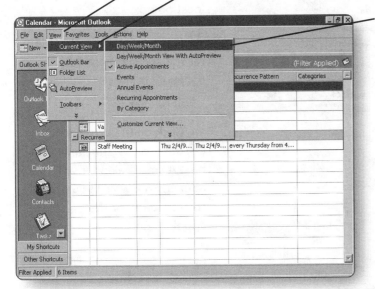

6. Click on **Day/Week/Month**. The standard calendar view will redisplay.

Setting Your Schedule

With Outlook you can schedule a one time appointment, an all day event, a recurring occasion, or even a meeting with coworkers.

Making an Appointment

An *appointment* is an entry to the Calendar that reserves time for an activity; appointments do not include other people. To make a new appointment, make sure you are viewing the Calendar.

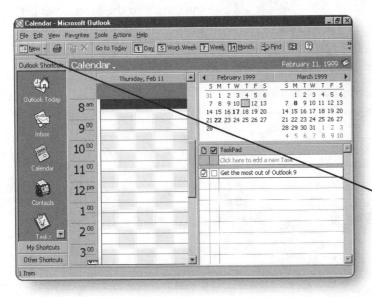

1. Click on the **New Appointment button**. The Appointment window will appear.

2. **Type** a **description** for the appointment in the Subject: text box. The text will display in the text box.

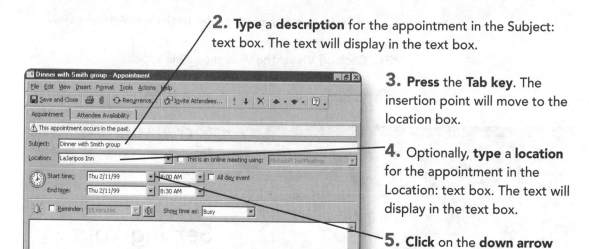

3. **Press** the **Tab key**. The insertion point will move to the location box.

4. Optionally, **type** a **location** for the appointment in the Location: text box. The text will display in the text box.

5. **Click** on the **down arrow** (▼) next to the Start time: list box. A small calendar will appear from which you can select a date for the appointment.

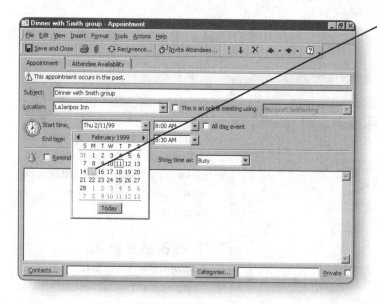

6. **Click** on the **date** for the appointment. Outlook will insert the date into the Start time: list box.

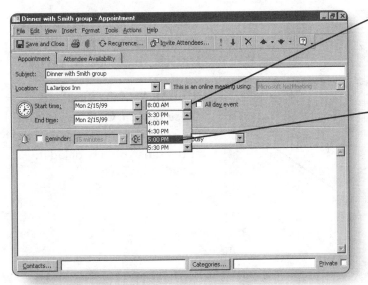

7. **Click** on **down arrow (▼)** the next to the Start time: list box. A list of available times will appear.

8. **Click** on a **start time** for the appointment. The selected time will display.

TIP

To set an end time, repeat steps 7 and 8 using the down arrows next to the End time: list boxes.

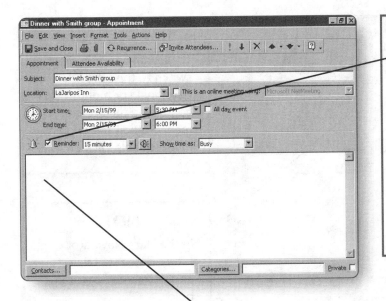

NOTE

Click to place a check mark in the Reminder: check box to tell Outlook to remind you of the appointment by playing a sound. If you do this, you can use the Reminder: list box to specify the amount of time prior to the appointment that Outlook will remind you.

9. **Click** in the **text box** at the bottom of the window. The blinking insertion point will appear.

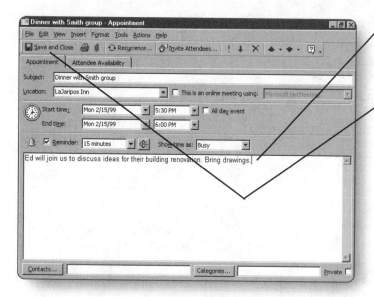

10. Optionally, **type** any **notes** about the appointment. The text will display in the text box.

11. Click on the **Save and Close button**. Outlook will save the appointment on the day and at the time you scheduled it.

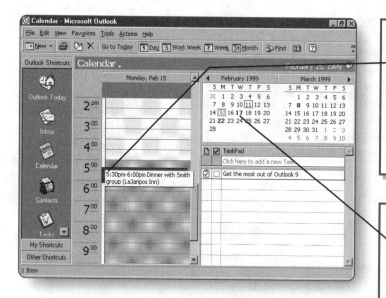

TIP

To view the appointment, switch to the scheduled day, week, or month view containing the appointment. To edit the appointment, double-click on it.

NOTE

In the Date Navigator, future dates containing appointments appear in bold.

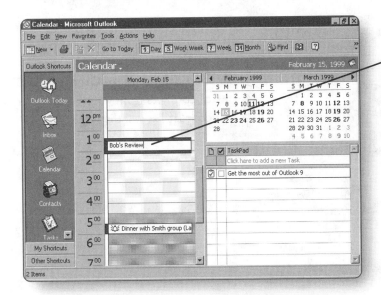

TIP

Another quick and easy way to schedule an appointment is to simply click on the desired time slot and type the appointment.

Scheduling a Meeting

Meetings are entries for which you schedule time and invite others to attend. When you invite others who are using Outlook, Outlook will let you look at their schedules and determine if they have free time at the proposed meeting time. When you schedule the meeting, you'll send an e-mail to each person and put a tentative activity on each person's Calendar.

If you want to invite someone who is not using Outlook, you won't be able to check for free time; however, if you have stored that person's e-mail address in your Outlook address book, you can send an e-mail requesting attendance.

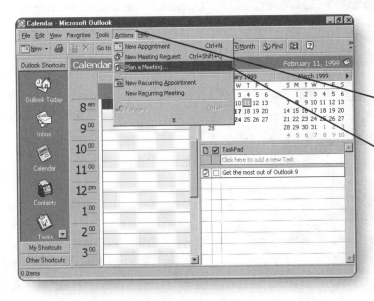

1. Click on **Actions**. The Actions menu will appear.

2. Click on **Plan a Meeting**. The Plan a Meeting dialog box will open.

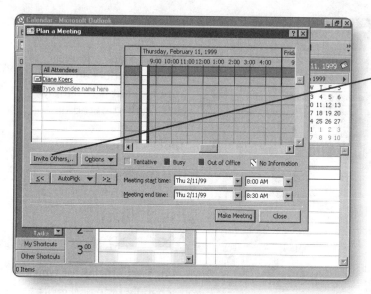

First, you can invite anyone in your Outlook contacts list.

3. **Click** on **Invite Others**. A list of contacts from your Outlook contact list will display.

4. **Click** on the **name** of the first person to attend the meeting. The person's name will be highlighted. Either a person will be required to attend the meeting, or their presence is optional.

5. **Click** on **Required or Optional**. The attendee's name will appear in the selected box.

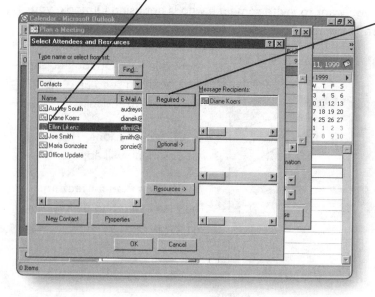

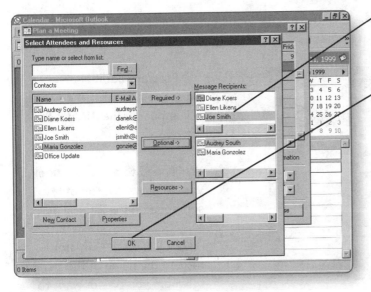

6. **Repeat these steps** for each attendee. Selected names will display in the boxes.

7. **Click** on **OK**. The dialog box will close.

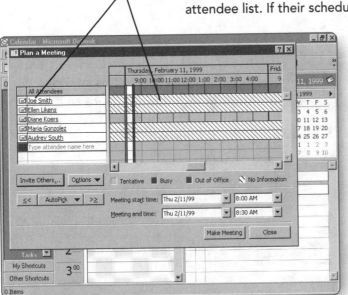

The people you selected will appear on the Plan a Meeting attendee list. If their schedules are not available (either because they are not using Outlook or because they are not on the network), you'll see diagonal lines through their schedule.

TIP

You can invite people to attend a meeting even if you don't have an e-mail address for them; you simply tell Outlook not to send an e-mail message.

8. Click the **mouse** in the next available line in the All Attendees list. The blinking insertion point will display.

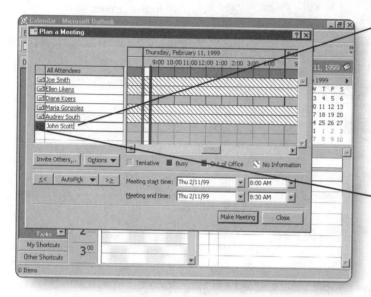

9. Type any additional **attendees' names**. The names will appear in the All Attendees list.

You'll need to advise Outlook if you don't want it to notify someone on the list.

10. Click on the **envelope** next to the name of the person to whom you *do not* want to send e-mail. A list box will open.

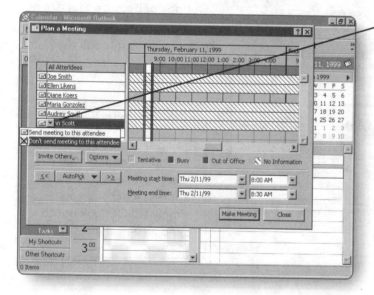

11. Click on the **Don't send meeting to this attendee**. Outlook will place an X over the envelope next to the attendee's name.

Now you need to set a meeting time.

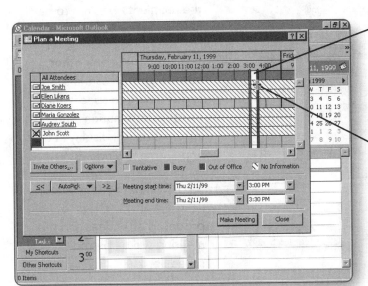

12. Click on the desired **meeting time**. A one-half hour increment of time will be blocked off.

TIP

Drag the time bars to increase or decrease the meeting length.

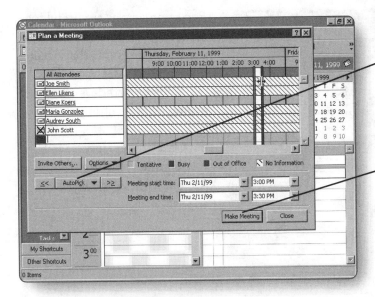

TIP

Optionally, click on AutoPick to let Outlook find a mutually available time for all attendees.

13. Click on **Make Meeting**. The appointment window will display.

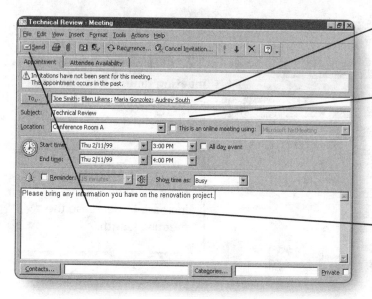

Notice that Outlook has placed the recipients who are to be notified in the To list.

14. **Complete any other notations**, such as the subject and location, to specify the meeting information. The information will display in the appointment window.

15. **Click** on **Send**. Outlook will send e-mail messages to the proposed attendees and the meeting will be placed on your schedule.

Creating Recurring Entries

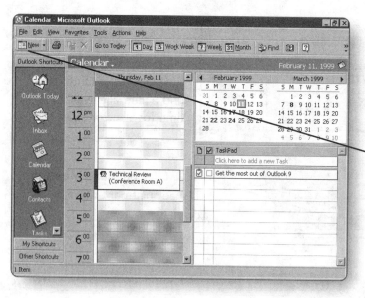

Recurring entries are useful for recording appointments, meetings, or events that occur on a regular basis. Weekly meetings or birthdays are good examples of recurring entries.

1. **Click** on the **New Appointment button**. The Appointment window will appear.

2. Type to complete **text boxes** for a subject, location, starting and ending time and any other notations to specify the event information. The information will display in the appointment window.

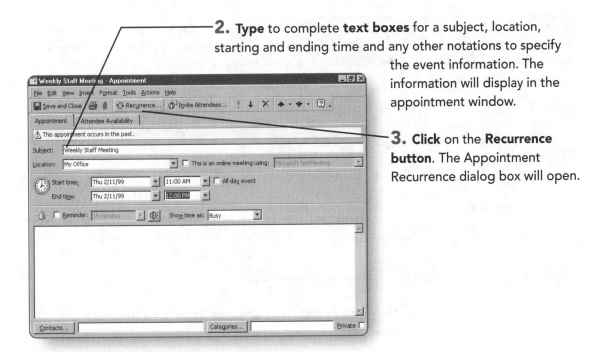

3. Click on the **Recurrence button**. The Appointment Recurrence dialog box will open.

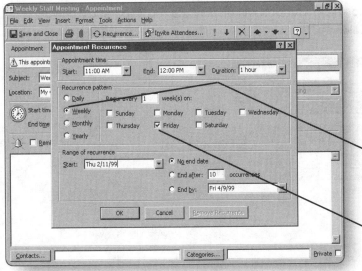

The Recurrence pattern choices on the right change, depending on the frequency you choose on the left side of the dialog box. After you choose a frequency, you must specify how often the entry will occur.

4. Click on a **Recurrence pattern**. The options for that pattern will display.

5. Click on the desired recurrence **options**. The options will be selected.

At the bottom of the dialog box, set the period over which the recurring entry will appear on your Calendar.

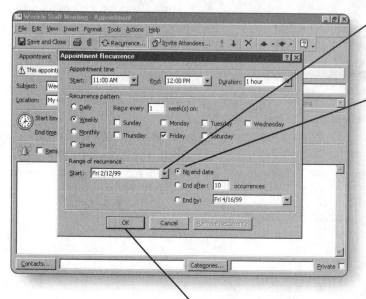

6. Click on the **down arrow** (▼) next to the Start: list box. A calendar will display.

7. Click on a **start date**. The date will display in the Start: list box.

8. Optionally, **specify** an **end date or** a total **number of occurrences**. The options will display in the Range of recurrence section.

9. Click on **OK**. The Recurring Appointment window will reappear.

10. Click on **Save and Close**. The Appointment window will close and Outlook will display the recurring entry on your Calendar.

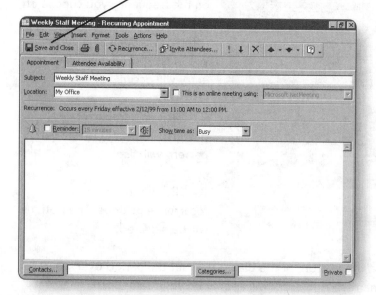

Editing an Appointment

If you need to reschedule an appointment, you can drag the appointment to the new date or time. If the appointment to be edited or deleted is a recurring appointment, Outlook will ask you if you want the change to affect all occurrences of the appointment or only the current one.

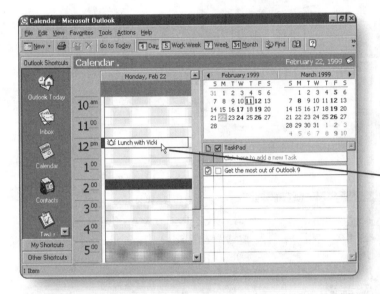

Moving to a Different Time

If you're moving your appointment to a different time the same day, move it in the day view.

1. Position the **mouse pointer** over an appointment to be moved. The pointer will be a white arrow.

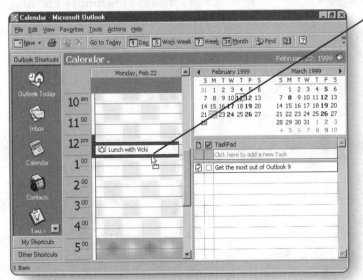

2. Drag the **event** to the desired time slot. The event will appear at the new time.

3. Release the **mouse button**. The event will be moved.

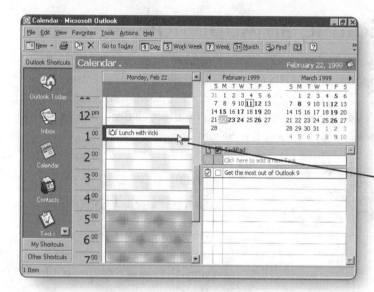

Moving to a Different Date

If your company picnic has been postponed to the next weekend, move it by using the Date Navigator.

1. **Position** the **mouse pointer** over the event to be moved. The pointer will be a white arrow.

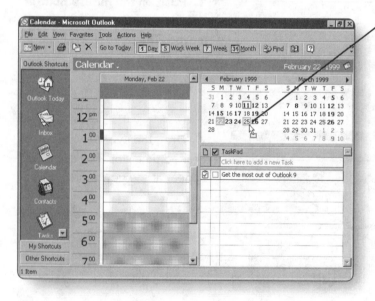

2. **Drag** the **event** to the desired day on the monthly calendar. The selected day will have a small box around it.

3. **Release** the **mouse button**. The event will be moved.

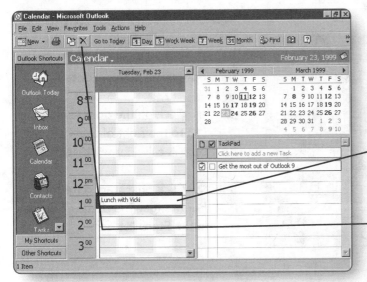

Deleting an Appointment

If you need to cancel an appointment, use the Outlook Calendar toolbar.

1. Click on the **appointment** to be deleted. The appointment will be selected.

2. Click on the **Delete Button**. The event will be deleted.

Printing the Calendar

You can print a daily, weekly, monthly, or tri-fold Calendar.

1. Click on **File**. The File menu will appear.

2. Click on **Print**. The Print dialog box will open.

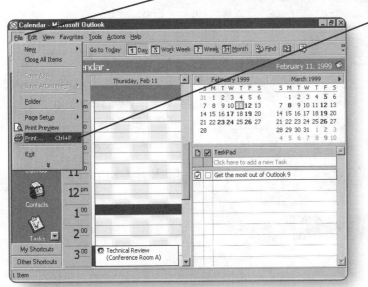

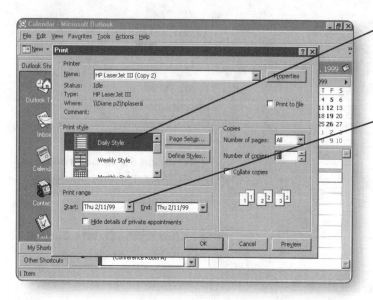

3. **Click** on a **Print style** (Daily, Weekly, Monthly, Tri-fold, or Calendar Details Style). The option will be highlighted.

4. **Click** on the **down arrow** (▼) to the right of the Start: list box. A calendar will display.

5. **Click** on a **start date** for the Print range. The date will display in the Start: list box.

6. **Click** on the **down arrow** (▼) to the right of the End: list box. A calendar will display.

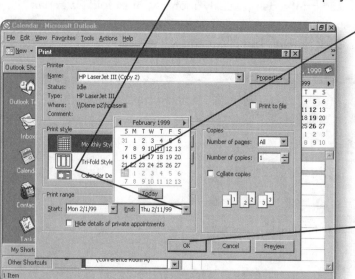

7. **Click** on an **end date** for the Print range. The date will display in the End: list box.

> **TIP**
>
> Click on Preview to preview your selection before printing.

8. **Click** on **OK**. Your Calendar will print.

22

Using Outlook to Keep Organized

Using the Tasks folder, you can create a To Do list to make sure things don't "fall through the cracks." The Notes folder provides a place where you can store miscellaneous information—perhaps the kind of information you usually would place on a sticky note. In this chapter, you'll learn how to:

- Work with a Task list
- Use the Notes folder to store miscellaneous information
- View the Outlook Today screen

Working with Tasks

A *task* is something you need to get done. It doesn't necessarily have a due date, but it is something you want to get done and don't want to forget. The Task List is frequently referred to as a To Do list.

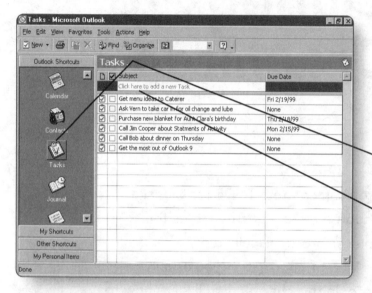

Creating a One-Time Task

Some tasks only need to be listed once whereas other tasks recur at regular intervals.

1. Click on the **Tasks shortcut**. The Tasks window will display.

2. Click on the **first line** of the Subject: text box to add a new task. A blinking insertion point will display.

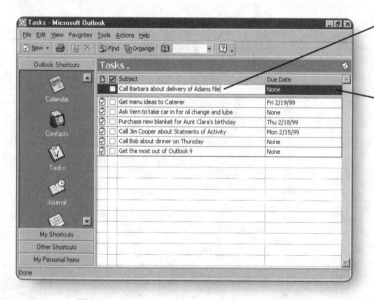

3. Type a **subject** for the task. The text will display in the Subject text box.

4. Click on the **Due Date text box**. A blinking insertion point will display with a down arrow (▾) next to it.

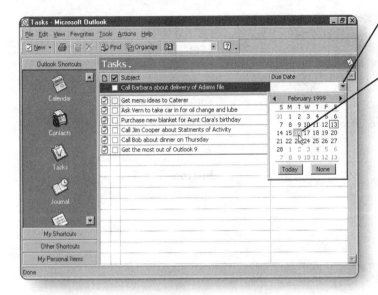

5. Click on the **down arrow** (▼). A calendar will display.

6. Click on a **date**. The date will display in the Due Date text box.

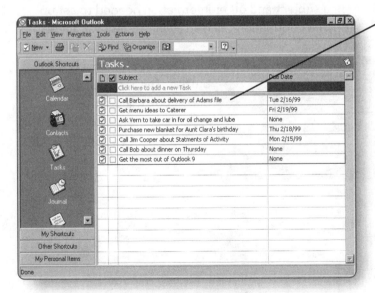

7. Press the **Enter key** or **click** in the **task list**. The task will be listed with any others you've created.

TIP

Optionally, double-click on a task to assign more information to it, such as a priority or reminder.

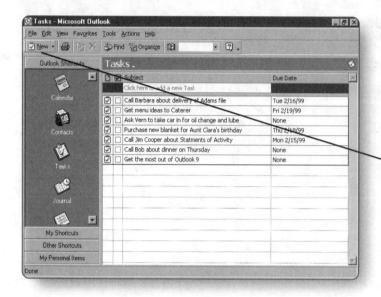

Creating Recurring Tasks

Sometimes, you need to do the same task at regular intervals, so set it up as a recurring task.

1. Click on the **New Task button**. The Task window will appear.

2. Type a **subject** and other information needed to set up the task. The information will display in the Task windows.

3. Click on the **Recurrence button**. The Task Recurrence dialog box will open.

Setting options in the Task Recurrence dialog box is similar to the options you selected in the Outlook Calendar.

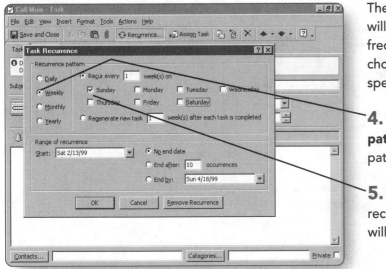

The Recurrence pattern choices will change depending on the frequency you choose. After you choose a frequency, you must specify how often it will occur.

4. **Click** on a **recurrence pattern**. The options for that pattern will be selected.

5. **Click** on the desired recurrence **options**. The options will be selected.

Near the bottom of the dialog box, set the time period over which the recurring entry will appear on your Task list.

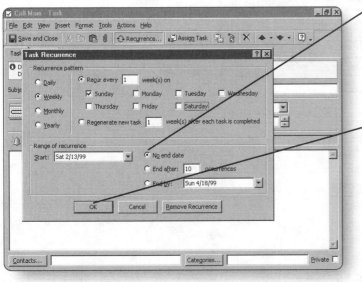

6. Optionally, **specify** an **end date** or a total **number of occurrences**. The options will be selected in the Range of recurrence section.

7. **Click** on **OK**. The Task Recurrence dialog box will close and the Task window will reappear.

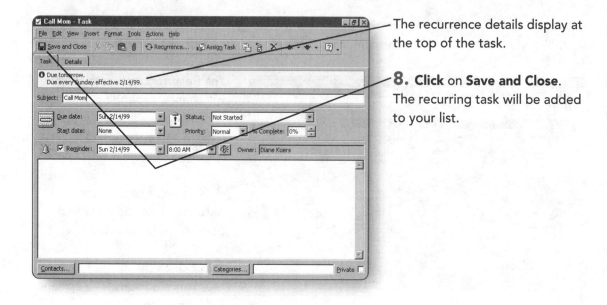

The recurrence details display at the top of the task.

8. **Click** on **Save and Close**. The recurring task will be added to your list.

Printing a Task List

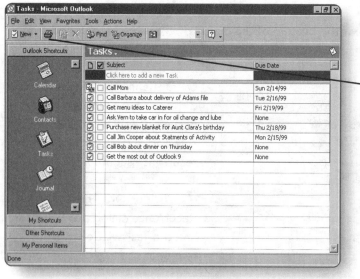

You may want to create a paper copy of your Task list to carry with you.

1. Click on the **Print button**. The Print dialog box will open.

2. Click on a **Print style** for your list. The option will be highlighted.

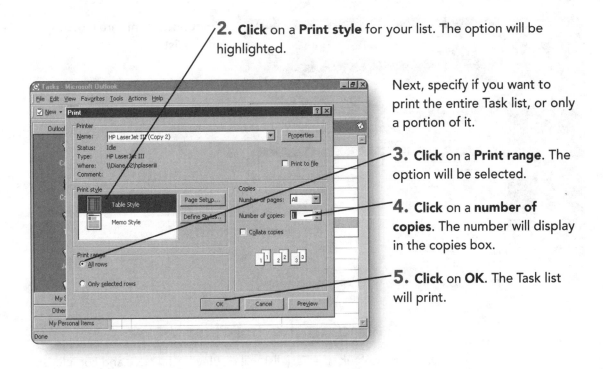

Next, specify if you want to print the entire Task list, or only a portion of it.

3. Click on a **Print range**. The option will be selected.

4. Click on a **number of copies**. The number will display in the copies box.

5. Click on **OK**. The Task list will print.

Completing a Task

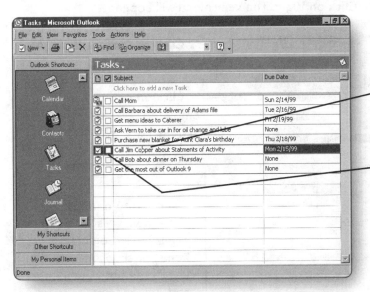

When a task is complete, you'll want to check it off your To Do list.

1. Click on the **completed task**. The task will be highlighted in the Task List.

2. Click in the **check box** just to the left of the subject. A check mark will display in the check box.

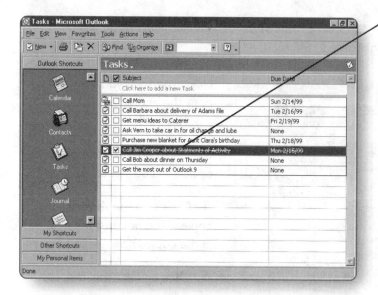

Completed items are crossed off the list.

Changing the Task List View

By default, the Task list will display both active and completed items. You may only want to see active items. With Outlook, you can filter the display of your tasks.

1. **Click** on **View**. The View menu will appear.

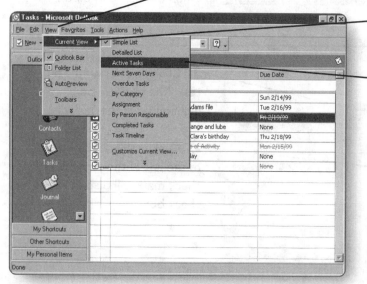

2. **Click** on **Current View**. A submenu will appear.

3. **Click** on **Active Tasks**. All completed tasks will disappear from the list.

TIP

You can return to the Current View list and display only Completed items, or choose Simple List to see both Complete and Active items.

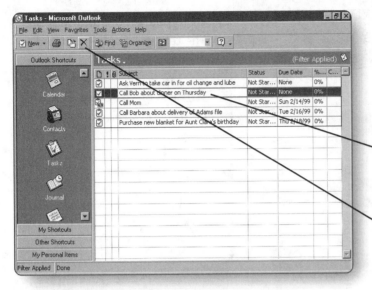

Deleting a Task

If you change your mind or no longer need to accomplish a certain task, you can delete it from the list.

1. Click on the **task** to be deleted. The task will be highlighted.

2. Click on the **Delete button**. The task will be removed from the list.

Making Notes

Think of the Notes window in Outlook as your electronic sticky notepad. Here you can record ideas you have, conversations you want to remember, and any other miscellaneous information that just doesn't fit into any other category.

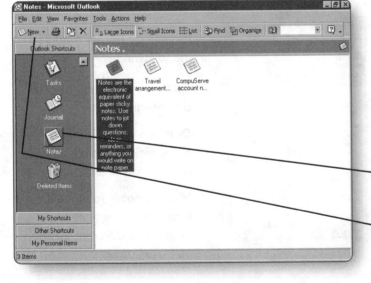

1. Click on the **Notes shortcut**. The Notes window will appear.

2. Click on the **New Note button**. A small "sticky note" window will appear.

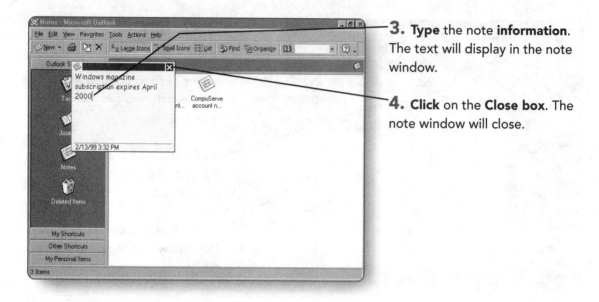

3. Type the note **information**. The text will display in the note window.

4. Click on the **Close box**. The note window will close.

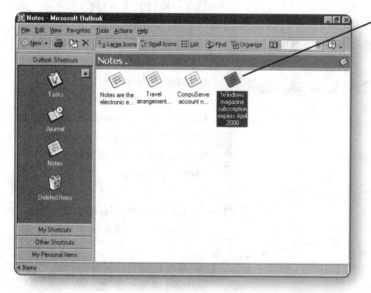

The note will appear in the Notes window.

Notes can be further modified in the following ways:

- **Edit a note**. To edit a note, double-click on it.

- **Delete a note**. To delete a note, click on it once and then press the Delete key.

- **Move a note**. To move a note, click on it once and drag it to a different location on the window.

Looking at the Outlook Today Screen

Outlook includes a feature called Outlook Today that gives you an overall list of things you need to get accomplished for today or in the near future.

1. **Click** on the **Outlook Today icon**. The Outlook Today window will appear.

Items included are your Calendar appointments, Tasks, and e-mail messages to be sent or read.

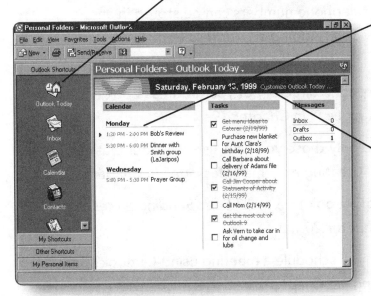

TIP

Click on Customize Outlook Today to modify the display and contents of your Outlook Today window. Make any changes then click on Save Changes.

Part V Review Questions

1. What is Outlook? *See "Getting Started with Outlook" in Chapter 18*

2. When you add a folder to the Outlook bar, which group is it added to? *See "Adding a Folder in Outlook" in Chapter 18*

3. How many different telephone numbers can be stored in an Address Book Entry? *See "Adding an Address Book Entry" in Chapter 19*

4. How can you print a phone directory of your address book entries? *See "Printing a Contact List" in Chapter 19*

5. Can e-mail be sent to only those you have listed in your Outlook Address Book? *See "Creating an E-mail Message" in Chapter 20*

6. Do you have to start Outlook to e-mail? *See "Sending a Message via Office Mail" in Chapter 20*

7. What happens when you schedule a meeting using Outlook? *See "Scheduling a Meeting" in Chapter 21*

8. Is a birthday a recurring event? *See "Creating Recurring Entries" in Chapter 21*

9. What does Outlook call a To Do list? *See "Working with Tasks" in Chapter 22*

10. What is Outlook's version of a sticky note? *See "Making Notes" in Chapter 22*

PART VI

Using Access

23

Creating an Access Database

The Access application of Office 2000 includes a powerful but easy-to-use database. There is one major difference between Access and Word, Excel, and PowerPoint; Access only allows you to have one database open at a time. In this chapter, you'll learn how to:

- Understand database terms
- Create a database using a wizard
- Add and edit records
- Find records
- Print standard reports

Understanding Database Terms

Before you can really work with a database, you should become familiar with some terms that are used in Access.

- **Database.** A *database* is a collection of information that is similar in nature. A telephone book, a list of your videos, and an inventory list are all examples of a database.

- **Records.** A *record* is all the information about one item. For example, in an address book, the entire sheet of information about Diane Koers would be the record.

- **Fields.** *Fields* are categories of information. In the Address Book, Last Name would be a field, Fax Number would be a field and so forth.

- **Tables.** A *table* is a matrix, similar in appearance to a spreadsheet, that's used to store database information. All databases require at least one table, whereas many databases require several tables, linked together; such as one to store a client's address and telephone numbers and another one to track all the phone calls made to the client.

- **Forms.** A *form* is used for easy data entry. Forms usually display one record at a time.

- **Queries.** A *query* is a subset of data that meets certain criteria. An example might be a query of all clients named Smith who live in the city of Chicago. Queries are also known as *filters*.

- **Reports.** A *report* summarizes data in a format suitable for printing. Mailing labels are an example of a report.

Using the Database Wizard

The fastest, easiest method to create a database is to start with one of the databases available from the Access Wizard.

1. Open the **Access** application. Use one of the methods you learned in Chapter 1, "Welcome to Office 2000." The Microsoft Access dialog box will open.

2. Click on the **option button** to Access database wizards, pages, and projects. The option will be selected.

3. Click on **OK**. The New dialog box will display.

Access provides many different sample databases.

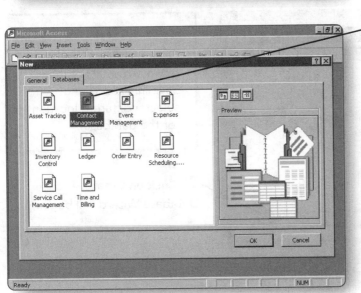

4. Click on the **database sample** you want to use. The database will be highlighted.

NOTE

For this chapter and the next one, you'll be working with the Contact Management database. Please be aware that if you select a different database, your screens will look a little different.

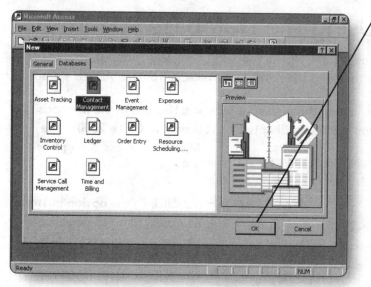

5. Click on **OK**. The File New Database dialog box will open.

An Access database must be named and saved before it is even created.

6. Type a **file name**. The file name will display in the File name: text box.

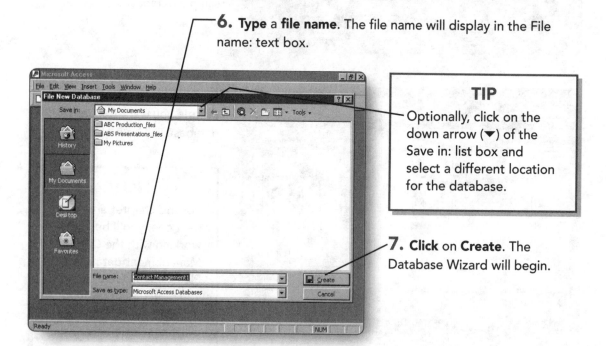

TIP

Optionally, click on the down arrow (▼) of the Save in: list box and select a different location for the database.

7. Click on **Create**. The Database Wizard will begin.

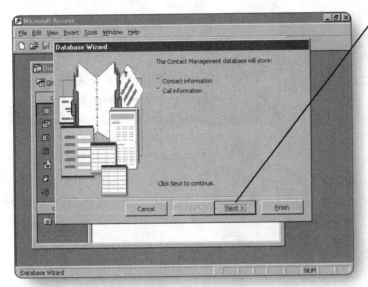

8. Click on **Next**. The next page of the Wizard will display.

A list of predefined tables in the database will display.

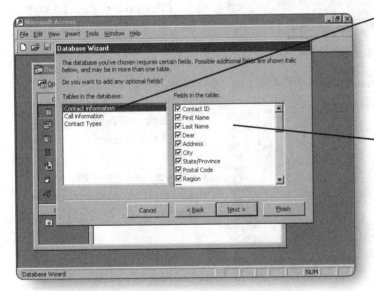

A list of the fields to be included in each table will display.

You can deselect any fields that you do not want in your database.

9. Click on any **field names** that you don't want to use. The check mark beside the field names will be removed.

TIP

Don't deselect any field that says ID (Contact ID, Call ID, or Contact Type ID). These are the fields that tie all the database information together.

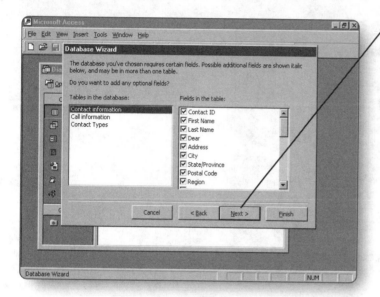

10. Click on **Next**. The next page of the Wizard will display.

You now need to select a background appearance for your database. These backgrounds do not print; they are for decorative purposes only.

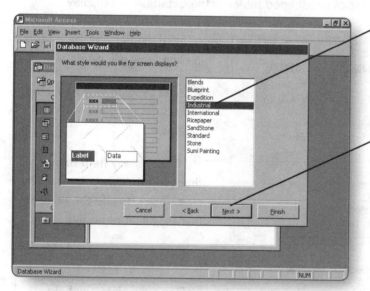

11. Click on a **style**. The style name will be highlighted and a sample will display in the preview box on the left of the screen.

12. Click on **Next**. The next page of the Wizard will display.

Next, you need to determine the overall appearance for your reports.

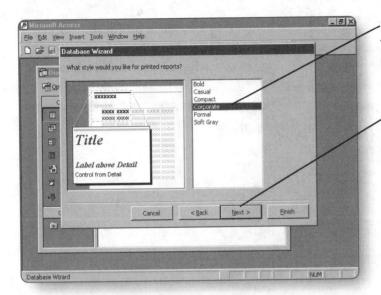

13. Click on a **report style**. The style name will be highlighted and a sample will display in the preview box.

14. Click on **Next**. The next page of the Wizard will display.

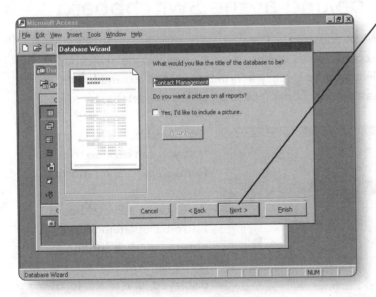

15. Click on **Next**. The final page of the Wizard will display.

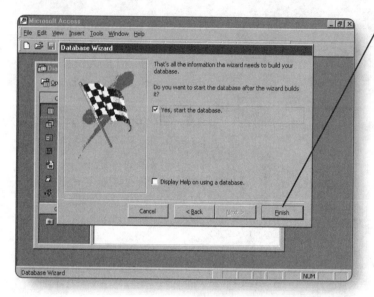

16. Click on **Finish**. The Database Wizard will close. After a few moments, the database will be created and the opening screen of the database will display.

Looking at the Switchboard

When you use the Database Wizard to create your database, Access creates an opening screen called the *Switchboard*. The Switchboard is really a form that acts as a menu for you to easily move from place to place in your database.

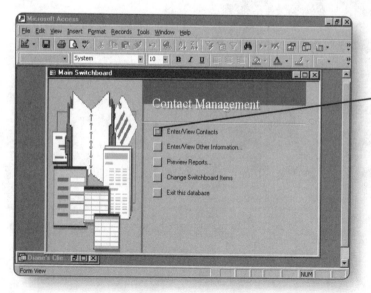

The Switchboard has buttons that you can click on to open forms, tables, and reports.

1. Click on a **Switchboard button**. Depending on which button you click and the particular Switchboard that is displayed, one of the following actions will take place.

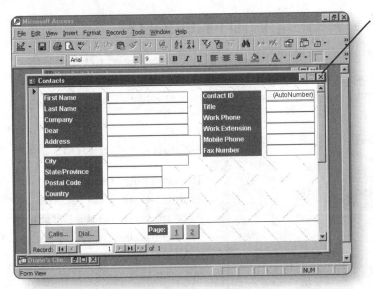

• A database screen (such as this form) will display. Click on the Close box to return to the Main Switchboard.

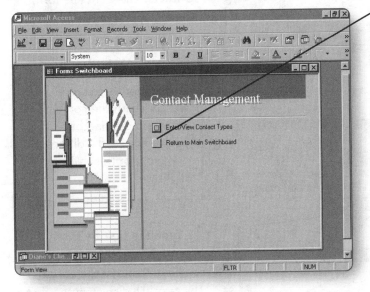

• A different Switchboard will appear with further options. Click on Return to Main Switchboard to return to the Main Switchboard.

• A dialog box will open. Click on Cancel to return to the Main Switchboard.

• The current database will close. You'll need to reopen the database to display the Main Switchboard.

Working with Records

To successfully use your database, you'll need to be able to add, edit, and delete records. You'll also want to be able to quickly locate information in the database.

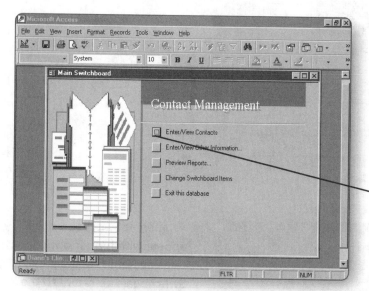

Adding Records

The data entry form is the easiest way to enter records. Because you used the Database Wizard to create your database, a data entry form is automatically created for you.

1. Click on **Enter/View Contacts**. The Contacts form will display with a blank entry.

> ### NOTE
> Remember that you're working with the contact management database. If you've selected a different one, your options will vary slightly.

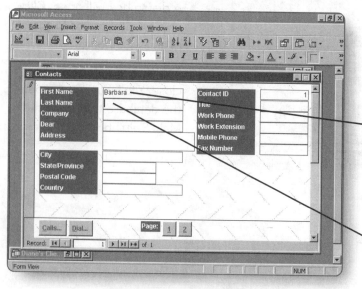

2. Type the **first field** of information. In this example, it's the First Name of the contact. The text will display in the first field box.

3. Press the **Tab key**. The insertion point will move to the next field.

4. **Type** the **next field** of information. The text will display in the second field box.

5. **Repeat steps 3 and 4** until all fields that you want to fill out are completed.

6. **Click** on the **New Record button**. A new blank record will appear for you to fill out.

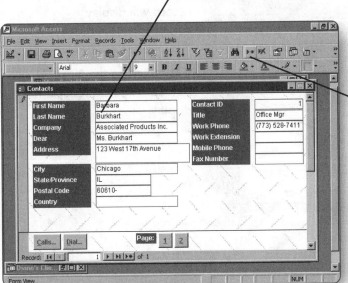

NOTE

A database is different from many other types of files in that you don't have to keep clicking on the Save button. The database is automatically saved each time you add or edit a record.

Viewing Records

Once you have your records entered, you'll want to be able to look at them. Access gives you two distinct views to use when viewing records: Form View and Datasheet View.

Navigating Around in a Form

Form View allows you to see one record at a time.

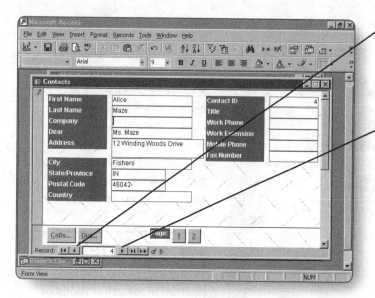

1a. **Click** on the **Previous Record button**. The previous record will display.

OR

1b. **Click** on the **Next Record button**. The next record will display.

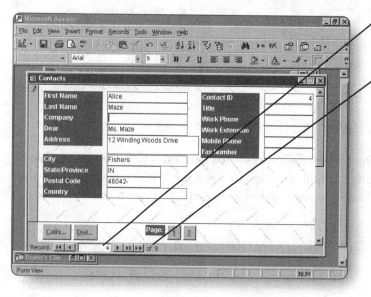

This counter is showing which record is currently displayed.

This counter is showing the total number of records.

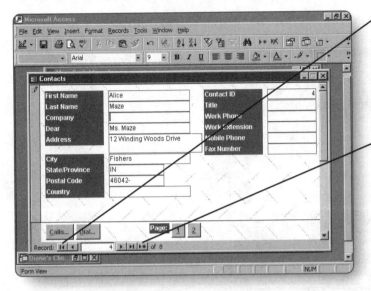

2a. **Click** on the **First Record button**. The first record you entered in your database will display.

OR

2b. **Click** on the **Last Record button**. The last record of your database will display.

Viewing from the Datasheet

In Datasheet view, you'll see many records on a sheet similar to an Excel spreadsheet.

1. **Click** on **View**. The View menu will appear.

2. **Click** on **Datasheet View**. The records will display in Datasheet View.

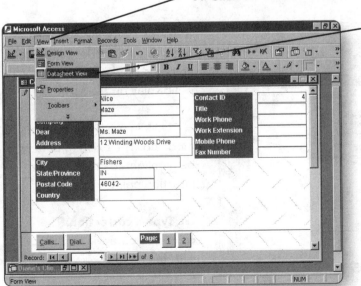

3. Click on **View**. The View menu will appear.

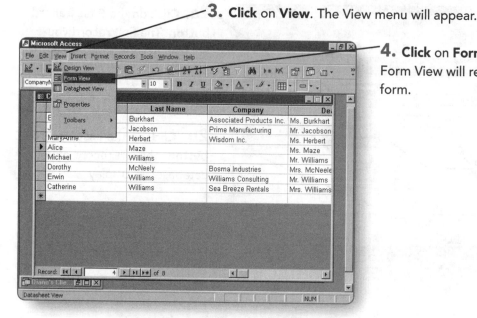

4. Click on **Form View**. The Form View will return to the form.

Editing Records

Editing a record is as easy as locating a record and typing a correction.

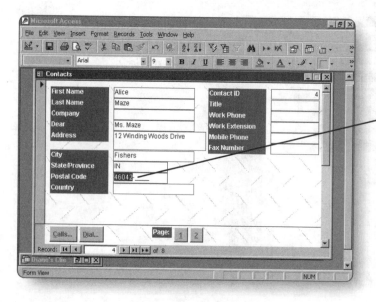

1. Click on the **navigation buttons** until the record to be edited is displayed. The record will display on the screen.

2. Click in the **field** to be modified. The existing data will be highlighted or a blinking insertion point will appear.

3. Type a **correction**. The corrected data will be saved with the record.

Deleting Records

If you need to delete a record from your database, the entire record will be deleted.

1. Display the **record** to be deleted. The record will display on the screen.

2. Click on the **Delete button**. A confirmation message will appear.

The message you see may vary, but if any of the information in this record is tied to other tables in the database (*relationships*), the message will warn you that deleting this record will also affect those tables.

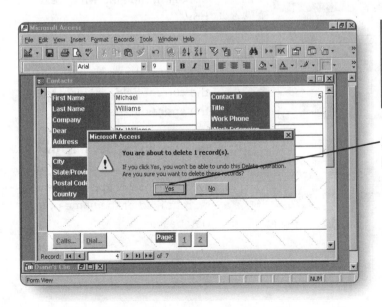

NOTE

Deleting a record cannot be undone.

3. Click on **Yes**. The record will be deleted.

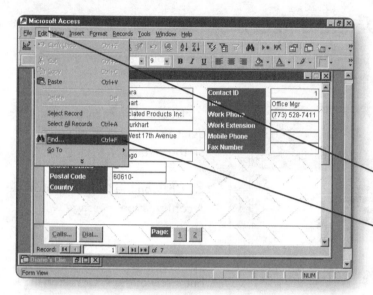

Finding Records

When many records have been entered, you may want to quickly locate one of them. Use the Find function to track down your record.

1. Click on **Edit**. The Edit menu will appear.

2. Click on **Find**. The Find and Replace dialog box will open.

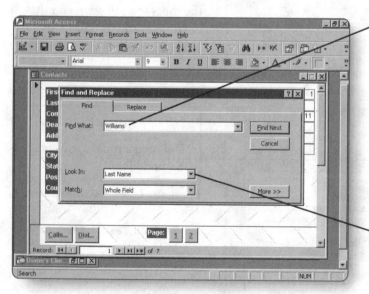

3. Type a piece of **information** related to the record you're searching for. The text will appear in the Find what: text box.

You'll need to tell Access where to look for the text—either in the current field, or to search the entire database.

4. Click on the **down arrow** (▼) next to the Look In: list box. Two options will appear: the current field or the name of your database.

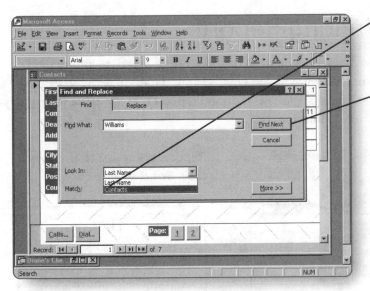

5. Click on an **option**. The selection will display in the Look In: text box.

6. Click on **Find Next**. The record with the first occurrence of the matched text will display.

7a. Click on **Cancel** if this is the record you're searching for. The Find and Replace dialog box will close.

OR

7b. If you need to search further, **click** on **Find Next**. The next occurrence will display.

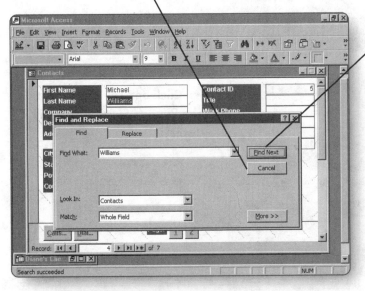

Printing Reports

Most of us will need all or some of the database information in printed form. If you created your database with the Wizard, you'll have some pre-designed reports that can provide useful summary information.

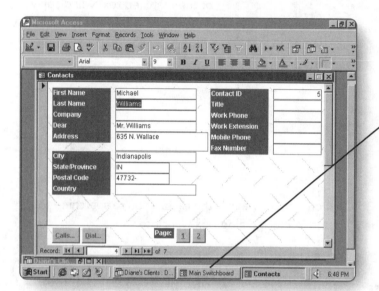

Reports are accessed from the Main Switchboard.

> ## TIP
> A quick way to access the Switchboard is to click on it from the Windows taskbar.

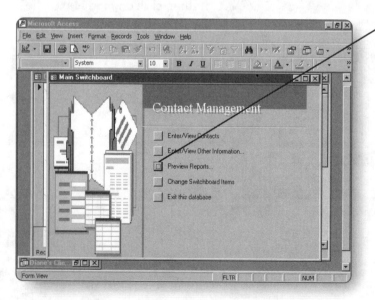

1. Click on **Preview Reports**. The Reports Switchboard will display.

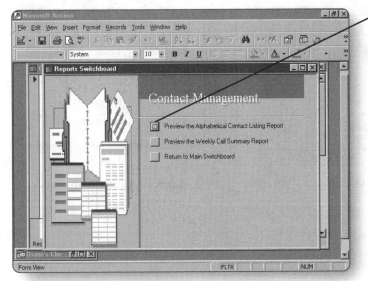

2. **Click** on a **report**. The report will appear on your screen.

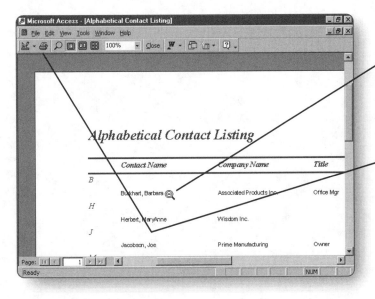

TIP
Click on the report to magnify it and then click again to return the view to normal size.

3. **Click** on the **Print button**. The report will be printed.

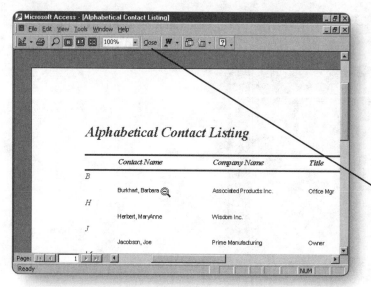

File   Edit   View   Tools   Window   Help

100%   Close

Alphabetical Contact Listing

Contact Name	Company Name	Title
B		
Burkhart, Barbara	Associated Products Inc.	Office Mgr
H		
Herbert, MaryAnne	Wisdom Inc.	
J		
Jacobson, Joe	Prime Manufacturing	Owner

Page: 1

Ready   NUM

TIP

Optionally, click on File, select Print to display the Print dialog box, and make specific selections on print specifications.

4. Click on **Close**. The view will return to the Reports Switchboard.

24

Modifying an Access Database

Sometimes a database created with the Wizard provides everything you need, but other times, you find yourself wishing for more reports, additional fields, or other tables and forms. Each database can be modified to meet your needs. In this chapter, you'll learn how to:

- Add and delete fields from a table
- Modify a form
- Create a query
- Create mailing labels

Modifying Table Structure

Whether you're going to add a new table or modify an existing one, you'll need to work with a window called the Database window. The Database window has been hiding behind your Main Switchboard window.

When a table is first created, you may not know exactly which fields you want and where you want them placed. You can choose to modify the structure of an existing table.

Adding Fields to a Table

Add as many additional fields as you need. In our Contacts Management database, you'll add a field for the contact's birthday.

1. Click on **Window**. The Window menu will appear.

2. Click on a **Database**. The name of the database will precede the word "Database." The Database window will display.

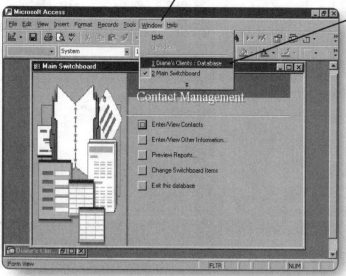

3. Click on **Tables**. The database tables will be listed.

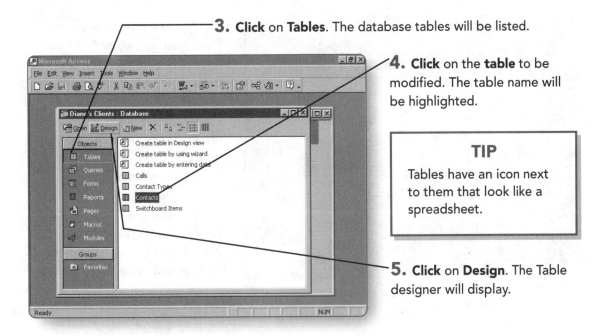

4. Click on the **table** to be modified. The table name will be highlighted.

TIP

Tables have an icon next to them that look like a spreadsheet.

---

5. Click on **Design**. The Table designer will display.

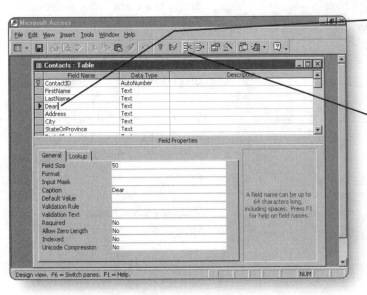

6. Click on the **grid** at the row where you want the new field to be located. A blinking insertion point will display.

7. Click on the **Insert Rows button**. A blank row will be inserted above the position of the insertion point.

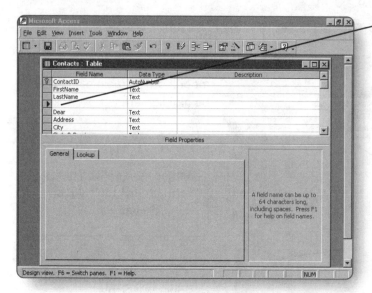

8. Type a **name** for the new field. Field names cannot have any spaces in them. The text will display in the Field Name column.

9. Press the **Tab key**. The insertion point will jump to the Data Type column.

You'll need to tell Access what type of data is going to be placed in this field. Examples include text, date, or numbers.

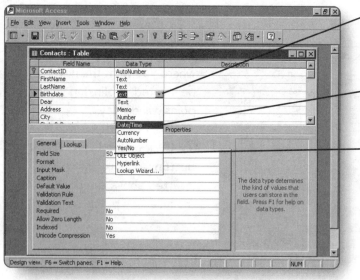

10. Click on a **down arrow** (▼) under the Data Type. A list of choices will display.

11. Click on a **Data Type**. The drop-down list will close.

The options in the Field Properties area will change according to the Data Type you select.

You may want to set some specific formats for the field.

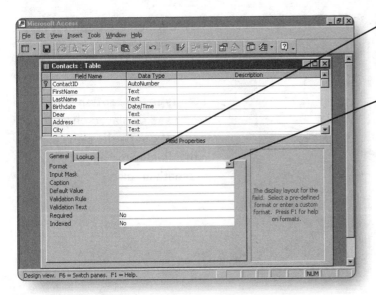

12. Click in the **Format: list box area.** A down arrow (▼) will appear.

13. Click on the **down arrow** (▼) at the right of the Format: list box. A list of choices will display.

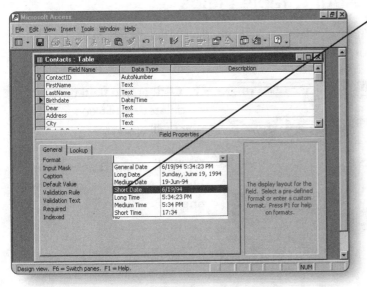

14. Click on a **format**. The format will display in the Format: list box area.

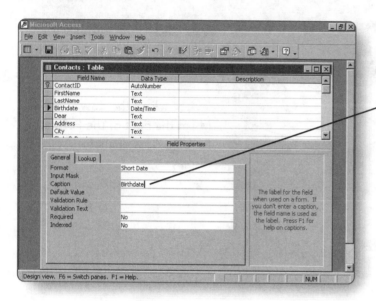

15. Click on the **Caption: text box area**. A blinking insertion point will display.

16. Type the **caption** you'd like to see displayed on your forms. It can be the same as the actual field name or you can call it something else.

Deleting Table Fields

When you delete a field, you'll also delete any record data stored in the field.

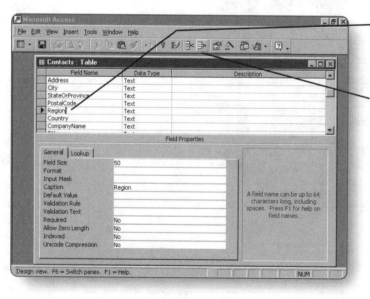

1. Click on the **field name** to be deleted. A blinking insertion point will appear.

2. Click on the **Delete Rows button**. A confirmation box will open.

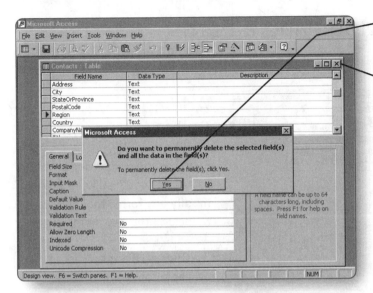

3. Click on **Yes**. The field and its data will be deleted.

4. Click on the **Table Close box**. A warning message will display.

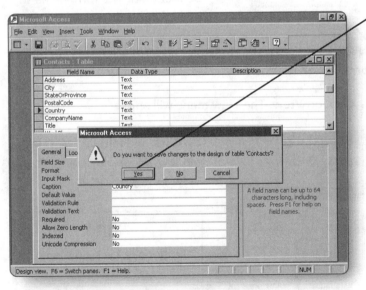

5. Click on **Yes**. The Database window will redisplay.

Modifying a Form

You may want to modify a form.

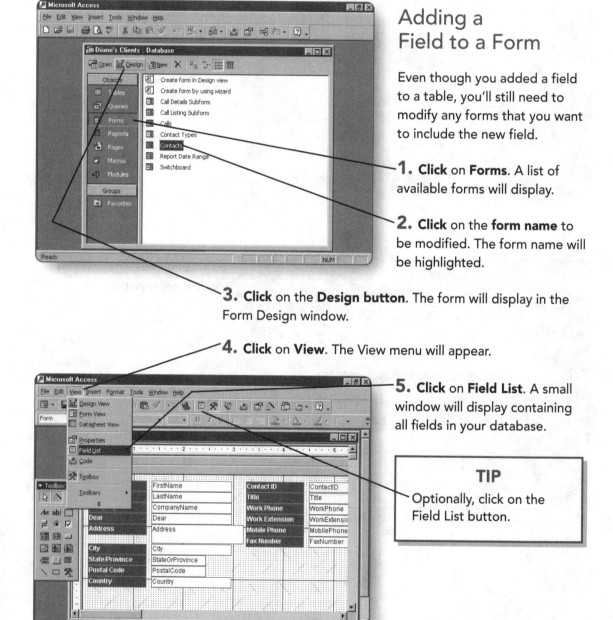

Adding a Field to a Form

Even though you added a field to a table, you'll still need to modify any forms that you want to include the new field.

1. **Click** on **Forms**. A list of available forms will display.

2. **Click** on the **form name** to be modified. The form name will be highlighted.

3. **Click** on the **Design button**. The form will display in the Form Design window.

4. **Click** on **View**. The View menu will appear.

5. **Click** on **Field List**. A small window will display containing all fields in your database.

TIP

Optionally, click on the Field List button.

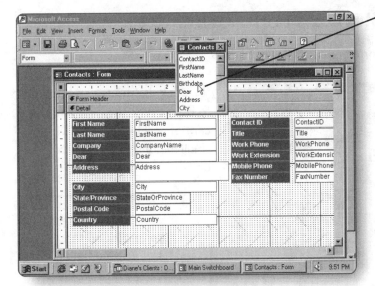

6. Position the **mouse pointer** over the field name that you want to add to the form.

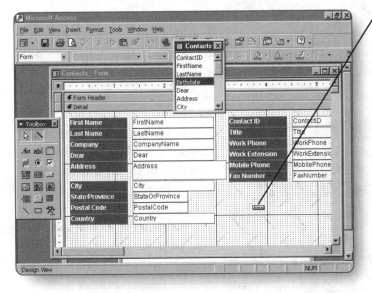

7. Press the **mouse button** and drag the **field name** onto the form. The mouse pointer will look like a small rectangular box.

8. Release the **mouse button**. The field will be placed on the form along with the caption you created earlier.

Moving a Form Field

Form fields can easily be moved.

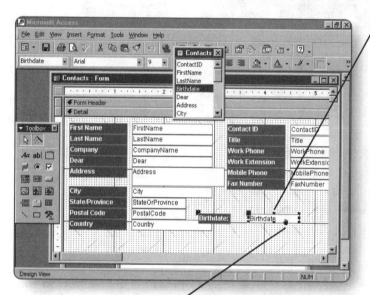

1. Click the **mouse** on the field to be moved. The field and the caption will be selected with small handles around each object.

TIP

Be sure to click on the field, not just the field caption. Clicking on the caption will select only the caption, not both field and caption.

---

2. Position the **mouse pointer** on the bottom edge of the field. The mouse pointer will turn into a small black hand.

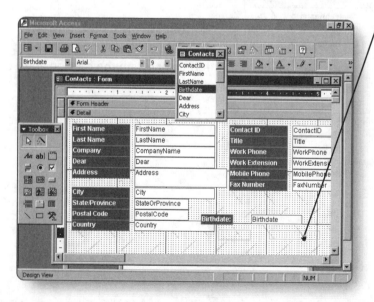

3. Press the **mouse button** and **drag** the **field** and its caption to the new position. A dotted box will indicate the new position.

4. Release the **mouse button**. The field will be moved.

Deleting a Field from a Form

When deleting a field from the form, no data will be lost.

1. Click the **mouse** on the field to be deleted. The field and the caption will be selected with small handles around each object.

2. Press the **Delete key**. The field and its caption will be removed from the form.

When you've finished making changes to the form design, you'll need to close the form window.

3. Click on the **Close box**. A warning message will display.

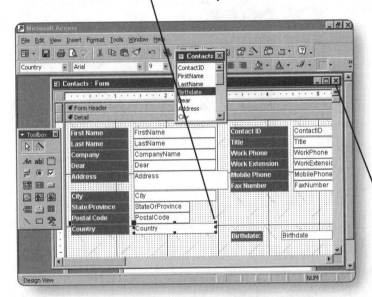

4. Click on **Yes**. The form designer will close and the Database window will redisplay.

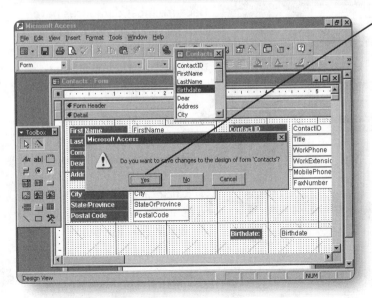

Creating Mailing Labels

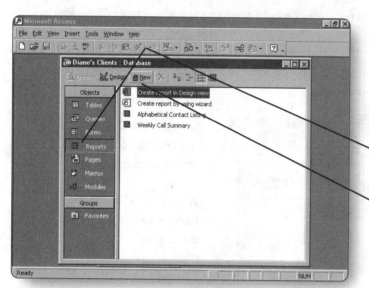

One popular use of a database is to create mailing labels for each record in your database. Access includes a Label Wizard to assist you in setting up your labels.

1. **Click** on **Reports**. A list of current reports is displayed.

2. **Click** on **New**. The New Report dialog box will display.

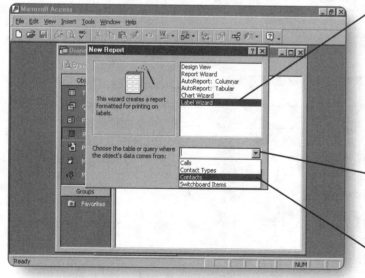

3. **Click** on **Label Wizard**. Label Wizard will be highlighted.

Because most databases have several tables in them, you'll need to indicate which table has the fields that you will use to create labels.

4. **Click** on the **down arrow** (▼) to choose the table. A list of existing tables will display.

5. **Click** on the **table** you want to use. The table name will display in the text box.

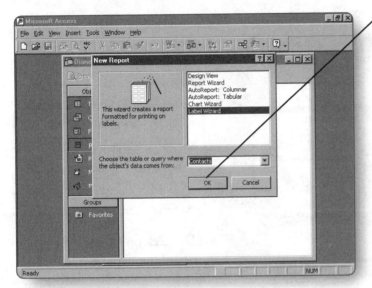

6. Click on **OK**. The first screen of the Label Wizard will display.

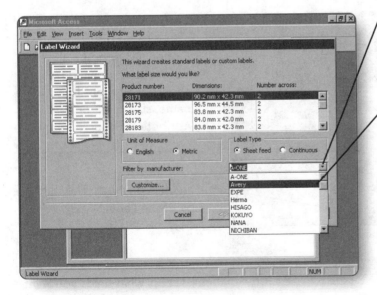

7. Click on the **down arrow** (▼) at the right of Filter by manufacturer. A list of label brands will display.

8. Click on the **label brand** you're going to use. The brand name will display.

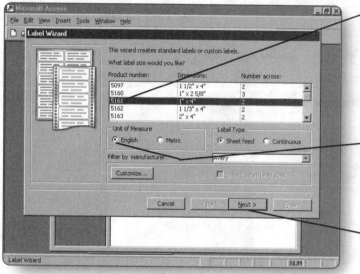

9. Click on the label **product number** you're going to use. A description of the labels will be displayed.

TIP

Click on English to see label sizes in inches instead of metric measurements.

10. Click on **Next**. The second page of the Label Wizard will display.

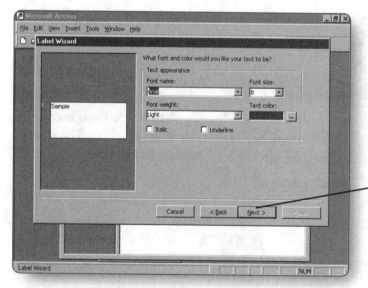

TIP

Optionally, from the various drop-down boxes, choose a different font name, size color, or attribute for your labels.

11. Click on **Next**. The third page of the Label Wizard will display.

On this screen, you'll need to tell Access what fields you want to place on the label.

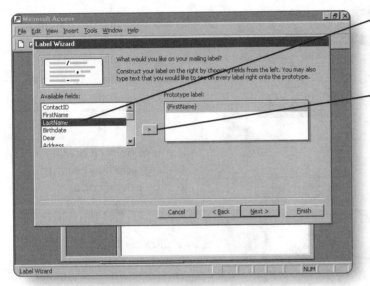

12. Click on the **first field** that you want to include. The field name will be highlighted.

13. Click on the **right arrow**. The field name will be added to the label layout.

14. Continue adding any desired **fields**. The fields will be added to the label layout.

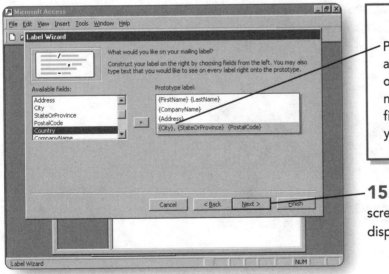

NOTE

Press any spaces, type any punctuation or text, or press the Enter key as needed to make sure the fields are placed where you want them.

15. Click on **Next**. The next screen of the Label Wizard will display.

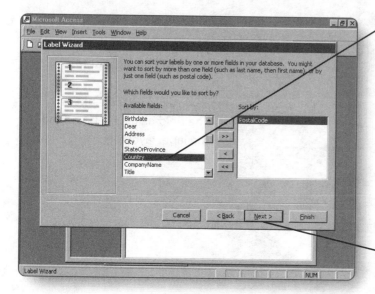

16. Double-click on a **field** to sort your labels in the Available fields: list box. The field name will display in the Sort by: area.

> **TIP**
>
> If you're doing a bulk mailing, you may want to sort by postal code.

17. Click on **Next**. The final screen of the Label Wizard will display.

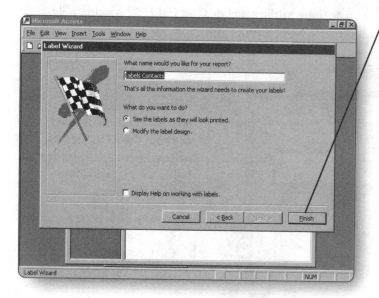

18. Click on **Finish**. The labels will be previewed on your screen.

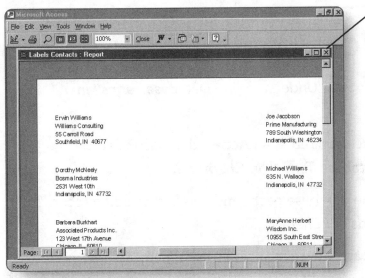

19. Click on the **Close box**. The Preview window will close and the Database window will redisplay.

Notice that the Labels have been added to your report list.

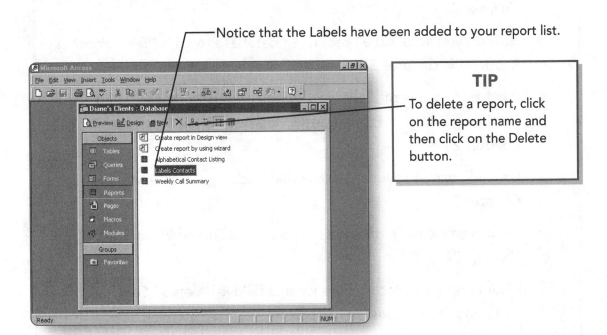

TIP

To delete a report, click on the report name and then click on the Delete button.

Part VI Review Questions

1. What is a database? *See "Understanding Database Terms" in Chapter 23*

2. How many tables are required in an Access database? *See "Understanding Database Terms" in Chapter 23*

3. What happens to the database each time you add or edit a record? *See "Adding Records" in Chapter 23*

4. Which Access database view allows you to see many records together on the same page? *See "Viewing from the Datasheet" in Chapter 23*

5. How do you access the predefined database reports? *See "Printing Reports" in Chapter 23*

6. What is the name of the Window you need to work with when modifying Tables or Forms? *See "Modifying Table Structure" in Chapter 24*

7. Can field names include spaces? *See "Adding Fields to a Table" in Chapter 24*

8. What is an example of data type? *See "Adding Fields to a Table" in Chapter 24*

9. What happens to record data when a field is deleted? *See "Deleting Table Fields" in Chapter 24*

10. What feature is included with Access to help you create mailing labels? *See "Creating Mailing Labels" in Chapter 24*

PART VII

Office and the Web

25

Working on the Web

You can use most of your Office 2000 applications — Word, Excel, and PowerPoint — to work on the Web. Each of these applications contains a Web toolbar that can launch your Web browser and take you to the Web sites you designate. In this chapter, you'll learn how to:

- Search the Web
- Display your start page
- Access a favorite Web site
- Access a specific Web site
- Get help on Office applications

Searching the Web

You can search the Web from an Office 2000 application. The search page you will see is sponsored by Microsoft; and, from it, you'll have access to the most popular search engines for the Web.

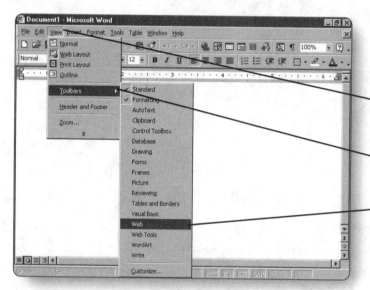

1. Start any **Office application**. The application will appear on the screen.

2. Click on **View**. The View menu will appear.

3. Click on **Toolbars**. The Toolbars menu will appear.

4. Click on **Web**. The Web toolbar will appear.

NOTE

Don't confuse the Web toolbar with the Web Tools toolbar. The Web Tools toolbar is used to design Web pages.

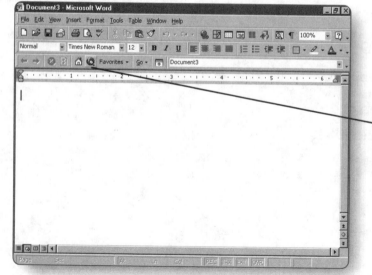

5. Click on the **Search the Web button**. You may be prompted to connect to your Internet Service Provider.

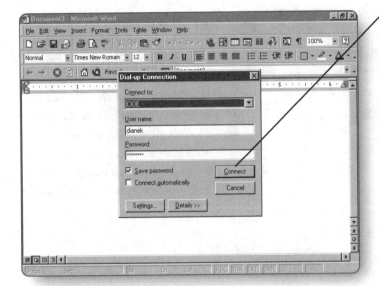

6. Click on **Connect**. You will be connected to your Internet Service Provider.

After you log on to the Internet through your Internet Service Provider, your Web browser will appear, showing the Microsoft-sponsored Web page.

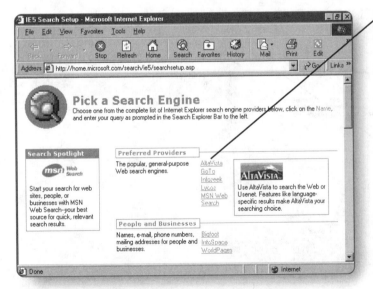

7. Click the **link** for the Search Engine you want to use. The search engine page will appear in a new frame at the left of your browser window.

TIP

Some favorite search engines are AltaVista and MSN Web.

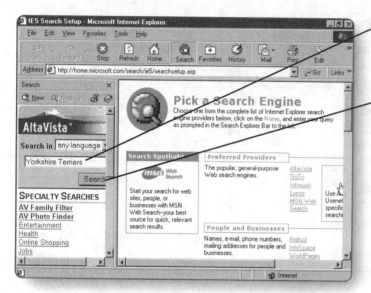

8. Type the **topic** for which you want to search. The text will appear in the search text box.

9. Click on **Search**. The search engine will display the number of Web sites that contain information related to the word(s) for which you searched. Each response is referred to as a *hit*.

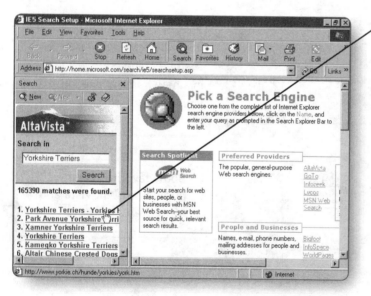

10. Click on the **response** that looks most interesting. Internet Explorer will jump to that Web page.

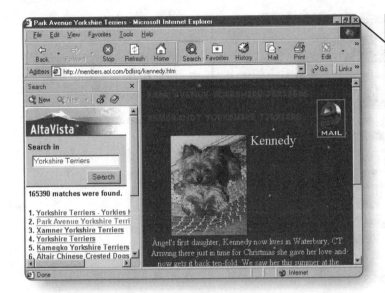

TIP

After you finish using the Web, you'll probably want to log off the Internet and return to work in your Office 2000 application. Simply click on the Internet Explorer Close box.

Displaying Your Start Page

You can access your Internet start page (the page that opens first whenever you log on to the Internet) from inside an Office 2000 application.

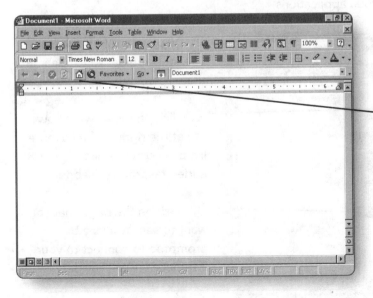

1. If not already displayed, **display** the **Web toolbar**. The Web toolbar will appear on the screen.

2. Click on the **Start Page button**. You may be prompted to connect to your Internet Service Provider. After you log on to the Internet through your Internet Service Provider, your Web browser will appear, showing your start page on the Internet.

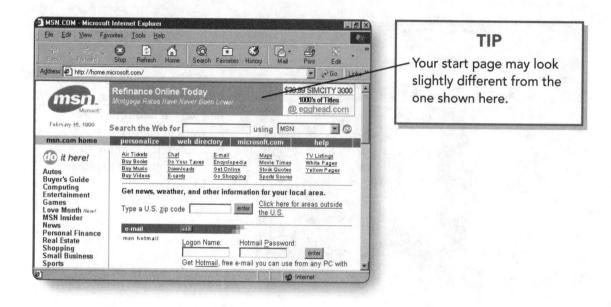

TIP

Your start page may look slightly different from the one shown here.

Viewing a Favorite Page

As you probably know from using your Web browser, you can store your favorite places that you know you'll want to visit again. You can access a favorite Web site from within Office 2000 applications.

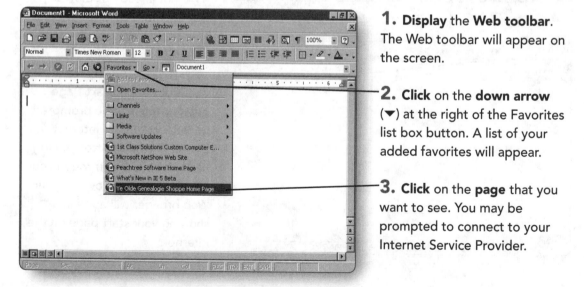

1. **Display** the **Web toolbar**. The Web toolbar will appear on the screen.

2. **Click** on the **down arrow** (▼) at the right of the Favorites list box button. A list of your added favorites will appear.

3. **Click** on the **page** that you want to see. You may be prompted to connect to your Internet Service Provider.

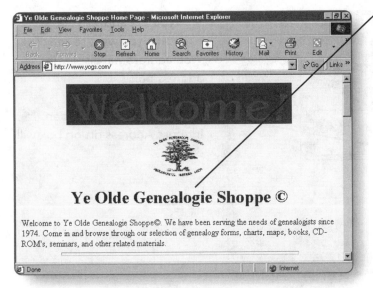

After you log on to the Internet through your Internet Service Provider, your Web browser will appear, showing the Internet page you chose from the Favorites list.

Checking Out a Specific Web Address

There you are, working in Office, and somebody comes along and says, "Check out this Web site." You can surf the Web without leaving your Office application.

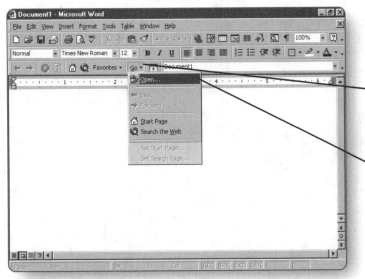

1. Display the **Web toolbar**. The Web toolbar will appear on the screen.

2. Click on the **down arrow** (▼) at the right of the Go list box button. A menu will appear.

3. Click on **Open**. The Open Internet Address dialog box will open.

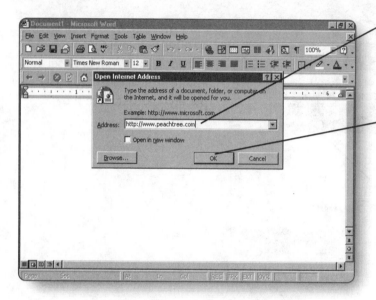

4. Type the **address** of the page that you want to see. The Web address will display in the address box.

5. Click on **OK**. The Open Internet Address dialog box will close.

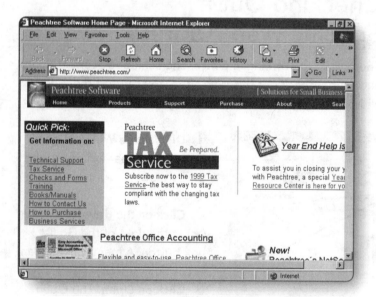

After you log on to the Internet through your Internet Service Provider, your Web browser will appear, showing the Internet page for which you typed the address.

26

Saving Office Documents as Web Documents

In Word, Excel, and PowerPoint, you can create documents that can be published as Web documents. Office programs let you create a document as you normally would and then, when you save the document as a Web document, the application automatically inserts the appropriate Hypertext Markup Language (HTML) tags so you can use the document on the Internet. In this chapter, you'll learn how to:

- Save a Word document as a Web document
- Save an Excel workbook as a Web document
- Save a PowerPoint presentation as a Web document

Saving an Existing Document as a Web Document

When a document is saved as a Web document, Office will insert the HTML tags for you—you won't even see them.

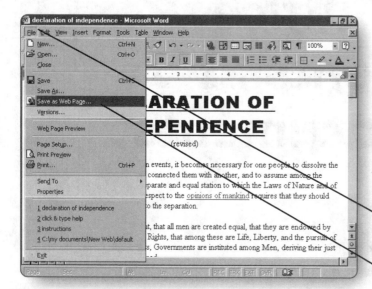

You don't need to create HTML documents from scratch if you want to use a document you've already created.

1. Open or **create** the Word, Excel or PowerPoint **document** you want to save as a Web page. The document will display on the screen.

2. Click on **File**. The File menu will open.

3. Click on **Save As Web Page**. The Save As dialog box will open.

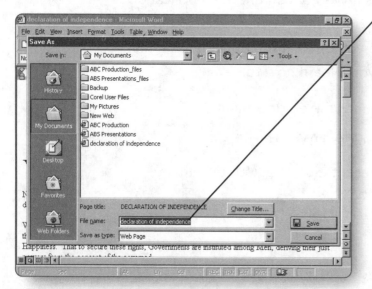

4. Type a **name** for the file. The name will display in the File name: text box.

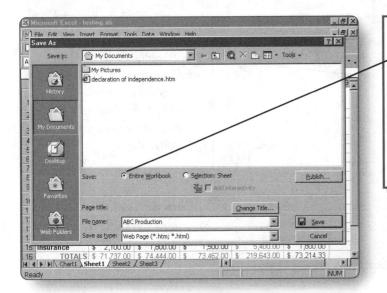

NOTE

When using Excel, you can save the entire workbook or just the current page. Click on an option to the right of the Save: area. The option will be selected.

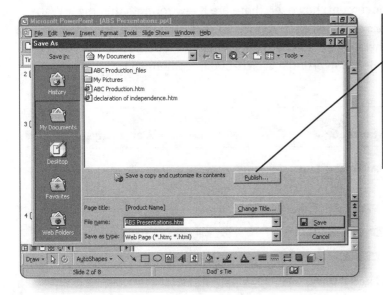

TIP

PowerPoint will assume you want to save all the slides in the presentation unless you click on the Publish button and select which slides to include.

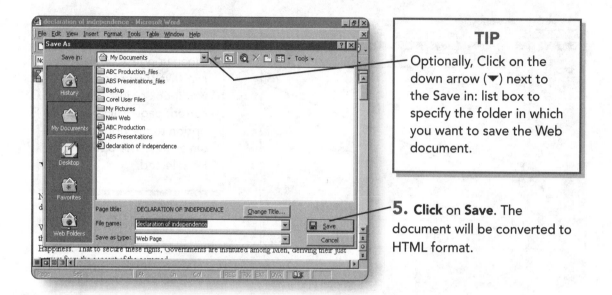

TIP

Optionally, Click on the down arrow (▼) next to the Save in: list box to specify the folder in which you want to save the Web document.

5. Click on **Save**. The document will be converted to HTML format.

Most Word formatting choices are acceptable in a Web document; however, there are a few formats that most Web Browsers cannot support. The following table lists a few of the specialized character formats that do not convert properly when converting a Word 2000 document to HTML.

Format	Reaction in a Web Browser
Animated Text	No animation and will appear as italicized text
Emboss or Engrave	Will turn into a light gray shaded text
Shadowed Text	Text will become bold
Character borders	No border around text
Special Underlining	Appears as a single underline
Color underline	Black underline
Small Caps	All Caps

If you have any of the non-supported formats in your Word document, a dialog box will advise you what will happen to the non-supported formats.

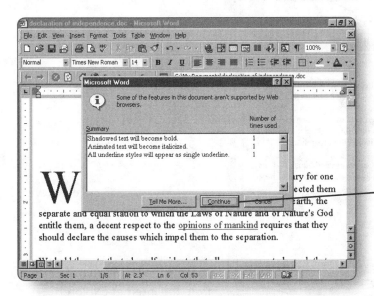

6. Click on **Continue**. The conversion will continue and the document will be displayed in Word's Web Layout view.

Viewing the Document in Internet Explorer

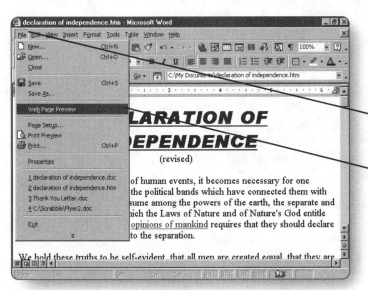

Now that the document has been saved as HTML, it's time to see what it looks like in Internet Explorer.

1. Click on **File**. The File menu will appear.

2. Click on **Web Page Preview**. The Internet Explorer window will display and you'll see the document as viewed through Internet Explorer.

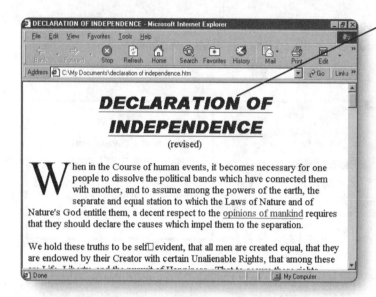

This is the Word document as viewed in Internet Explorer.

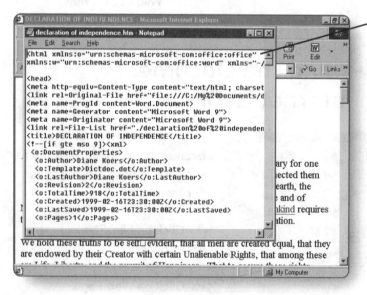

To view the HTML source code, from the Internet Explorer window, click on View, Source. A window will open with all the HTML tags. Aren't you glad you have Office to do all this work for you?

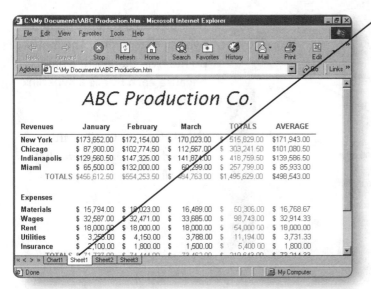

If you elected to save your entire Excel workbook when you saved to HTML, Internet Explorer (and most Web browsers) will display the worksheet very similarly to the way they are displayed in the Excel program. Tabs will be placed along the bottom of the screen to view the different worksheet or chart pages.

In PowerPoint, the HTML document includes two frames: an Outline frame and a Slide frame. By default, the Outline frame only includes the slide titles, not the text.

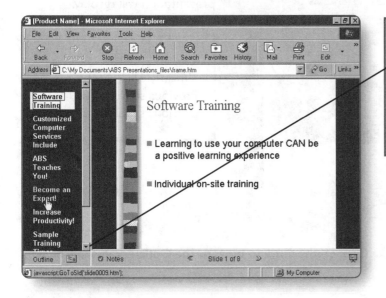

NOTE

If your outline is longer than will fit on the screen, a vertical scroll bar will display for the Outline frame.

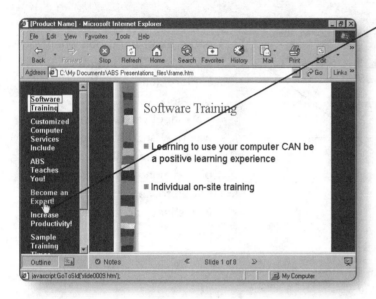

3. Position the **mouse pointer** over an outline title. The mouse pointer will change to a hand because each title is a hyperlink to that slide.

4. Click on an **Outline title**. The slide associated with that title will display.

5. Click on the **Next Slide arrow**. The next slide in the presentation will display.

TIP

Similarly, click on the Previous slide arrow. The previous slide will display.

6. Click on the **Outline button**. The Outline frame will hide.

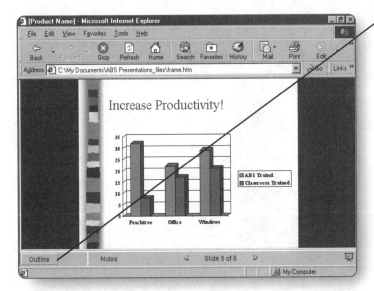

7. Click on the **Outline button** again. The Outline frame will redisplay.

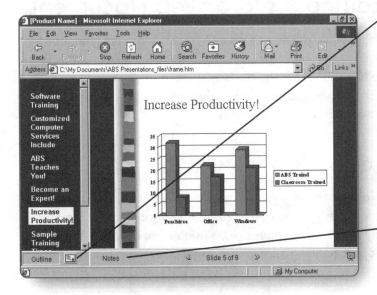

8. Click on **Expand/Collapse Outline**. The Outline text will display in full.

TIP

Click on Expand/Collapse Outline again to display only titles.

---

9. Click on **Notes**. A speaker notes frame will display.

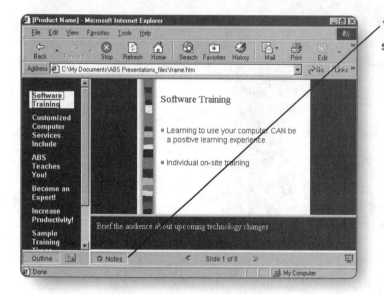

10. **Click** on **Notes** again. The speaker notes frame will hide.

Editing a Word Web Document

After you've previewed your Microsoft Word document as a Web document, you may find you want to make changes to it. Editing the text in the document is the same as any other Word document, but Word includes some special effects that are quite nice for Web pages.

Adding Scrolling Text

Scrolling text on a Web page provides quite a dramatic effect. Unfortunately, not all Web browsers support scrolling text. Any surfer who happens to be using a browser that doesn't support scrolling text will see regular text.

To create scrolling text, you'll need to use the Web Tools toolbar.

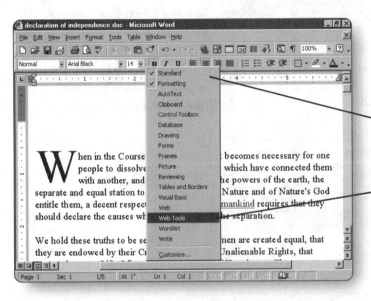

1. Open the **Word document** that will include scrolling text. The document will display on the screen.

2. Right-click on any **toolbar button**. A shortcut menu will appear.

3. Click on **Web Tools**. The Web Tools toolbar will display.

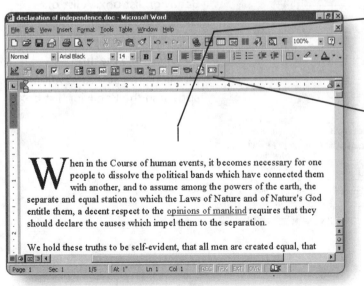

4. Click the **mouse pointer** at the location you want the scrolling text. The blinking insertion point will appear.

5. Click on the **Scrolling Text tool** from the Web Tools toolbar. The Scrolling Text dialog box will open.

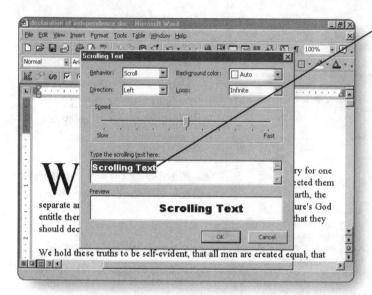

6. Select the words **Scrolling Text** in the Type the scrolling text here: text box. The text will be highlighted.

7. Type the **text** you want to appear. The new text will replace the original text.

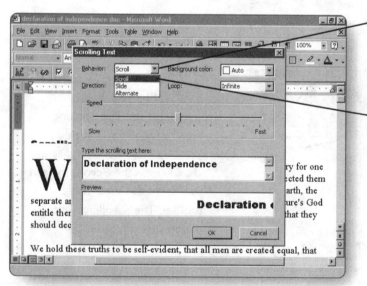

8. Click on the **drop-down arrow** (▼) to the right of the Behavior: list box. A list of choices will appear.

9. Click on a **method** of scrolling. The selection will appear in the Behavior: list box.

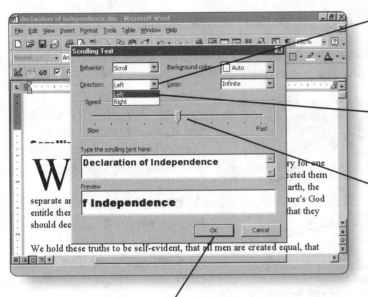

10. Click on the **down arrow** (▼) to the right of the Direction: list box. A list of choices will appear.

11. Click on a **direction** for the text to scroll. The selection will appear in the Direction: list box.

12. Drag the **speed knob** to the left or right. Dragging to the left will slow down the speed of the scrolling text, whereas dragging to the right will increase the speed.

13. Click on **OK**. The Scrolling Text dialog box will close and you will return to your Web page.

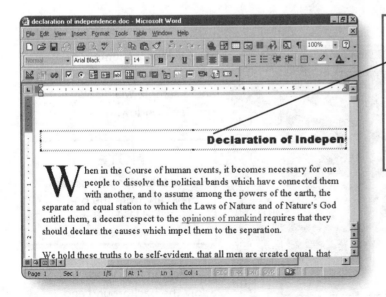

TIP

You can now further edit the scrolling text object. Click on the appropriate choices from the Standard toolbar to edit size, font, or color.

Using a Web Theme

Themes are a collection of background colors/patterns, bullet styles, line styles, heading styles, and font styles. When you select a theme, you make available, in your document, all the styles associated with the theme. Most people use themes when designing Web pages.

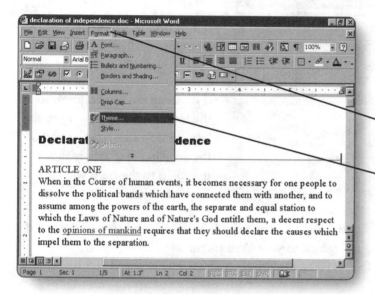

1. Click on **Format**. The Format menu will appear.

2. Click on **Theme**. The Theme dialog box will open.

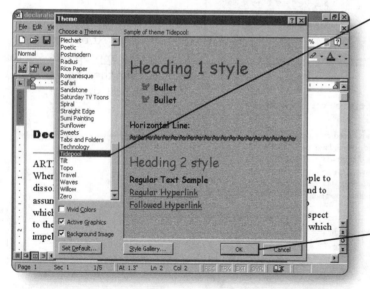

3. Click on a **theme**. The theme name will be highlighted and a sample will display in the preview window.

NOTE

Your selection of themes may vary from the ones displayed in this figure.

4. Click on **OK**. Word will apply the background and other formatting choices to the document.

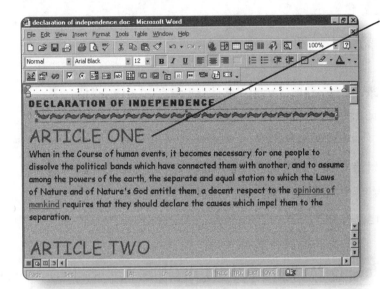

Notice the changes to the headings, backgrounds, and horizontal line.

Publishing Web Documents

You've created your Web documents; now the issue becomes how to make your Web pages accessible to your company's Intranet or on the Web.

You'll need to save your Web pages and their related files (the graphics, lines, bullets, and so on) to a *Web folder*, which is a shortcut to a Web server. The Web server must support Web folders. This varies between servers so you'll need to check with your system administrator or Internet Service Provider.

Part VII Review Questions

1. Which Office applications contain a Web toolbar that can launch your Web browser and take you to the Web sites you designate. *See "Working on the Web" in Chapter 25*

2. Which toolbar should be displayed to access the web from Office applications? *See "Searching the Web" in Chapter 25*

3. What is an Internet start page? *See "Displaying Your Start Page" in Chapter 25*

4. Can you access your favorite Web places from an Office Application? *See "Viewing a Favorite Page" in Chapter 25*

5. What must be inserted into a document to be able to read it on the Internet? *See "Saving Office Documents as Web Documents" in Chapter 26*

6. What happens to Word's animated text when the document is saved as a Web document? *See "Saving an Existing Document as a Web Document" in Chapter 26*

7. By default, how many frames appear when viewing a PowerPoint presentation in Internet Explorer? *See "Viewing the Document in Internet Explorer" in Chapter 26*

8. Describe how to view a Web document you have created in an Office program using your Internet browser. *See "Viewing the Document in Internet Explorer" in Chapter 26*

9. Which toolbar must be displayed in order to create scrolling text? *See" Adding Scrolling Text" in Chapter 26*

10. When do most people use Word's themes feature? *See "Using a Web Theme" in Chapter 26*

PART VIII

Appendixes

A

Streamlining Office Activities

The Microsoft Office Shortcut bar contains a series of toolbars that help speed up your work. For example, using these toolbars, you can quickly open Office documents or create new Office documents or access, from any Office program, a shortcut on your Desktop.

You can also speed up your work in Office 2000 through the use of hyperlinks. By using hyperlinks, you can work in one Office document and open another Office document with just one click. In this chapter, you'll learn how to:

- Use the Office Shortcut Bar
- Customize the Office Shortcut Bar

Working with the Office Shortcut Bar

The Office Shortcut Bar provides you with quick access to the resources you use most often on your computer. When you first see the Office Shortcut Bar, it will appear at the top your screen, but you can move it. By default, the Office Shortcut Bar remains visible at all times, regardless of the program(s) in which you are working. However, you can hide it, making it available but not always visible. You can also close it.

Understanding and Using the Office Shortcut Bar

If your Office Shortcut bar does not automatically display when you start your computer, you'll need to select it from the menu.

1. **Click** on **Start**. The Start menu will appear.

2. **Click** on **Programs**. The Programs submenu will appear.

3. **Click** on **Microsoft Office Tools**. The Microsoft Office Tools submenu will appear.

4. **Click** on **Microsoft Office Shortcut Bar**. A dialog box will open unless this is the first time you have accessed the Office Shortcut Bar.

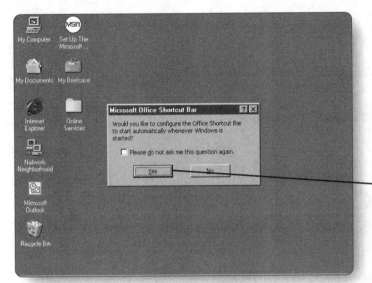

If this is the first time you access this feature, the Office installer will begin in Maintenance Mode. You'll need the Office 2000 installation CD-ROM to add the Office Shortcut Bar. When installation has been completed, repeat steps 1 through 4.

5. Click on **Yes**. The Office Shortcut Bar will launch.

The Office Shortcut Bar will appear, by default, at the top of your screen. It automatically fits into the title bar of your programs.

- **The Control Menu.** You'll click here to do any customizing to the shortcut bar.

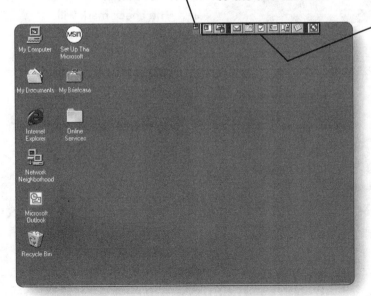

- **Shortcut Bar Buttons.** You'll click on these to make various applications launch; those provided by Microsoft and some of your own you'll add later in this chapter.

To make the Office Shortcut Bar easier to use, you may want to enlarge it.

6. Right-click on the **control menu**. A shortcut menu will appear.

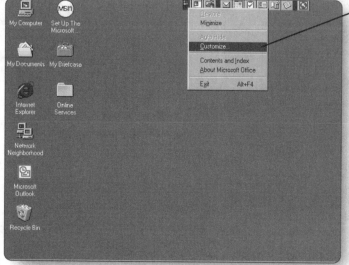

7. Click on **Customize**. The Customize dialog box will open.

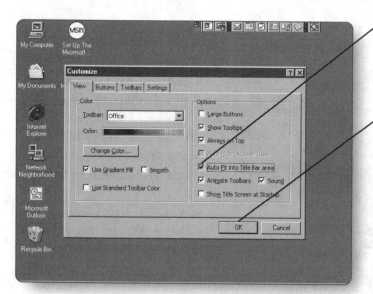

8. Click on the **check box** next to the Auto Fit into Title Bar area. The check mark will disappear from the check box.

9. Click on **OK**. The shortcut bar will enlarge to fill the top of your screen.

The Office Shortcut Bar contains buttons to help you quickly get whatever you need.

Click on these buttons to create new Office documents and to open existing Office documents.

Click on these buttons to create new Outlook events.

Click on this button to open Microsoft FrontPage.

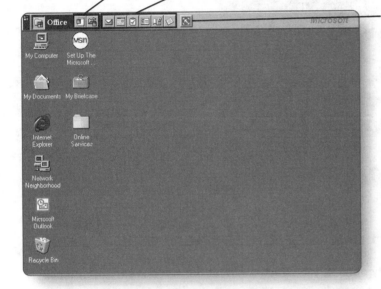

Moving the Office Shortcut Bar

You can place the Office Shortcut Bar anywhere onscreen.

1. Move the **mouse pointer** onto a gray area on the shortcut bar. Make sure you're not pointing at any buttons.

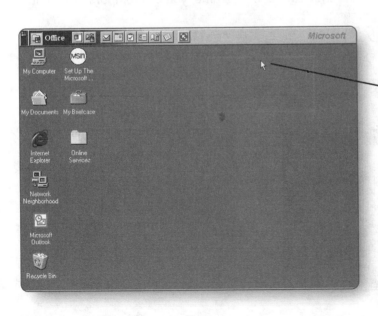

2. Drag the **shortcut bar** to a new location. A red box indicates the new position.

TIP

For best results, move the shortcut bar to an edge of your screen. The box will change shape from an almost square box to a long thin rectangular box.

3. Release the **mouse button**. The shortcut bar will appear wherever you drop it.

Hiding the Office Shortcut Bar

By default, the Office Shortcut Bar will appear onscreen all the time. If you aren't using Auto Fit and you don't want to see the shortcut bar all the time, you can temporarily hide it.

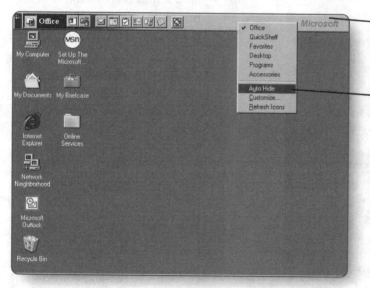

1. Right-click on any gray area of the **Shortcut Bar**. The shortcut bar menu will appear.

2. Click on **Auto Hide**. The shortcut menu will disappear.

Your Desktop will adjust itself as though the Office Shortcut Bar were not there. Some shortcuts might not be entirely visible.

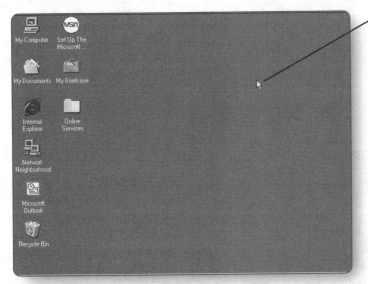

3. Point the **mouse anywhere** on the Desktop except on the shortcut bar. The Office Shortcut Bar will roll up into an edge of the screen and disappear.

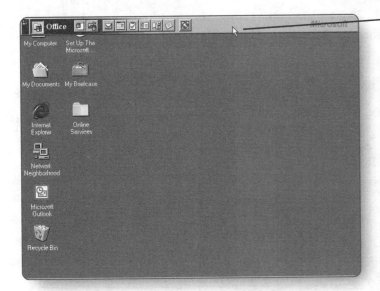

4. Move the **mouse pointer** to the location where the Office Shortcut Bar used to appear. The Office Shortcut Bar will reappear and remain visible as long as the mouse pointer stays somewhere over it.

NOTE

If you hide the Office Shortcut Bar, it will cover some portion of your screen when it reappears.

TIP

If you decide that you prefer to see the Office Shortcut Bar at all times, move the mouse pointer to the edge of the screen so that you can see the Office Shortcut Bar. Then, repeat steps 1 and 2. When the Office Shortcut Bar menu appears in step 1, you'll see a check mark next to Auto Hide. Repeating step 2 removes the check mark.

Closing the Office Shortcut Bar

If you're working on a project that won't require the shortcut bar, you can close it so it's not visible. You can make the closing of the Office Shortcut bar temporary or permanent.

1. Right-click on the **Office Shortcut Bar menu**. The Office Shortcut Bar menu will appear.

2. Click on **Exit**. A message box will display.

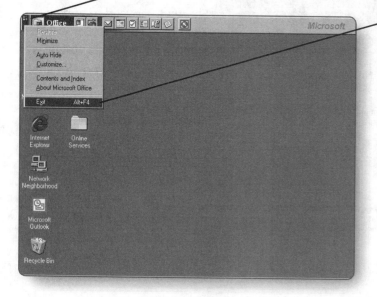

3a. **Click** on **Yes**. The shortcut bar will close but will reappear the next time you restart your computer or if you choose Start, Programs, Startup, and Microsoft Office.

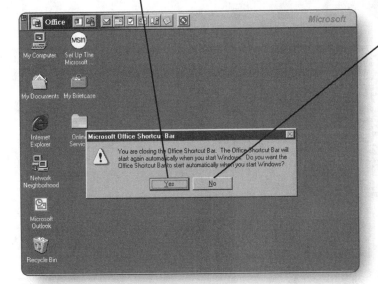

OR

3b. **Click** on **No**. The shortcut bar will close and will not reappear the next time you restart your computer.

TIP

If you choose no, and then decide you want to restart the Office Shortcut Bar, click on Start, Programs, Microsoft Office Tools, and then choose Microsoft Office Shortcut Bar.

Customizing the Office Shortcut Bar

Do you have a program, folder, or document that you use all the time and you want to place it on one of the toolbars on the Office Shortcut Bar? You can add a button to a toolbar. To add a button to a toolbar, that toolbar must be visible. Use the steps in the previous task to display the toolbar on which you want to add a button.

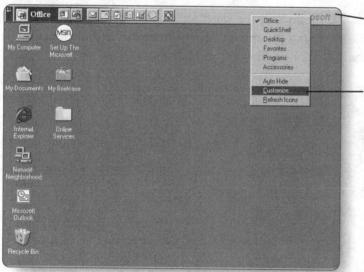

1. **Right-click** on the **gray area** of the Office Shortcut Bar. A shortcut menu will appear.

2. **Click** on **Customize**. The Customize dialog box will open.

3. **Click** on the **Buttons tab**. The Buttons tab will come to the front.

4. **Click** on **Add File**. The Add File dialog box will open.

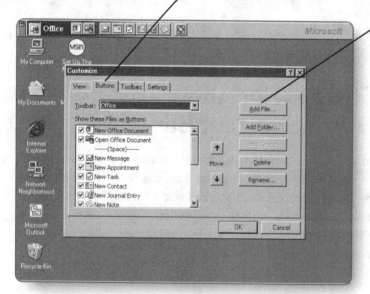

TIP

Buttons that appear on the selected toolbar have a check mark next to them.

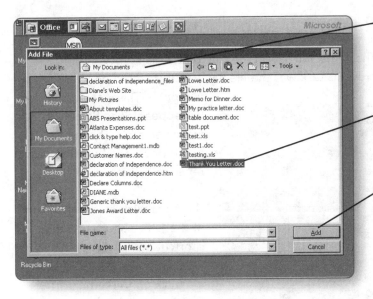

5. **Navigate** to the **folder** containing the file or program for which you want to add a button.

6. **Click** on the **file** for which you want to add a button. The file will be selected.

7. **Click** on **Add**. The Add File dialog box will close.

The Customize dialog box will reappear with the file you chose appearing as a button at the top of the list.

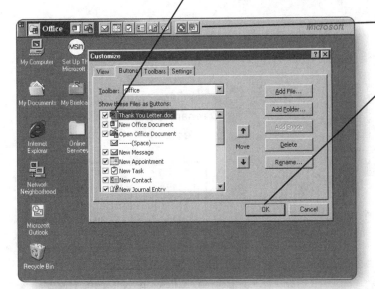

A button for the file will also appear at the end of the toolbar.

8. **Click** on **OK**. The Customize dialog box will close, and you'll have a new button on the toolbar.

Renaming a Toolbar Button

The name you saw in the Customize dialog box in the previous task was the file name as it is stored on your computer. This is the name that will appear in the ScreenTip when you move the mouse pointer over the button. You can rename the button.

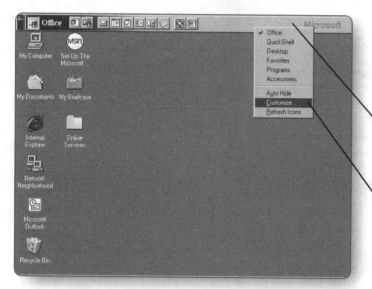

1. Right-click on the **gray area** of the Office Shortcut Bar. A shortcut menu will appear.

2. Click on **Customize**. The Customize dialog box will open.

3. Click on the **Buttons tab**. The Buttons tab will come to the front.

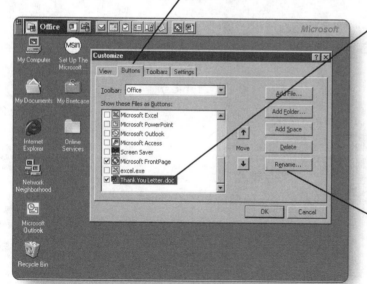

4. Click on the **file** you want to rename. The file will be selected.

TIP

The file might appear at the end of the list.

5. Click on **Rename**. The Rename dialog box will open.

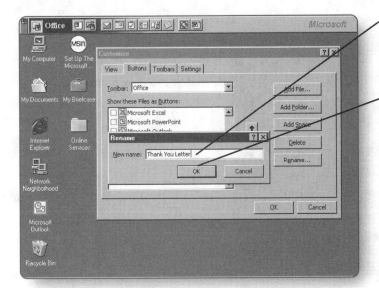

6. Type a new **name**. The new name will replace the existing name.

7. Click on **OK**. The Rename dialog box will close.

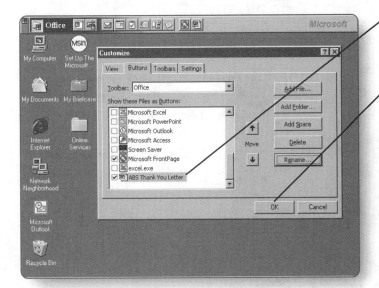

The Customize dialog box will reappear and the button will be renamed.

8. Click on **OK**. The Customize dialog box will close.

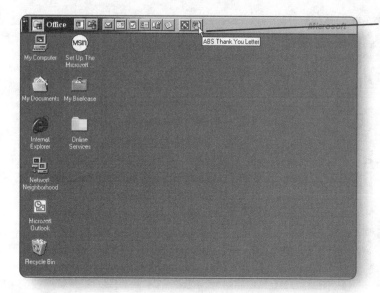

9. Move the **mouse pointer** over the button to see its ScreenTip. The ScreenTip will match the new name you supplied.

Moving a Toolbar Button

You can place toolbar buttons anywhere on the toolbar.

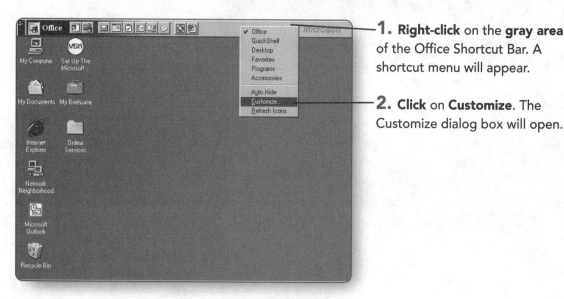

1. Right-click on the **gray area** of the Office Shortcut Bar. A shortcut menu will appear.

2. Click on **Customize**. The Customize dialog box will open.

3. Click on the **Buttons tab**. The Button tab will come to the front.

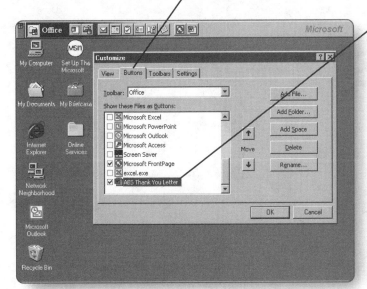

4. Click on the **file name** for the button you want to move. The file name will be highlighted.

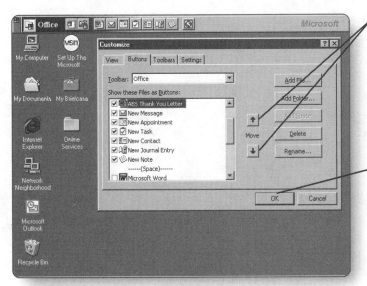

5. Click on the **Move arrows** in the direction you want to move. Each time you click, the button will move up or down (depending on which direction you choose) in the Customize dialog box and on the toolbar.

6. Click on **OK**. The Customize dialog box will close and the button will appear in its new location on the toolbar.

B

Office 2000 Installation

Installing Office 2000 is typically very quick and easy. In this appendix, you'll learn how to:

- Install Office 2000 on your computer
- Choose which Office components you want to install
- Detect and repair problems
- Reinstall Office
- Add and remove components
- Uninstall Office 2000 completely
- Install content from other Office CDs

Installing the Software

The installation program for the Office 2000 programs is automatic. In most cases, you can simply follow the instructions onscreen.

NOTE

When you insert the Office 2000 CD for the first time, you may see a message that the installer has been updated, prompting you to restart your system. Do so, and when you return to Windows after restarting, remove the CD and reinsert it so that the Setup program starts up automatically again.

---

1. **Insert** the **Office 2000 CD-ROM** into your computer's CD-ROM drive. The Windows Installer will start and the Customer Information dialog box will open.

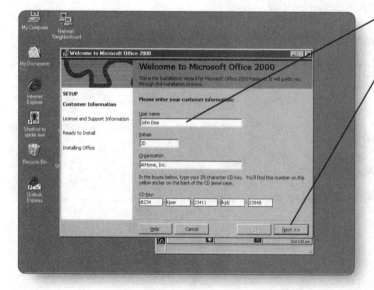

2. **Type** all of the **information** requested.

3. **Click** on **Next**. The End User License Agreement will appear.

NOTE

You'll find the CD Key number on a sticker on the back of the Office CD jewel case.

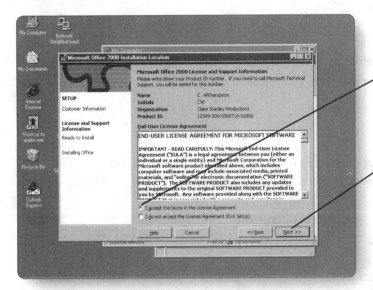

4. **Read** the **License Agreement**.

5. **Click** on the **I accept the terms in the License Agreement option button**. The option will be selected.

6. **Click** on **Next**. The Ready To Install dialog box will open.

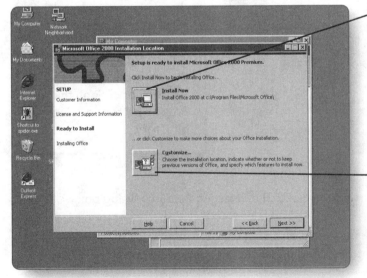

7a. **Click** on the **Install Now button.** Use this option to install Office on your computer with the default settings. This is the recommended installation for most users.

OR

7b. **Click** on the **Customize button**, if you want to choose which components to install or where to install them. The Installation Location dialog box will open. Then see the next section, "Choosing Components," for guidance.

8. **Wait** while the **Office software** installs on your computer. When the setup has completed, the Installer Information box will open.

9. Click on **Yes**. The Setup Wizard will restart your computer. After your computer has restarted, Windows will update your system settings and then finish the Office installation and configuration process.

Choosing Components

If you selected option 7b in the previous section, you have the choice of installing many different programs and components.

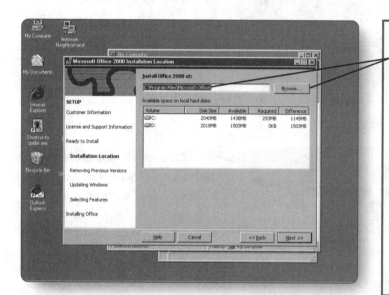

NOTE

For a custom installation, you have the option of placing Office in a different location on your computer. It is recommended that you use the default installation location. If you want to install Office in a different directory, type the directory path in the text box or click on the Browse button to select a directory.

1. Click on **Next**. The Selecting Features dialog box will open.

2. Click on a **plus sign (+)** to expand a list of features. The features listed under the category will appear.

3. Click on the **down arrow (▼)** to the right of the hard drive icon. A menu of available installation options for the feature will appear.

4. Click on the **button** next to the individual option, and choose a setting for that option:

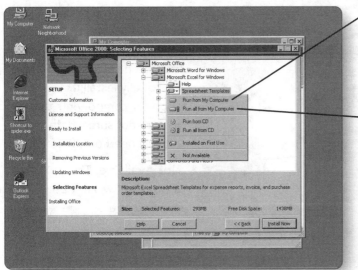

- **Run from My Computer**. The component will be fully installed, so that you will not need the Office CD in the CD-ROM drive to use it.

- **Run all from My Computer**. The selected component and all the components subordinate to it will be fully installed.

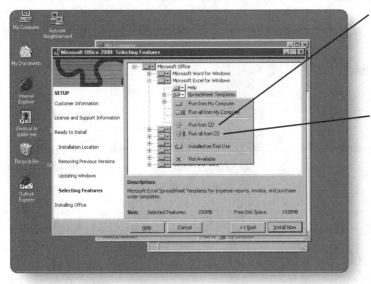

- **Run from CD**. The component will be installed, but you will need to have the Office CD in the CD-ROM drive to use it.

- **Run all from CD**. The selected component and all the components subordinate to it will need to have the Office CD in the CD-ROM drive to use it.

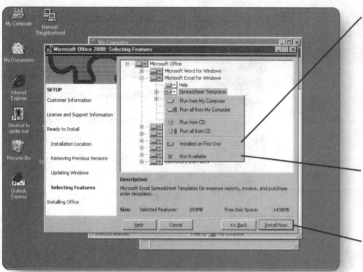

● **Installed on First Use**. The first time you try to activate the component, you will be prompted to insert the Office CD to fully install it. This is good for components that you are not sure whether you will need or not.

● **Not Available**. The component will not be installed at all.

5. Click on **Install Now**. The Installing dialog box will open.

In a Custom installation, you'll be asked whether you want to update Internet Explorer to version 5.0. Your choices are:

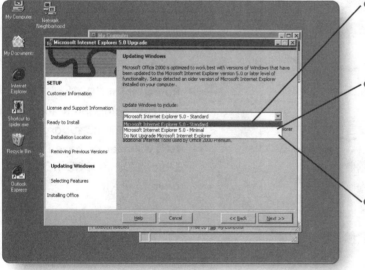

● **Microsoft Internet Explorer 5.0—Standard**. This is the default, and the right choice for most people.

● **Microsoft Internet Explorer 5.0—Minimal**. This is the right choice if you are running out of hard disk space but still would like to use Internet Explorer 5.0.

● **Do Not Upgrade Microsoft Internet Explorer**. Use this if you don't want Internet Explorer (for example, if you always use another browser such as Netscape Navigator, or if you have been directed by your system administrator not to install Internet Explorer 5).

Working with Maintenance Mode

Maintenance Mode is a feature of the Setup program. Whenever you run the Setup program again, after the initial installation, Maintenance Mode starts automatically. It enables you to add or remove features, repair your Office installation (for example, if files have become corrupted), and remove Office completely. There are several ways to rerun the Setup program (and thus enter Maintenance Mode):

- Reinsert the Office 2000 CD. The Setup program may start automatically.

- If the Setup program does not start automatically, double-click on the CD icon in the My Computer window.

- If double-clicking on the CD icon doesn't work, right-click on the CD icon and click on Open from the shortcut menu. Then double-click on the Setup.exe file in the list of files that appears.

- From the Control Panel in Windows, click on the Add/ Remove Programs button. Then on the Install/Uninstall tab, click on Microsoft Office 2000 in the list, and finally, click on the Add/Remove button.

After entering Maintenance Mode, choose the button for the activity you want. Each option is briefly described in the following sections.

Repairing or Reinstalling Office

If an Office program is behaving strangely, or refuses to work, chances are good that a needed file has become corrupted. But which file? You have no way of knowing, so you can't fix the problem yourself.

If this happens, you can either repair Office or completely reinstall it. Both options are accessed from the Repair Office button in Maintenance Mode.

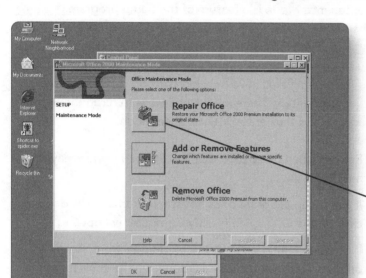

1. **Click** on the **Repair Office button** in Maintenance Mode.

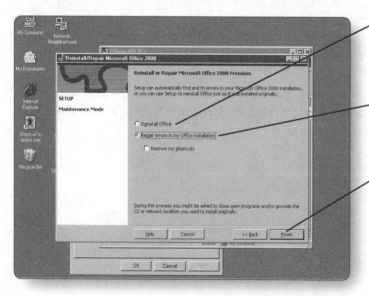

2a. **Click** on **Reinstall Office** to repeat the last installation.

OR

2b. **Click on Repair errors in my Office installation** to simply fix what's already in place.

3. **Click** on **Finish**. The process will start.

TIP

You can also repair individual Office programs by opening the Help menu in each program and clicking on Detect and Repair. This works well if you are sure that one certain program is causing the problem, and it's quicker than asking the Setup program to check all of the installed programs.

Adding and Removing Components

Adding and removing components works just like selecting the components initially.

1. Click on the **Add or Remove Features button** in Maintenance Mode. The Update Features window will appear. This window works exactly the same as the window you saw in the "Choosing Components" section earlier in this appendix.

NOTE

Some features will attempt to automatically install themselves as you are working. If you have set a feature to be installed on first use, attempt to access that feature. You will be prompted to insert your Office 2000 CD, and the feature will be installed without further prompting.

Removing Office from Your PC

In the unlikely event that you should need to remove Office from your PC completely, click on Remove Office from the Maintenance Mode screen. Then follow the prompts to remove it from your system.

After removing Office, you will probably have a few remnants left behind that the Uninstall routine didn't catch. For example, there will probably still be a Microsoft Office folder in your Program Files folder or wherever you installed the program. You can delete that folder yourself.

CAUTION

If you plan to reinstall Office later, and you have created any custom templates, toolbars, or other items, you may want to leave the Microsoft Office folder alone, so that those items will be available to you after you reinstall.

Installing Content from Other Office CDs

Depending on the version of Office you bought, you may have more than one CD in your package. CD 1 contains all the basic Office components, such as Word, Outlook, PowerPoint, Excel, Access, and Internet Explorer. It may be the only CD you need to use.

The other CDs contain extra applications that come with the specific version of Office you purchased. They may include Publisher, FrontPage, a language pack, or a programmer and developer resource kit. Each of these discs has its own separate installation program.

The additional CDs should start their Setup programs automatically when you insert the disk in your drive. If not, browse the CD's content in My Computer or Windows Explorer and double-click on the Setup.exe file that you find on it.

C

Using Keyboard Shortcuts

You may have noticed the keyboard shortcuts listed on the right side of several of the menus. You can use these shortcuts to execute commands without using the mouse to activate menus. You many want to memorize these keyboard shortcuts. Not only will they speed your productivity, but they will also help decrease wrist strain caused by excessive mouse usage. In this appendix, you'll learn how to:

- Get up to speed with frequently used keyboard shortcuts
- Use keyboard combinations to edit text

Learning the Basic Shortcuts

Trying to memorize all these keyboard shortcuts isn't as hard as you may think. Windows applications all share the same keyboard combinations to execute common commands. Once you get accustomed to using some of these keyboard shortcuts, try them out on some of the other programs.

Common Office Shortcuts

The following table shows you a few of the more common keyboard shortcuts that you may want to use when working with documents, spreadsheets or other Office applications.

To execute this command	Do this
Use Help	Press F1
Use the What's This? Button	Press Shift+F1
Create a new document	Press Ctrl+N
Open a different document	Press Ctrl+O
Switch between open documents	Press Ctrl+F6
Save a document	Press Ctrl+S
Print a document	Press Ctrl+P
Close a document	Press Ctrl+W
Cut selected text or objects	Press Ctrl+X
Make a copy of selected items	Press Ctrl+C
Paste the copied or cut items	Press Ctrl+V
Undo an action	Press Ctrl+Z
Redo an action	Press Ctrl+Y
Make the menu bar active	Press F10 or Alt

Using Word Shortcut Keys

Word has many shortcuts available to speed up data entry and formatting.

To execute this command	Do this
Highlight an entire word	Press Ctrl+Shift+Right Arrow
Highlight an entire line	Press Shift+End
Highlight a paragraph	Press Ctrl+Shift+Down Arrow
Select an entire document	Press Ctrl+A
Go to a specific page	Press Ctrl+G
Spell check a document	Press F7
Find text in a document	Press Ctrl+F
Replace text in a document	Press Ctrl+H
Change the font	Press Ctrl+Shift+F
Change the size of the font	Press Ctrl+Shift+P
Make selected text bold	Press Ctrl+B
Make selected text italic	Press Ctrl+I
Make selected text underlined	Press Ctrl+U
Remove character formatting	Press Ctrl+Spacebar
Single space a paragraph	Press Ctrl+1
Double space a paragraph	Press Ctrl+2
Set 1.5 line spacing	Press Ctrl+5
Center a paragraph	Press Ctrl+E
Left align a paragraph	Press Ctrl+L
Right align a paragraph	Press Ctrl+R
Left indent a paragraph	Press Ctrl+M
Remove paragraph formatting	Press Ctrl+Q

Using Excel Shortcuts

Whether you need to move around in the large Excel spreadsheet or make your data look great, Excel has shortcuts to make the process faster.

To execute this command	Do this
Move to the row beginning	Press Home
Move to the worksheet beginning	Press Ctrl+Home
Move down one screen	Press Page Down
Move up one screen	Press Page Up
Move left one screen	Press Alt+Page Up
Move right one screen	Press Alt+Page Down
Move to next sheet in workbook	Press Ctrl+Page Down
Move to previous sheet	Press Ctrl+Page Up
Complete a cell entry	Press Enter
Start a new line in the same cell	Press Alt+Enter
Fill the selected cell range with the current entry	Press Ctrl+Enter
Fill data down	Press Ctrl+D
Fill data to the right	Press Ctrl+R
Edit a cell entry	Press F2
Start a formula	Press = (equal sign)
Insert the AutoSum Formula	Press Alt+= (equal sign)
Enter the date	Press Ctrl+; (semicolon)
Enter the time	Press Ctrl+Shift+: (colon)
Display the Format Cells dialog box	Press Ctrl+1

To execute this command	Do this
Apply currency format	Press Ctrl+Shift+$
Apply percentage format	Press Ctrl+Shift+%
Apply general number format	Press Ctrl+Shift+~
Apply date format	Press Ctrl+Shift+#
Apply time format	Press Ctrl+Shift+@
Apply number format	Press Ctrl+Shift+!
Apply outline border	Press Ctrl+Shift+&
Hide Rows	Press Ctrl+9
Hide Columns	Press Ctrl+0 (Zero)
Unhide Rows	Press Ctrl+Shift+((opening parenthesis)
Unhide Columns	Press Ctrl+Shift+) (closing parenthesis)
Select an entire column	Press Ctrl+Spacebar
Select an entire row	Press Shift+Spacebar
Select an entire worksheet	Press Ctrl+A
Extend selection one cell	Press Shift+arrow key
Extend the selection to the last used cell on the worksheet (lower right corner)	Press Ctrl+Shift+End

Using PowerPoint Shortcuts

Powerful PowerPoint presentations can be created using many of the available shortcut keys.

To execute this command	Do this
To move to the next title or body text placeholder	Press Ctrl+Enter
To move to the beginning of a text box	Press Ctrl+Home
To center a paragraph of text	Press Ctrl+E
To left align a paragraph	Press Ctrl+L
To right align a paragraph	Press Ctrl+R
To change font	Press Ctrl+Shift+F
To change font size	Press Ctrl+Shift+P
To apply bold formatting	Press Ctrl+B
To apply italics formatting	Press Ctrl+I
To apply underline formatting	Press Ctrl+U
To promote a paragraph	Press Alt+Shift+Left Arrow
To demote a paragraph	Press Alt+Shift+Right Arrow
To select all objects in the slide view	Press Ctrl+A
To select all slides in the slide sorter view	Press Ctrl+A
To select all text in the outline view	Press Ctrl+A
To advance a slide in a slide show	Press N
To return to the previous slide in a slide show	Press P
To display a black screen during a slide show	Press B
To return from a black screen	Press B during a slide show
To display a white screen during a slide show	Press W
To return from a white screen during a slide show	Press W
To see a list of slide show controls during a slide show	Press F1

Using Outlook Shortcuts

Like the other Office applications, Outlook includes shortcuts to speed up your tasks whether it's working with E-mail, editing a To Do list or scheduling a meeting.

To execute this command	Do this
To display the address book	Press Ctrl+Shift+B
To switch to the Inbox	Press Ctrl+Shift+I
To switch to the Outbox	Press Ctrl+Shift+O
To create or open an appointment	Press Ctrl+Shift+A
To create or open a contact	Press Ctrl+Shift+C
To create or open a message	Press Ctrl+Shift+M
To create or open a task	Press Ctrl+Shift+K
To create or open a note	Press Ctrl+Shift+N
To dial a contact	Press Ctrl+Shift+D
Reply to a mail message	Press Ctrl+R
Mark a message as read	Press Ctrl+Q
Add bullets to a message	Press Ctrl+Shift+L
Increase indent of text	Press Ctrl+T
Decrease indent of text	Press Ctrl+Shift+T
Apply Bold to text	Press Ctrl+B
Apply Italics to text	Press Ctrl+I
Apply Underline to text	Press Ctrl+U
Left align text	Press Ctrl+L
Center align text	Press Ctrl+E
View 1 day on the calendar	Press Alt+1
Switch to week view	Press Alt+- (hyphen)
Switch to month view	Press Alt+= (equal sign)
Go to the next day	Press the right arrow key
Go to the previous day	Press the left arrow key
Go to the same day in the next week	Press Alt+down arrow

Using Access Shortcuts

Whether you need to move from one view to another or enter data, Access includes shortcuts to assist you.

To execute this command	Do this
To switch to Form View from Design View	Press F5
To switch from Edit mode and Navigation Mode	Press F2
To select the next field	Press Tab
To select a column in Datasheet View	Press Ctrl+Spacebar
To select all records	Press Ctrl+A
To enter the current date	Press Ctrl+; (semicolon)
To enter the current time	Press Ctrl+: (colon)
To insert the value from the same field in the previous record	Press Ctrl+' (apostrophe)
To add a new record	Press Ctrl++ (plus sign)
To delete the current record	Press Ctrl+- (minus sign)

Glossary

+   Addition operator.

–   Subtraction operator.

=   Initiates all formulas.

*   Multiplication operator.

/   Division operator.

>   Greater than operator.

<   Less than operator.

<>   Not equal to operator.

:   Range operator.

=AVERAGE. An Excel function that calculates the average of a list of values. SYNTAX: =AVERAGE(*list*)

=COUNT. An Excel function that counts the non-blank cells in a list of ranges. SYNTAX: =COUNT(*list*)

=MAX. An Excel function that finds the largest value in a list. SYNTAX: =MAX(*list*)

=MIN. An Excel function that finds the smallest value in a list. SYNTAX: =MIN(*list*)

=SUM. An Excel function that adds a range of cells. *See also* AutoSum. SYNTAX: =SUM(*list*)

Absolute reference. In a formula, a reference to a cell that does not change when copying the formula. An absolute reference always refers to the same cell or range. It is designated in a formula by the dollar sign ($).

Active cell. The selected cell, in a worksheet. Designated with a border surrounding the cell.

Address Book. Stores names, addresses, and phone numbers in one handy location.

Address. A named reference to a cell, based on its location at the intersection of a column and row; for example, the cell in the fourth row of the second column has an address of B4.

Alignment. The position of data in a document, cell, range, or text block; for example, centered, right-aligned, or left-aligned. Also called *justification*.

Animation. The adding of movement to text that is displayed on the screen.

Applet. A small software program provided with Word that enables the user to perform additional operations, such as WordArt, for enhanced text effects.

Appointment. An entry in the Outlook calendar that spans less than one day to which no other individuals are invited.

Array. A contiguous set of cells in a worksheet.

Attributes. Items that determine the appearance of text such as bolding, underlining, italics, or point size.

AutoCorrect. A feature of Office that automatically corrects common spelling mistakes (changes "teh" into "the").

AutoFormat. AutoFormat enables the user to apply pre-defined sets of formatting to a table's (or worksheet's) text, rows, and columns.

AutoSum. A function that adds a row or column of figures by clicking on the AutoSum button on the Excel toolbar. Same as *=SUM*.

AutoText. A feature of Word that enables the user to save a set of text which is inserted into the document after a word or phrase is typed.

Axis. A line that forms a frame of reference for the chart data. Most charts have an x-axis and a y-axis. In a graph, one of two value sets (*see also* x-axis and y-axis).

Bar chart. A type of chart that uses bars to represent values. Normally used to compare items.

Bold. A style applied to text to make the font lines thicker.

Bookmark. Used to mark a place in a document to locate it quickly.

Border. A line surrounding paragraphs, pages, table cells, or objects.

Break. An instruction embedded in a Word document that indicates a change, such as a Page Break, to start a new page.

Browser. A software program especially designed for viewing Web pages on the Internet.

Bullet. A small black circle or other character that precedes each item in a list.

Cell Reference. A method of referring to a cell in a formula by listing the location of its row and column intersection.

Cell. The area defined by a rectangle at which a row and column intersect in an Excel worksheet or a Word table.

Chart. A graphic representation of numerical data. Also called *graph*.

Choose. To use the mouse or keyboard to pick a menu item or option in a dialog box.

Circular reference. A cell that has a formula that contains a reference to itself.

Click on. To use the mouse to pick a menu item or option in a dialog box.

Clip art. Ready-made line drawings that are included with Office in the Clip Art Gallery. These drawings can be inserted into Office documents.

Clip Gallery. A collection of clip art, pictures, and sound files that comes with Office.

Clipboard. An area of computer memory where text or graphics can be temporarily stored.

Close button. Used to shut down or exit a dialog box, window, or application.

Column. A set of cells running vertically down a worksheet. Or, vertical divisions of text on a page.

Comment. To add annotations to a document or spreadsheet cell. Comments do not print.

Compound Formula. A formula, usually in a spreadsheet, that has multiple operators. An example might be A2*C2+F4.

Contact. An entry that appears in an address book.

Copy. To take a selection from the document and duplicate it on the Clipboard.

Cut. To take a selection from the document and move it to the Clipboard.

Data form. A place where data, such as data used in a mail merge operation, is stored in individual records.

Data series. In charts, elements that represent a set of data, such as pie segment, line, or bar.

Data source. In a Word mail merge, the information that is used to replace field codes with personalized information, such as names and addresses.

Data type. The category of numerical data, such as currency, scientific, or percentage.

Data. Information, which can be either numerical or textual.

Database. A file composed of records, each containing fields together with a set of operations for searching or sorting.

Datasheet View. A view in a database where many records display in a table format.

Default. A setting or action predetermined by the program unless changed by the user.

Desktop. The main area of Windows where files and programs are opened and managed.

Dialog box. A box that appears that displays warnings, messages, or requests information from the user.

Document. A letter, memo, proposal, or other file that is created in an Office application.

Drag-and-drop. A method of moving text or objects by clicking on an object with a mouse, dragging it to a new location, and releasing the mouse button to drop it into its new location.

Drop Caps. A large dropped initial capital letter. Frequently used in the first line of newsletter articles.

E-mail. Messages sent electronically.

Equation. *See* Formula.

Event. An entry in the Outlook calendar that spans an entire day.

Export. The ability to copy data from one program to another.

Field. A piece of information used in a database.

Field. In a form letter, a field is a placeholder for corresponding data.

File format. The arrangement and organization of information in a file. File format is determined by the application that created the file.

File. Information stored on a disk under a single name.

Fill (color). A formatting feature used to apply color or a pattern to the interior of an object, such as a cell.

Fill Data. A function that allows Excel to automatically complete a series of numbers or words based on an established pattern.

Fill Handle. A block at the bottom-right corner of the active cell in a worksheet that is used to fill cells as it is dragged across them with a pattern of data.

Fill. An action in Excel that automatically completes a series of numbers based on an established pattern.

Filter. Settings to ensure that only cells meeting certain criteria are displayed in the worksheet.

Financial functions. Functions (stored formulas) that are used with money, such as payments and interest rates.

Find. An Office feature used to locate characters in an Office document.

Flip. To turn an object on a page 180 degrees.

Font. A design set of letters, symbols, and numbers, also called a *typeface*.

Footer. Text repeated at the bottom of each page of a document or spreadsheet.

Footnote. Reference information that prints at the bottom of the page.

Form Design View. The view in a database that allows the structure of the database to be modified.

Form View. A view in a database where one record displays at a time.

Form. A type of database document with spaces reserved for fields to enter data.

Format painter. A feature of Word that enables the easy copying of all formatting that's applied to one set of text to any other.

Format. To change the appearance of text or objects with features such as the font, style, color, borders, and size.

Formula bar. The location where all data and formulas are entered for a selected cell.

Formula. An equation that instructs Excel to perform certain calculations based on numerical data in designated cells.

Freezing. The preventing of sections of a worksheet from scrolling off the screen when the page moves down.

Function. A series of predefined formulas used in spreadsheets. Functions perform specialized calculations automatically.

General format. A numerical type applied to numbers in cells.

Go To. A feature that allows the quick movement to a page or cell of the document based on criteria that is provided.

Gradient. A shading effect that moves from lighter to darker in such a way that it suggests a light source shining on the object containing the gradient.

Graph. Also called *chart*. A graph is a visual representation of numerical data.

Greater than. A mathematical operator that limits the results of a formula to be higher than a named number or cell.

Gridlines. The lines dividing rows and columns in a table or worksheet.

Handle. Small squares that appear when an object is selected and enable its resizing.

Header. Text entered in an area of the document for display at the top of each page of the document.

Hide. A feature of Excel that temporarily stops the displaying of designated cells in a worksheet.

Highlight. A feature that places colored highlighting onscreen for selected text.

HTML. The language used to create documents for publication on the Web.

Hyperlink. A created element that consists of an address to a location, such as a folder on a computer or Web page. When a

hyperlink is clicked, the screen will jump to the location defined in the hyperlink.

Icon. A graphic representation used on toolbars to represent the various functions performed when those buttons are clicked with a mouse.

IF function. A pre-defined formula indicating that a result is to occur only if some criteria is met. For example, this function could be used to indicate that "if the result of a sum is greater than 10, the result should appear in this cell."

Import. The ability to receive data from another.

Indent. To set text away from a margin by a specific distance; for example, at the beginning of a paragraph.

Italic. A font style that applies a slanted effect to text.

Justification. *See* Alignment.

Justify. A type of alignment that spreads letters on a line or in a cell evenly between the left and right margin or across selected cells.

Label. A descriptive text element added to a chart to help the reader understand a visual element. Also refers to row or column headings. Also any cell entry that begins with a letter or label-prefix character.

Landscape. A page orientation that prints a document with the long edge of the paper across the top.

Legend. In a chart, a box containing symbols and text that explains what each data series represents. Each symbol is a color pattern or marker that corresponds to one data series in the chart.

Less than. A mathematical operator that limits the results of a formula to be lower than a named number or cell.

Line spacing. The amount of space between lines of text.

Line style. Effects using width, arrows, and dashes that can be applied to a line.

Macro. A saved series of keystrokes that can be played back to perform an action.

Mail merge. A procedure that uses a form document, inserts placeholders for types of data (called fields), and merges that document with specific data to produce personalized mailings.

Maps. Representing data in charts with geographical maps rather than traditional chart elements such as bars and lines.

Margin. A border that runs around the outside of a document page in which nothing will print.

Mathematical functions. Functions that produce mathematical results, such as SUM and AVG.

Meeting. An entry in the Outlook calendar that spans less than one day to which others are invited.

Named ranges. Providing a name for a set of cells so that name can be used in formulas.

Notes (Speaker Notes). Additional text displayed alongside a printed slide to prompt the presenter.

Object. A picture, map, or other graphic element that can be placed in an Office document.

Office Assistant. A help feature for Microsoft Office products that allows the user to ask questions in standard English sentence format.

Office Shortcut Bar. A utility that ships with Microsoft Office. The Microsoft Office Shortcut Bar contains a series of toolbars that help speed up work by providing quick access to the resources most often used on the computer.

Open. To start an application, to insert a document into a new document window, or to access a dialog box.

Operator. The parts of a formula that indicate an action to be performed, such as addition (+) or division (/).

Orientation. The way a document prints on a piece of paper; landscape prints with the longer side of a page on top, whereas portrait prints with the shorter edge at the top.

Outline. A hierarchy of lines of text that suggests major and minor ideas.

Outlook bar. The panel that appears down the left side of the Outlook window. It contains shortcuts to the various sections in Outlook.

Page Break. A command that tells the application where to begin a new page.

Page Setup. The collection of settings that determine how the pages of the document are set up, including margins, orientation, and the size of paper on which each page will print.

Passwords. A word selected by an Excel user to protect a worksheet; once a sheet is protected, the correct password must be entered to modify that sheet.

Paste. To place text or an object previously placed on the Windows Clipboard (through cutting or copying) into an Office document.

Pattern. Shading and line arrangements that can be used to fill the center of an object.

Pie chart. A round chart type in which each pie wedge represents a value.

Plot. The area of a chart where data is drawn using elements such as line, bars, or pie wedges.

Point size. A unit of measurement used to indicate font size. One point is 1/72 inch in height.

Point. To move the mouse until the tip of the mouse pointer rests on an item.

Portrait. A page orientation where a document prints with the shorter edge of the paper along the top.

Print area. The portion of a worksheet that is designated to print.

Print Layout. A view in Word that is commonly used for arranging objects on a page and drawing.

Print Preview. A feature that allows the viewing of a document on the screen as it will appear when printed.

Properties. The characteristics of text, objects, or devices. Text properties might include font, size, or color.

Protect. To make settings so that only someone with the correct password can modify a document.

Queries. Used in a database, a subset of data that meets certain criteria.

Range name. An "English" name that identifies a range and that can be used in commands and formulas instead of the range address.

Range. A collection of cells, ranging from the first named cell to the last.

Recalculation. Used with manual calculation, recalculation is applied to a formula when data has changed to receive the new result.

Record. The collection of field information about one particular element. For example, Joe Smith's record might include field information such as name, address, and phone number.

Redo. A feature that allows the restoration of an action that was reversed using the Undo feature.

Reference. In a formula, a name or range that refers the formula to a cell or set of cells.

Relative. In a formula, making reference to a cell relative to the location of the cell where the formula is placed; if the formula cell is moved, the cell being referenced changes in relation to the new location.

Replace. An Office function that locates text or formatting and replaces it with different text or formatting.

Revisions. Highlighting effects applied to indicate any changes in text from one version of a document to another.

Right-aligned. Text that is lined up with the right side of a tab setting or document margin, as with a row of numbers in a column.

Rotate. To manipulate an object so that it moves around a 360 degree axis.

Row. A set of cells running from left to right across a worksheet.

Ruler. An on-screen feature provided to place text and objects accurately on a page.

Save. To take a document residing in the memory of the computer and create a file to be stored on a disk.

Save As. To save a previously saved document with a new name or properties.

Scroll bars. The bars on the right side and bottom of a window that allow vertical and horizontal movements through a document.

Selection bar. An invisible bar along the left side of a document. When the mouse pointer is placed in the bar, it can be used to select a single line or multiple lines of text.

Shading. A color that fills cells or an object.

Shadow. A drawing effect that appears to place a shadow alongside an object.

Shape. Item such as a circle, rectangle, line, polygon, or polylines in the document.

Sheet. *See* Worksheet.

Simple Formula. A formula, usually in a spreadsheet that has only one operator. An example might be B4+B5.

Slide Layout. The term used to refer to the general appearance of a slide and the elements it contains; for example, a bulleted list layout, a chart layout, or a title only layout.

Slide Sorter. A view in PowerPoint that allows the viewing of all slides together in one screen.

Slide. An element in a PowerPoint presentation, equivalent to a page.

Sort. To arrange data alphanumerically in either ascending (A–Z) or descending (Z–A) order.

Spelling checker. A feature that checks the spelling in a document against a dictionary, and flags possible errors for correction.

Spreadsheet. A software program used to perform calculations on data.

Start Page. The first Web page to appear after logging onto the World Wide Web.

Status bar. An area at the bottom of a window that provides information about the document, such as what page, line, and column that the pointer is currently resting in.

Style. A saved, named set of formatting such as color, size, and font that can be applied to text in a document.

SUM function. A saved, named function of addition that can be applied to cells by typing the term "SUM" in a formula.

Switchboard. In Access, the opening screen of a database.

Symbol. A typeface that uses graphics such as circles, percentage signs, or smiling faces in place of letters and numbers.

Syntax. The structure and order of the functions and references used in a formula.

Tab. A setting that can be placed along the width of a line of text that enables the pointer to quickly jump to that setting.

Table. A collection of columns and rows, forming cells at their intersection, to organize sets of data. Also a matrix, similar in appearance to a spreadsheet, that's used to store database information.

Tabs. Settings in the document that determine where the insertion point moves when the Tab key is pressed or the indent feature used.

Target cell. The cell where the results of a formula should be placed.

Task. An entry that is made in Outlook's To Do section.

TaskWizards. An interactive Help feature that prompts the user for key pieces of required information to complete a project.

Template. A pre-defined collection of formatting and style settings on which to base a new document.

Text box. A floating object containing text that can be created with the drawing feature of Office programs to place text anywhere in a document.

Text wrap. This feature forces newly entered text to wrap to the next line when the insertion point reaches the right margin.

Themes. A collection of background colors/patterns, bullet styles, line styles, heading styles, and font styles. Frequently used when designing Web pages.

Thesaurus. A feature used to find *synonyms* (words that are alike) and *antonyms* (words that are opposite).

Titles. Descriptive pieces of text frequently used in charts and spreadsheets.

Tool tip. A Help feature that displays the name of a tool in a small box when the pointer is over the tool.

Toolbars. Appears at the top of the application window and is used to access many of the commonly-used features of the Office applications.

Transitions. In PowerPoint, elements to add to a slide that determine the appearance of the transition from slide to slide.

Undo. A feature that allows the reversal of the last action performed. The user can undo actions by repeatedly using this feature.

Unhide. To reveal rows or columns previously hidden in a worksheet.

Unprotect. To remove password safeguards from a worksheet so that anyone can modify the worksheet.

Uppercase. A capital letter.

Value. An entry that is a number, formula, or function.

Variable. Cells that are changed to see what results from that change.

View. In software, various displays of documents or information that enable the performance of different tasks or see different perspectives on information; for example, the Outline view in Word.

Web Page Preview. The feature of Office that allows the viewing of a document in Internet Explorer as it would appear on the Web.

Web page. A document that appears after logging-on to the World Wide Web. Also called a Web document.

What's This? A part of the Help system; once it is selected, the pointer changes to a question mark. The user can click on any on-screen element to receive an explanation of that element.

Wizard. A feature that walks through a procedure step by step, and produces something, such as a table, letter, or chart, based on answers that are given to questions and selections made in Wizard dialog boxes.

Word count. A tally of the number of words in a document.

Word Processing. The ability to type, edit, and save a document.

Word Wrap. To allow text in a paragraph to automatically flow to the next line when it reaches the right margin.

WordArt. A feature that allows blocks of text to be manipulated into varying shapes and formats.

Workbook. A single Excel file containing a collection of Excel worksheets.

Worksheet. One of several pages in an Excel workbook.

World Wide Web. A series of specially designed documents—all linked together—to be viewed over the Internet.

Wrap. *See* Text Wrap.

X-axis. In a chart, a horizontal reference line marked in regular intervals to display the categories with descriptive labels.

Y-axis. In a chart, a vertical reference line marked in regular intervals to display the values of a chart.

Zoom. To enlarge or reduce the way the text displays onscreen. It does not affect how the document will print.

Index

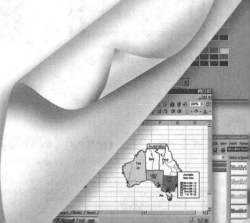